NOTABLE WOMEN OF PENNSYLVANIA

Now and not hereafter, while the breath is in our nostrils,
Now and not hereafter, ere the meaner years go by—
Let us now remember many honourable women,
Such as bade us turn again when we were like to die.

Rudyard Kipling in "Dirge of Dead Sisters"

NOTABLE WOMEN

of Pennsylvania

Edited by

GERTRUDE BOSLER BIDDLE

and SARAH DICKINSON LOWRIE

Committee of 1926

Philadelphia Sesquicentennial Celebration

UNIVERSITY OF PENNSYLVANIA PRESS

Philadelphia

1942

Dedicated to the Memory of

ELIZABETH PRICE MARTIN

This place of honor on so superlative a roll of
distinction is a proof in itself that her contemporaries
recognized her character and citizenship as their
standard of public spirit

FOREWORD

✝✝

THE inspiration for this volume grew out of the "Book of Honor," an illuminated record of notable Pennsylvania women which is now in the keeping of the custodians of Strawberry Mansion in Fairmount Park in Philadelphia. The Book of Honor consists of biographical essays prepared and gathered by the Committee of 1926, Philadelphia Sesquicentennial Celebration, and was presented to the Committee in 1932 by the late Cyrus H. K. Curtis, publisher of the Philadelphia *Ledger* in which the articles first appeared in print. Since that time the Book of Honor has been opened many times to add more names. This record has been further amplified to make up the contents of this book—an enduring tribute to the many women who have helped to build the state and nation.

It has taken a surprisingly long time to gather these names out of the past, and much patient delving to verify the biographical facts of the lives and deeds of these illustrious women who now, for the first time in a majority of instances, are gathered into the "company of those immortal dead," and recognized historically as leaders in thought and action beyond their own generation of neighbors and fellow citizens. The biographies have been constructed from documented records, tradition, sometimes from hear-say, by a variety of authors, and have passed muster before a group of historical experts. After publication in the *Ledger* such new evidence as came to light has been incorporated in the descriptions.

In the process of reviewing so many generations of Pennsylvanians to select those who should have an entry in the Book of Honor, two hundred and fifty candidates were proposed by biographers. The biographical details of some two hundred women could be verified sufficiently to include them in this historical record. When it is remembered that only recently have women been considered individuals in their own right, with special abilities of their own, it is remarkable that so many emerge from the obscurities of the past to take their place in the history of Pennsylvania.

To Mrs. J. Willis Martin and her High Street Committee of the

Sesquicentennial Celebration of 1926 belongs the credit for the conception of a Book of Honor of Pennsylvania women. Mrs. Edward W. Biddle, first vice-president of that Committee, through her spirited administrative ability and steadfastness of purpose, has successfully carried out the project in its present permanent form.

The several committees of judges who read the nominating articles and selected from among them those which later were placed in the Book of Honor at Strawberry Mansion were:

Hon. John S. Fisher	Late Governor of Pennsylvania
Dr. Hiram H. Shenk	Professor of American History, Lebanon Valley College
Dr. Frederic A. Godcharles	Former Director, State Library
Mr. Ernest Spofford	Former Librarian, Historical Society of Pennsylvania
Dr. C. F. Hoban	Curator, State Museum
Dr. George P. Donohue	Historian
Mrs. Samuel Semple	Titusville
Mr. Edward Robins	President, Historical Society of Pennsylvania
Dr. Julian P. Boyd	Former Librarian, Historical Society of Pennsylvania
Nicholas B. Wainwright	Assistant Librarian, Historical Society of Pennsylvania

SARAH DICKINSON LOWRIE

Philadelphia
March 1942

CONTENTS

ix

CONTENTS

CONTENTS

CONTENTS

CONTENTS

CONTENTS

xvi

CONTENTS xvii

MARIA VON LINNESTAU PRINTZ

early 1600's–?

⚜

THE great Gustavus Adolphus had long cherished a desire to establish a colony in America. His death in 1632 in the Thirty Years' War prevented the realization of this dream. Succeeding him, his daughter, Queen Christina, with her council of state, the wise Axel Oxenstierna as its chancellor, selected Johan Bjornsson Printz to carry out this project, giving him two ships, the *Fame* and the *Swan,* with one hundred souls and equipment for the expedition.

The honor of knighthood was bestowed upon him, and a wise and helpful order of instructions given him for his guidance in the ordering and governing of his colony. Accompanied by his six children and his newly married second wife, he arrived at Fort Christina, February 15, 1643.

Governor Printz selected a new site of strategic importance for the seat of the government farther up the Delaware at Tinicum Island. Here he erected a dwelling built of logs which was called Printzhoff, and a fortress of "hemlock beames laid one upon another" and mounted with four small cannon. This, in honor of the Swedish home city, he named New Gothenburg. Later, in 1646, a church was erected, in the tower of which was hung the bell brought from Sweden, which now hangs in Gloria Dei (Old Swedes') Church, Philadelphia.

Here his lady, the first Governor's wife of Pennsylvania, presided and lived the rigorous life of an early settler. The records have left little as to her personality, and we can only construct her as an individual by deduction. Her portrait is that of a woman of refinement and personal charm. That she was willing to brave the dangers of a perilous voyage to come to an unknown land, almost a savage one, speaks for her courage.

The responsibility of mothering and bringing up six children again bespeaks character. The management of a household such as Printzhoff was in itself a tremendous undertaking. There were no facilities such as lessen labors in our day, and the duties that fell to the lot of

women as enumerated below are appalling. We may suppose, as the
Governor's wife, our First Lady did not physically perform all these,
but as mistress of her home they came under her supervision. There
was a garden—the source of vegetable food; the cattle, milking, making butter and cheese; the spinning and weaving of cloth and linen
and wool; the keeping of nets and seines in order; the making of malt;
brewing of ale; baking and cooking. We must remember these duties
were performed in the most laborious manner. It seems impossible
that there could have been occasion or time for the wife of Governor
Printz to have given consideration to affairs of state and hospitality
such as her position demanded.

Maria Von Linnestau Printz must have been a clever as well as
diplomatic woman to have managed her husband, who comes down
to us in history as a man of unusual character, extremely difficult of
temper and exacting in all things. After about ten years of colony life
at Tinicum Island, Maria Von Linnestau Printz returned to the home
country with her husband and four of his daughters, arriving in
Sweden in the early spring of 1654.

HANNAMEEL CANBY PAXSON

ARMEGOT PRINTZ PAPEGOJA

1627?–1695

ARMEGOT PRINTZ, the eldest of five daughters of Governor Johan
Bjornsson Printz, accompanied her father to New Sweden in 1642.
About three years later she became the wife of Count Johan Papegoja.
There were intercessions from powerful sources to further this match.
Even Queen Christina added her strong approval. Armegot was not
of the marrying temperament, being a decided character of the earliest
independent woman. She at all times manifested a decision of purpose,
and force of action equal to our most modern times. Although the
name of Madame Papegoja was bestowed upon her, she preferred
to be called by her maiden name, Armegot Printz.

When the time came at the expiration of ten years, for her father,
the Governor, and his family to return to Sweden, Armegot remained

behind and carried on the management of her large estates with great efficiency and shrewd business acumen. Until her husband's return to Sweden in 1654, she was the power that directed and upheld him in the performance of his official duties.

After all the family had left the New World, Armegot moved to her father's estate at Tinicum Island. There she lived in great splendor for those times until Stuyvesant's army came up the Delaware to lay siege of New Sweden. Beautiful Printzhoff, the fortress, and the church, with all of the colony's holdings passed into the hands of the Dutch. Armegot's personal property suffered much during this time, but was later restored to her. She was obliged to take refuge at one of her estates, Printztorp, on the mainland near Upland. Here she engaged in the cultivation of her lands, and the raising of cattle. Only her cleverness and courage saved her from being victimized by the authorities in power. In 1660, upon being ordered to leave Tinicum Island, she complained that she could not "remove on account of her heavy buildings," also "because the Church stands there." Thus she gained permission to remain.

In May 1662 she sold Tinicum Island to De la Grange and his wife for six thousand florins, obtaining a draft on a Holland merchant for half the amount. After removing her personal property to Printztorp, she left for Sweden; but as the remainder of the money was not paid, she set sail again for New Sweden, where she obtained a judgment upon the verdict of a jury for the sum of three thousand florins. The widow of De la Grange was ordered not only to restore the Island to Madame Papegoja, and pay her costs, but also to pay the income which had been received from the place for the time she had lived upon it, and for the buildings which had been allowed to go to waste. Madame de la Grange appealed the case, but Armegot Printz again won out. The Governor confirmed the decision and empowered the sheriff "to put Armegot into possession of the said Island and stock thereon." During the litigation of this important early law case, which covered a period of two years, she lived at Printztorp. Her agriculture and cattle raising, especially at Printztorp, were successfully carried on, her great handicap being shortage of labor at harvest times. To remedy this she was obliged to seek far and near for farmhands.

In 1675 she removed to Tinicum Island, but the estate there had fallen into decay and Armegot was growing weary of the struggle.

She sold the Island about 1676 and removed to Sweden, where she died November 26, 1695.

Armegot Printz was a remarkable woman. She possessed great business ability and determination of character to a marked degree. That she was overbearing and self-willed, with a "temper that often flowed over," was due to an inheritance from a father who was all of these, in addition to many sterling qualities that made him the remarkable man he was.

HANNAMEEL CANBY PAXSON

LYDIA WADE

1646–1701

IN 1664 Lydia Wade, the first American hostess of William Penn, makes her initial appearance in history as a young London bride, her maiden name having been Lydia Evans. An early convert to the Quaker faith, she was then living in the Parish of St. Botolph. Her marriage with Robert Wade was solemnized at the Peel Meeting, in St. Johns Street, on June 28, 1664, on historic ground received from the Crown by the Knights of St. John of Jerusalem.

A few weeks after their marriage the young couple entertained as their guest the gay, young cavalier, William Penn, who had just returned, in his twentieth year, from a two-year sojourn in France. Two great calamities were to visit London within the next two years, the terrible Plague of 1665 and the Great Fire of 1666, but from both of these the Wades were fortunate enough to escape.

Lydia Wade took an active part in the affairs of Friends' Meetings in both England and Pennsylvania. In 1672 she was one of the signers of the epistle sent by London Friends to the women Friends in Barbadoes. In 1674 and 1676 she contributed liberally to aid poor women through the agency of the Women's Box Meeting of London.

She remained in England when her husband removed to America in 1675, but soon followed him to Upland, where she lived in Essex House and dispensed kindly hospitality. Among notables entertained at Essex House was William Penn's cousin, Captain William Markham, the Deputy Governor, who visited them in 1681. In 1682 the Wades were honored by a visit from Charles Calvert, Lord Baltimore, Proprietor of Maryland. Later in the same year William Penn enjoyed their hospitality from time to time. On his return to England in 1684, he sent them his "kind remembrance."

Her husband died in 1698. The following year she was one of those who greeted William Penn upon his return to Pennsylvania on the ship *Canterbury,* which landed at Chester, bearing on board his second wife, Hannah Callowhill, and his daughter, Laetitia.

Lydia died in 1701, leaving no children. Her will disclosed the charitable nature that characterized her life—one of generous philanthropy and unwavering devotion to religious and civic duty.

LYDIA SHARPLESS HAWKINS

CLOTILDE DE VALOIS ZELLER

1660?–1749

THE history of Clotilde Zeller, born De Reni of a cadet branch of the Valois family, a subject of France, but through the persuasion of Governor Keith and the astute Secretary Logan, of Philadelphia, a citizen of Pennsylvania in pioneer days, is a typical one of a European immigrant to these shores.

Born during the liberalism of the Edict of Nantes, when it was the fashion for ladies of high rank to be educated, Margaret de Valois, Countess d'Auvergne, in her chatelaineship at Le Mont Doré left a reputation for letters, while the Countess Clotilde de Valois de Reni, her many-times-removed cousin, fell in love with a scholar, for in her teens she married Jacques de Sellaire—or, if one knew the family across the border, Von Zeller of Castle Zellerstein Zurich and fled from France with him and their children after the revocation of the Edict of Nantes to Holland.

Shortly after their son's marriage in Holland the Zellers journeyed to England, and the Lady Clotilde, as she was recorded there, placed herself, her children, and husband under the protection of Queen Anne, who made them welcome not only in England but, should they choose, in her colonies across the sea. With many of their race and a considerable number of their own class and position, they gladly accepted the chance to begin again in a new world. Clotilde at this time was the sole head of her family, her husband having died, either in London or before their ship arrived at New York in June 1710.

These French immigrants, together with many of the Palatinate Germans who were coming to the Americas for the same reason—freedom to worship God according to their own conscience—had a bitter experience of scant welcome and indifferent choice of lands along the Hudson River. The Zellers and the French group which had placed themselves with the Lady Clotilde for protection and advice found even their second venture farther north, in the Dutch-English province at Schoharie, little to their comfort though they named their settlement L'Ésperance! It was at this juncture that Governor Keith of Pennsylvania paid them a visit and, impressed with their character and worth, invited them over to Pennsylvania by a well-known and already much-used route down the Susquehanna River.

Being French, and already twice warned, the Lady Clotilde was wary of promises. So Jean Henri, her eldest son, with an Indian guide was sent ahead to prospect. Perhaps it was she who stipulated rich lands, as well as clear titles, or perhaps Jean Henri, now in his thirties, was already aware of the soil from a farmer's standpoint. At all events he journeyed down the Susquehanna below where the great river branches at what is now Sunbury, paddled up a creek of some dimensions still known as the Swatara, and so across what is now the Lebanon Valley to a fertile region watered by the Tulpehocken, in which black walnut trees of great age and fine verdure flourished. In the country of Jean Henri Zeller's mother's people, the French tradition was that black walnuts meant fertility and a deep soil. So armed with this assuring promise young Zeller journeyed by foot and canoe back to the Schoharie in northern New York and made his report to his mother and her party.

They accepted the good sign at once, rafts were built, provisions were packed, utensils, canoes, and baggage were assembled, and the contingent set forth, arriving at the Mill Creek region not far from the present Newmanstown and the larger settlement of Womelsdorf in 1723.

Here the Zellers built a fort to protect themselves and their neighbors and procured deeds for land from three Penns—John, Thomas, and Richard. Somewhat later, they helped to start the first church of that vicinity. Under pressure of Indian raids they rebuilt, in 1745, their log fort with stone outside and plaster over wattles inside, placing over the door the carved emblem of their faith, and the family crest as knights of the Holy Roman Empire. About this time the Zeller name was Germanized—Heinrich Zeller—for the America all about them was German, in speech and behavior.

Clotilde de Valois, who saw all this and much else come to pass, lived to be past eighty, and to remain a personage long remembered in her family, a tradition of dignity, of authority, and of exalted if shadowy backgrounds, remaining extant generation after generation.

SARAH D. LOWRIE

HANNAH PENN

1664-1733

It is a fact recalled by few that for six years of Pennsylvania's history as a province the reins of government were held by a woman. This signal honor and responsibility fell to the lot of Hannah Penn, second wife of William Penn, the founder of the Province, and, because of the wisdom and ability with which she discharged her great trust, as well as her inherent nobility of character, her name deserves to shine conspicuously in the annals of the Commonwealth.

The first wife of William Penn was Gulielma Maria Springett, the daughter of Sir William Springett and Mary, daughter of Sir John Proud. They were married on April 4, 1672, at King's Farm, Chorley Wood, one of the few houses connected with the life of William Penn which remains standing. After twenty-one years of happy married life, on February 23, 1694, the fragile "Guli" expired in her husband's arms at the age of forty-nine. Of the seven children born of this union only three survived, and it was not to them, but to the children of Penn's second marriage, that the Province descended.

Penn had been released from his imprisonment as a Jacobite suspect on November 30, 1693, three months before the death of his first wife, and on August 20, 1694, he was reinstated in the government of the Province of Pennsylvania. During the latter months of 1695, he began to manifest an affectionate regard for Hannah, daughter of Thomas Callowhill, a respectable and well-to-do merchant of Bristol, England. Penn's only surviving daughter, Laetitia, now a girl of seventeen, ardently aided the courtship. On March 4, 1696, he was married to Hannah Callowhill in the old Broadmead Meeting at Bristol. After the wedding they went to Worminghurst, which Penn had inherited from his first wife, where they lived until 1697, when they made their home for a time in Bristol.

On December 3, 1699, seventeen years after his first visit to the Province of Pennsylvania, Penn returned to it, bringing with him Hannah, and his daughter Laetitia, now a young woman of twenty-one. They first lived at the house of Edward Shippen, on Second Street, north of Spruce, in Philadelphia, afterwards known as "The Governor's House," removing a month later to the famous "Slate Roof House" on Second Street at the corner of Norris Alley. Here, on January 29, 1699, was born their first child, John, known in history as "The American." When one year old, this child was described by Isaac Norris as "a comely, lovely babe, who has much of his father's grace and air. I hope he will not want a good portion of his mother's sweetness, who is a woman extremely well beloved here, exemplary in her station, and of excellent spirit."

In her duties as housekeeper, Hannah Penn manifested rare prudence and good judgment, qualities that later stood her in good stead when the burdens of the provincial government rested upon her shoulders. Her devotion to her husband is shown in a letter to James Logan, provincial secretary, near the end of November, 1700, after Penn's return from the prolonged six weeks' session of the Assembly at New Castle, ill from exertion and exposure. She writes:

My husband has been, for some time, especially the two days past, much indisposed with a feverish cold; his sweating last night relieved him, but not so as to be capable of going to town without great hazard of his health, which has prevailed with him to stay till tomorrow, when, if better, he intends not to fail of being in town; wherefore he would have the Council to adjourn, from day to day, till they see him. Also would have thee tell Thomas Story to read over the laws carefully, and observe their shortness and other defects, with memoranda of directions, especially those about courts of justice, marriage, law of property, unreasonable alienation of fines, etc., and what time thou canst spare he would have thee employed on the same subject.

Her days at Pennsbury, the elegant estate of the Proprietor, were happy, as were those of Marie Antoinette at the Petit Trianon, and, like the latter, they presaged a sad and stormy future. Complications with the Crown made it imperative that Penn return to England in defense of his rights. On November 3, 1701, he embarked with his wife, his daughter Laetitia, and his infant son, John, on board the ship *Dalmahoy.*

Hannah Penn had made an excellent impression upon the Province. Isaac Norris, previously quoted, writes of her:

She is beloved by all (I believe I may say in its fullest extent), so is her leaving us heavy and of real sorrow to her friends; she has carried under and through all with a wonderful evenness, humility, and freedom; her sweetness and goodness have become her character, and are, indeed, extraordinary. In short, we love her, and she deserves it.

The next eight years brought nothing but turmoil and vexation to William Penn. His efforts to sell his province to the Crown met with failure, his debts increased, and the exorbitant demands of Philip Ford, the Quaker manager of his estates in Great Britain, led to his confinement for debt in the Fleet Street Prison. At the end of nine months his friends secured his release, but he was a broken man, and after several strokes of paralysis died on July 30, 1718.

During the last six years of his life, while he was too weak in body and mind to attend affairs of government, Hannah administered not only her large household, but the government of the Province of Pennsylvania. None has risen to say that she failed in either direction. In 1716, when the Council joined in an address to the Proprietor asking the recall of Charles Gookin, Deputy Governor, Mrs. Penn received the appeal, and with great good judgment appointed Sir William Keith, a Scotch nobleman, whose administration proved very popular with the people. During his term of office, paper money was first issued by the Province, and Hannah was enabled to pay off her husband's debts and mortgages.

William and Hannah Penn had seven children. Three died in childhood; the daughter Margaret (1704–1750) married Thomas Freame;

and three sons, John (1699–1746), Thomas (1701–1775), and Richard (1705–1771), succeeded to the proprietorship under the final settlement of their father's will.

Two months after her husband's death, Hannah had made her will, dated September 11, 1718. In it she is described as "Hannah Penn, Widow, the relict of William Penn, late of Ruscombe in the county of Berks." She divided her personalty and estate into six parts. The oldest son, John, was left three-sixths, with the direction that he should pay his sister, Margaret, two thousand pounds on her marriage or when she reached the age of twenty-one. Three-sixths went to the other sons, Thomas, Richard, and Dennis, the latter of whom died before his mother.

Hannah Penn, who since the incapacity of her husband had proved herself such a capable and prudent executive, died on December 20, 1733, aged sixty-nine years, after suffering for some time from a stroke of paralysis. Her body was laid beside that of William Penn in the graveyard of the old Jordan Meetinghouse in Buckinghamshire, England.

During her husband's active life, she had shared his cares and trials cheerfully and uncomplainingly, and after his decline in health and mentality, she gravely bore these burdens alone. Born and raised amidst wealth, her closing years were a hard struggle for existence. Once her resources were so low that she wrote to her son Thomas, then fourteen years of age, that she had been compelled to draw on him for ten pounds. Cheerless as was her life under these conditions, history does not record that she ever expressed a regret over her lot, or that she failed to face every situation that arose with courage, fortitude and good judgment. She lived at a crucial time in the history of Pennsylvania, and her life, so rich in the elements of character, so loyal in its devotion to duty, belongs to the Commonwealth as an inspiration and a model to its womanhood for all time to come.

WILLIAM HOMER AMES

HANNAH LLOYD

1666–1726

᙮᙮

HANNAH LLOYD, daughter of Pennsylvania's first chief magistrate under William Penn, was the first woman representative appointed to the General Meeting of Ministers of the Society of Friends.

Born at Dolabran, North Wales, July 21, 1666, she was the eldest of ten children. Her father, Thomas Lloyd, was a staunch and upright Quaker who at one time suffered eight years' imprisonment for the sake of his faith. It was the search for religious liberty that brought him, with his entire family, to this country in 1683, to take up his residence in Philadelphia and become the faithful assistant and right-hand man of William Penn.

Shortly after the arrival of the Lloyds in the new land, Mrs. Lloyd died and the care of the entire household devolved upon the shoulders of seventeen-year-old Hannah. However, Thomas Lloyd married again and for several years made his home in New York. It was here that Hannah met John Delavall, a young merchant of that city, who fell in love with her and asked her to marry him. But Delavall was not a Friend, and the Quaker maid refused to marry outside her faith. As a result of this the young man was eventually converted and received into the Society of Friends. They were married on March 31, 1686. Delavall later became a minister and preached the religion of his adoption until his death on June 10, 1693.

Except for the fact that she was active in charitable works little is known of Hannah Delavall's life during the years that followed, until August 1700, when she married again. Her second husband, Richard Hill, was also a merchant who, although born in Maryland, had resided for some time in London.

In the year 1704 Hannah is mentioned in the Meeting of Ministers in Philadelphia, after which traces of her attendance at meetings were frequent. That she was a brave and dauntless woman, zealous in her determination to spread the Gospel, is testified by the fact that she traveled fearlessly through the wilderness, preaching and lending aid, both spiritual and physical, to all with whom she came in contact. Her memorial says:

Though not large in appearance, yet with great modesty and soundness of expression, "her doctrine dropped as the dew, and distilled as the small rain." She traveled in the service of the Gospel to New England and divers other parts of this continent, and was also concerned for the good order and discipline of the church, having for a number of years served in the station of clerk of the Women's Monthly, Quarterly, and Yearly Meetings, wherein she gave satisfaction.

During the latter part of her life she was in poor health, but despite the fact remained active in charity up to the time of her death, December 25, 1726, at the age of sixty.

S. HARBERT HAMILTON

LAETITIA PENN

1678-1746

AN English girl who spent less than two years in America might well have her title questioned to a place among the notable women of Pennsylvania. The fact, however, that this girl was the daughter of the great Proprietor himself and was here with him throughout his second visit to Philadelphia gives her a unique place in the annals of the Colony. This is all the more true in view of her ownership of extensive property, a part of which is now included in one of the most famous historic sites of the world.

Laetitia was the daughter of William Penn and his first wife, Gulielma Maria Springett. She was born in Sussex at Worminghurst, the home that Gulielma had inherited from her father, Sir William Springett. Shortly before Penn sailed for America in 1682 he sent a letter to his wife in which he calls her "the love of my youth and the joy of my life." At the same time he wrote to each of his three children a letter on one sheet of paper which is preserved in the Historical Society of Pennsylvania. That to his little daughter reads, "Dear Letitia, I dearly love ye and would have thee sober, learn thy book, and love thy Brothers. I will send thee a pretty Book to learn in Ye Lord bless thee and make a good woman of thee."

The years passed. Laetitia had not yet grown to womanhood when her mother died, so that it was with a stepmother she accompanied her father to Pennsylvania in 1699. For a month they lived at the home of Edward Shippen, on Second Street, above Spruce, and then moved to the "Slate Roof House." The house that had been completed in time to be Penn's home during the latter part of his first visit now seemed too small and plain, though the grounds extended from Front to Second and halfway from High to Chestnut streets. In 1701 Penn conveyed this house and "great lot" to Laetitia.

Tishe, as her father calls her in his letters of this time, was probably a lively and self-willed young lady. Watson tells of at least one "playful freak." She must have soon tired of the new life, however, for Penn wrote Logan in 1701, "I cannot prevail on my wife to stay, and still less on Tishe. I know not what to do."

When the Penns left Philadelphia soon afterward the Friends' Meeting gave her a certificate stating that she "hath well behaved herself here . . . being well inclined, courteously carriaged, and sweetly tempered in her conversations amongst us, and also a diligent comer to Meetings." Not many months had passed before the news came that she was to marry William Aubrey, a merchant of London, whereupon one William Masters made a great to-do over what he claimed was her engagement to him. Logan warns Penn of the jilted suitor's indignant departure for London, and Penn writes in high dudgeon of those who were "striving for William Masters." After Laetitia's marriage, August 20, 1702, her brother wrote that "Masters made a mighty noise here, but it lasted not long." Years later, Laetitia's nephew, Richard Penn, when Governor of Pennsylvania, married Mary Masters, the daughter of her old suitor, and lived in the handsome brick house built by the bride's mother, later to be known as Washington's Mansion.

William Penn soon had reason to regret his daughter's choice of a husband, for William Aubrey fairly hounded him for the payment of Laetitia's dowry of £2,000. As Penn said in a letter to Logan, "Both son and daughter clamor, she to quiet him." In his will Penn left her ten thousand acres of land. Among her holdings were Mount Joy Manor, comprising the greater part of what is now Valley Forge Park, and Steyning Park Manor. The latter has been marked by the Pennsylvania Historical Commission as fifteen thousand five hundred acres patented by William Penn, for "Fatherly Love" and one beaver skin yearly to his daughter, Laetitia Penn, October 23, 1701. Today a site within the boundaries of this old grant is occupied by the town of Kennett Square.

By 1731 Laetitia Aubrey was a childless widow. Her will made in 1744 left money and plate to nephews and nieces, while all her American estate was bequeathed for life to William Penn, 3rd, and after him to his daughter, Christiana Juliana, later Mrs. William Gaskill. At the time of her death in 1746 she was living in Spitalfields, London. Her grave is with that of her family in the quiet burying ground of Jordan's.

ANNA LANE LINGELBACH

GRACE GROWDON LLOYD

1679–1760

GRACE GROWDON was born in 1679, in Bucks County in the home of her father, Joseph Growdon, Speaker of the Assembly and one of the most powerful leaders in the Colony.

On March 31, 1697, the eighteen-year-old daughter of Speaker Growdon became the bride of David Lloyd in Friends' Meeting. Their first and only child, Thomas Lloyd, Jr., was born on January 27, 1698, at the southwest corner of Second and Moravian streets, Philadelphia. This was said to have been the first brick house in the city. It was erected by the Griscom heirs nearly opposite the "Slate Roof House," built by Samuel Carpenter and occupied a few months later by Governor Penn and his little son John.

On June 2, 1701, when young Thomas was three and a half years old, Mrs. Lloyd made a short visit to Maryland, leaving the child with her housekeeper. While she was away the child was punished by being shut in a dark closet, and terror caused convulsions from which he died. This sorrow seems to have caused them to build the house in Chester, on Edgemont Avenue, which still stands. But Mr. Lloyd was too busy to leave Philadelphia, and they continued in their Second Street home until 1710, when they took up residence in Chester. They were living there seven years later when Mr. Lloyd was made Chief Justice under Governor Keith. As the Chief Justice owned most of the waterfront from the creek northward they soon began preparation of a mansion, which was erected in 1721 on Welsh Street and was one of the most notable houses in the colony. Here they lived until the Chief Justice died in 1731.

They had a housekeeper, Jane Fenn Hoskins, who was a talented and earnest Quaker preacher, and ten years after the Chief Justice's death Mrs. Lloyd adopted her as a daughter and gave her and her husband the mansion, reserving only a small part for herself.

Grace Growdon Lloyd died at eighty-one in July 1760. In her will, a notable instrument, she gave about a thousand dollars to Penn Charter School in Philadelphia to be used for poor children; she provided that certain of her Negroes should be freed when thirty years old. Two others she set free at once, and provided a burial ground for Negro Quakers.

BURTON ALVA KONKLE

MARGARET WATSON

before 1683–?

THE land of William Penn was governed with wisdom and clear judgment, though at times ignorance and prejudice sought to lead the way to violence. In February 1683–84 the minutes of the Provincial Council record the only case of witchcraft noted in the Colony.

Margaret Watson was "examined and about to be proved a witch," whereupon the Council ordered that Neels Watson should give bail in fifty pounds for his wife's further appearance before the Judges. Then the Council again being met, a Grand Jury was present and Governor Penn gave them their charge. Many witnesses attested to spells of witchcraft, to all of which Margaret had pleaded guilty.

The jury retired and finally brought in a verdict of "having the *common* fame of a witch but not guilty in manner and *forme* as she stands Indicted." Thus ended the only trial for witchcraft in Pennsylvania. William Penn himself presided at the trial. His calm judgment saved the day and Margaret Watson was freed.

MARY ALLEN CALEY

MADAME MONTOUR
1684?–1752?

EARLY pages in the history of the Provincial and Proprietary governments of Pennsylvania contain many descriptions of the cruelties and depredations of the Indians; of hostilities against the red men upon the part of the white settlers and of numerous councils held by representatives of the French, English, and Indians.

Naturally interpreters were essential at all such conferences, and it is an interesting fact that one of the most intelligent and influential interpreters during the early half of the eighteenth century was a woman—Madame Montour. History credits her with having guided hostile Indian chiefs and belligerent white settlers toward many an amicable adjustment of their difficulties.

Mr. Frederic A. Godcharles, in his *Daily Stories of Pennsylvania*, says that there has always been a question of doubt as to her birth. She claimed to be a half-breed Indian descended from a French nobleman and an Indian woman, probably a Huron. He further states his conclusion that she was born previous to the year 1684, being possibly a French Canadian without any admixture of Indian blood, and that for some reason she preferred the life and dress of her adopted people. In Appleton's *American Biography* it is stated that she was a half-breed supposed to have been the daughter of Count de Frontenac, Governor of New France. When she was ten years old, it is said she was captured by the Iroquois, and was afterward adopted by a Seneca tribe. At all events she later married a young Seneca chief named Roland Montour and became the mother of five children.

She first appeared as an official interpreter at an important council in Albany in 1711, summoned by the French and British authorities and the chiefs of the Six Nations. In Philadelphia in 1727 she served as the official interpreter at a great conference between the Deputy

Governor, Patrick Gordon, and the Provincial Council on the one hand, and the chiefs of the Six Nations on the other.

Though her course as interpreter was always without prejudice to the interests of the Indians, she was uniformly loyal to the Proprietary government of Pennsylvania. Two of her sons, Henry and Andrew, became prosperous citizens of that commonwealth. Andrew at an early age followed his mother's example and became an official interpreter. Like her, he served the Proprietary government faithfully. His ability and loyalty received generous recognition through large land grants in what are now Northumberland and Lycoming counties.

In 1734 Madame Montour was living in a village in Lycoming County. She was present at the great treaty at Lancaster in 1744. Always upon such occasions her refined manners and attractive personality secured for her many courtesies. She was a woman of fearless courage and of undoubted ability, the proof of the latter lying in the fact that an acceptable interpreter for such occasions as she served required a knowledge of both the French and English languages and of numerous Indian dialects.

Mr. Godcharles believed that she died in 1752 at the home of her son Andrew. This son during the French and Indian War was captain of a company of Indians in the English service, later rising to the rank of major. Before this time the French had put a price of five hundred dollars on his head.

Pennsylvania's appreciation and lasting gratitude for the patriotic services of Madame Montour and her two sons is fittingly expressed through the bestowal of their name upon Montour County.

GERTRUDE BOSLER BIDDLE

MARIA FERREE

before 1685–1716

MARIA FERREE was a devout woman who lived in the vicinity of La Fere in France in the latter part of the seventeenth century. Her husband, Daniel Ferree, was a silk manufacturer, a man of wealth and high position. In 1685, the time immediately following the revocation of the Edict of Nantes, when many of the Huguenots fled persecution, the Ferrees left under cover of darkness and reached Strasbourg. After a stay there, they moved on to Lindau in Bavaria, also a free city.

Upon her husband's death, her son Daniel had married Anna Marie Lenninger, her daughter Catharine was married to Isaac LeFever, and the family as a unit took preliminary steps to go to America. With the necessary certificates of standing and passports, Madame Ferree and her family went to England by way of Holland. Shortly after their arrival, she met William Penn. Before him she laid her problem regarding a home in the New World; he arranged for her to be presented to Queen Anne, who had already shown great sympathy for the refugees. Penn granted her a tract of two thousand acres in what is now Lancaster County, Pennsylvania.

After a six months' stay in London, the Ferrees embarked for America, joining a party of fifty-four which had obtained a patent of naturalization and permission to colonize in America. On their arrival in New York, they went to Esopus, about a hundred miles up the Hudson. They were accompanied by some friends who meant to settle there. The Ferrees expected to tarry until they could find a convenient way to go on to Pennsylvania but several years elapsed before they were able to continue their journey.

After a long, tiresome trip over the new country, the Ferrees reached the crest of a hill overlooking the valley of the Pequea. It was on a lovely May evening in 1712. The Indians they met were friendly and talked to them in their broken English; they were some of those who had traded with William Penn. They took the newcomers to their chief, Beaver, who, to show his friendliness, offered them his wigwam. The next day on the great flats of Pequea they met the chief of that branch of the Conestoga Indians.

All the final arrangements for taking possession of the land granted to Madame Ferree by William Penn were arranged by Martin Kendig, who went before the commissioners requesting that the two thousand acres toward the Susquehanna be granted and confirmed by patent to Maria Warenbuer, Madame Ferree, widow.

Not long after her arrival in Pequea, Madame Ferree invested in a plot of ground as a burial place for the settlement. This is still in existence and is known as Carpenter's Graveyard, near Paradise. Although she spent many long years finding a haven, she lived only four years after she had come into her estate in the New World; however, her shining faith, her great courage, and her ability to overcome apparently unsurmountable obstacles have given us a splendid example of a woman's accomplishments more than two hundred years ago.

Her descendants number many well-known men and women, jurists, scholars, ministers, teachers, soldiers and men of affairs in the business world: Major General John F. Reynolds, who made the gallant stand at Gettysburg; Admiral Winfield Scott Schley, of Santiago fame; Judge O. E. LeFevre, of Denver; Judge Landis, of Lancaster; Barr Ferree, former secretary and director of the Pennsylvania Society of New York, were among her distinguished descendants who could look back with pride to their remarkable ancestor.

Mrs. J. W. Happer

QUEEN ALIQUIPPA

late 1600's–1754

Like Pocahontas, Queen Aliquippa, for whom the town of Aliquippa in Beaver County is named, was the daughter of a chief. Whether she came from the Mohawk or the Seneca tribe is a matter of dispute among the writers of Indian history, but it is known that she was married while very young to either a Conestoga chief or a Seneca chief who settled among the Conestogas. That her husband was one of the leaders who signed the famous treaty with William Penn is quite likely, for the friendship of Queen Aliquippa and her family with the great Quaker is known to have extended over a period of years and was so strong that it induced the couple to travel many miles with their young son Canachquasy to New Castle, Delaware, in 1701, where they bade farewell to Penn at the time of his final departure for England.

After the death of her husband, Queen Aliquippa took his place at the head of the tribe. Her home was at the present site of McKees Rocks. Here Celeron mentions visiting her on one of his trips, and reports that she ruled with great authority. Brunot's Island, near Pittsburgh, was formerly called Aliquippa Island and was for a time the home of her tribe.

When Washington went to western Pennsylvania he found her camped at the mouth of the Youghiogheny River. He presented her with gifts and was asked by her to take her son into the white men's councils. Washington did so with befitting ceremony, giving him the English name of Colonel Fairfax, which greatly delighted the aged queen. She was at Great Meadows during Washington's ill-fated campaign, remaining steadfastly loyal to the English settlers, as did her son. After the surrender she went to Aughwick with the other Indians of the Ohio, still retaining her interest and friendliness for the followers of Penn. She died soon after, for on December 23, 1754, George Croghan, then in charge of Indian affairs at Aughwick, reported to the Colonial authorities, "Alequeapy, the old quine is dead."

MARY APPLEGATE THOMPSON

SARAH FINNEY

about 1692–1743

☙❧

THE first settler upon the present site of Reading, Pennsylvania, was Joseph Finney, son of Samuel Finney the elder, a distant relative of William Penn, who accompanied the founder upon his second voyage to Pennsylvania. Upon the return of Samuel Finney to England his son Joseph remained in Pennsylvania, and in 1712 married Sarah, who afterward became the "Widow Finney," so often referred to in early property recitals concerning the site of the town of Reading.

Joseph and Sarah Finney had two sons, Samuel and John. It is probable that the family moved to the Reading location in 1733, and here both Joseph Finney and his son Samuel died in 1734. Letters of administration were taken out upon both decedents by the widow and surviving son, John, but no inventory was filed, which suggests that there was little property except the lonely house and 150 acres on the Schuylkill. Neither of the sons married, so when John Finney died in 1738 his part of the tract passed to his two sisters, Anne and Rebecca.

The Widow Finney continued to occupy her home in the wilds after the death of her husband and son. She must have been a woman of great hardihood and resource to dwell so long in that remote outpost of settlement. In the documents which she executed she made her mark, so she probably was illiterate.

But here was the only point of civilization in the neighborhood for ten years, and during that time travelers and surveyors described the site of Reading as "Widow Finney's." Indeed, but for the insistence of the proprietors upon the English appellation the place might have taken the permanent name of "Finney's."

Before the purchase of her tract by the Penns the Finneys had cleared part of the land and planted an orchard, but most of the plain upon which the city proper now stands was covered with virgin timber. A ferry has been installed near the ford where the rough, stony trail of the Tulpehocken Road crossed the Schuylkill by the island to the south of the present Penn Street Bridge; twenty miles to the westward were the Tulpehocken settlements, while northward the savage wilderness stretched away to the French settlements on the St. Lawrence.

Richard Hockley and Richard Peters, the Proprietor's agents, later made the preliminary survey for the town of Reading, and in much of the correspondence relative to the plotting out of the town lots the name of the Widow Finney is prominent.

She died in November 1743, a picturesque pioneer figure, in the midst of the negotiations of the Proprietor in England about his far-away project of a town which has now become one of Pennsylvania's great manufacturing cities.

J. BENNETT NOLAN

ESTHER SAY HARRIS

about 1697–1757

PROBABLY there was no woman who more courageously went out to meet the hard and often dangerous adventures of a pioneer's wife and who lived her part with more fortitude than did the youthful bride of John Harris. Her home was made in the heart of the wilderness in a strategic spot at the crossing of Indian trails. Naturally the location and her husband's Indian trade made this home more or less of a storm center, and later, when the Indian wars came on, a refuge for those settlers who had ventured farther north and west. Many traditions have been handed down of this sturdy, resourceful, well-poised woman—Esther Say.

She, a "lady of superior intelligence and extraordinary energy," was born in Yorkshire, England, and came to Pennsylvania to the home of her kinsman, Edward Shippen, the first Mayor of Philadelphia. There she met her friend John Harris, also from Yorkshire, whom she married in Old Christ Church, in Philadelphia, about 1717.

John Harris, a friend of William Penn and a brave and daring man, had secured a commission to trade with the Indians on the east bank of the Susquehanna River as early as 1705, but had made no permanent settlement. Upon his marriage he took his bride into what is now Chester County, then moving on into Lancaster County and finally settling at Peixton about 1719. The name was soon changed to Harris Ferry and later to Harrisburg.

There in a beautiful spot near the mouth of the present Paxtang Creek as it empties into the Susquehanna River, he dug his well, built his house and sheds, and enclosed all in a stout stockade. At this place where the trails crossed he developed a large trade with the Indians. As time went on his house became a stopping place for travelers and traders.

Esther Say Harris, his wife, took a full share with her husband in the exciting life of this frontier post. It is greatly to be regretted that so few records were kept of the pioneer women so that we have few recorded dates for her. But the historians—Egle, Morgan and Hazzard—have agreed upon the authenticity of the following facts. In this wilderness home she bore and reared five children: Elizabeth, born in 1720, later married to John Findley; Esther, born in 1722, and married to Dr. William Plunkett, of Carlisle and later of Sunbury; John, Jr., born in 1726, the founder of Harrisburg; William, born in 1730; Samuel, born in 1733, and David, born in 1737. When her third child and first son, John, Jr., was eleven months old, she took him, alone some authorities assert, to Philadelphia to be baptized in Old Christ Church, since she was a devout Episcopalian.

The mansion house, situated on the river bank, was surrounded by a stockade for security against Indians. An English officer was at the house one night when by accident the gate of the stockade had been left unfastened. The officer, clothed in his regimentals, was seated with Mr. Harris and his wife at the supper table when an Indian entered the gate of the stockade, thrust his rifle through one of the portholes of the house and pointed it at the officer. The night being damp, the gun simply flashed. Instantly Mrs. Harris clapped the candle out with her hands to prevent the Indian aiming a second time.

One time she sent her servant, an Irish girl, to the attic for a piece of meat. On her return Mrs. Harris noted that the girl had left her lighted candle behind. When asked what she had done with it the girl replied that she had set it down on a keg of black sand. This happened to be a keg of powder. Mrs. Harris instantly went to the attic, cautiously slipped her hands—one on each side—under the candlestick, coolly lifted it out most carefully so no sparks should fall, brought it down, and then reproved the girl for her carelessness.

Several times during the trying days of the Indian raids, when the men collected to man the fort or go up the river to meet the Indians, Mrs. Harris had ridden down toward Lancaster to warn the people that the Indians were coming. Upon one occasion she rode bareback, as there had not been enough time to saddle her horse, and returned without having had a fall. At times she went alone through the wilderness as far as Philadelphia, to give warning and secure aid. The famous ride of Paul Revere rather pales in comparison when one visualizes what the dangers of such a ride must have been for a woman riding alone before 1748.

John Harris died in 1748 at Harris Ferry. Esther Say Harris married William McChesney in 1752 and lived across the Susquehanna River in what is now Newberry Township, York County. She died in 1757 and is probably buried in Silver Spring Church graveyard, though there is no record, nor any stone to mark her grave.

MARGARET L. MACLAY
ANNA A. MACDONALD

SUSANNA WRIGHT

1697–1784

᙭

Susanna Wright was born in 1697, in Lancashire, England. The daughter of a prominent Quaker, John Wright, she followed her family to this country about 1714 and settled with them in Chester County, Pennsylvania.

She had been well educated and possessed an excellent mind which she continued to develop and cultivate in her New World home. Deborah Norris Logan, a good judge of people, wrote of her:

She was small in person and had never been handsome, but had a very penetrating, sensible countenance, and was truly polite and courteous in her address and behavior. She was well acquainted with books; had an excellent memory; and a clear and comprehensive judgment. She spoke and wrote the French Language with great ease and fluency. She had a knowledge of Latin, and could read Italian, and had made considerable attainment in many of the sciences.

Her brilliant mind and vivacious character attracted the men of culture of the times to her father's home in Chester. She corresponded with James Logan, Charles Norris, Samuel Blunston, Benjamin Franklin, and many other prominent men, exchanging and receiving thoughts and opinions on literature, politics, foreign affairs, agriculture, and the many needs of the New World.

In 1722, after her invalid mother had died, her family moved to the banks of the Susquehanna where their friends, Robert Barber and Samuel Blunston, had preceded them. In this remote frontier settlement Susanna assumed the responsibility of her father's household.

Although Samuel Blunston was by rumor a suitor for her hand, she never married. However, the relationship between them was very close, and in his last feeble years she virtually managed his affairs. Upon his death he left her all his possessions for her lifetime. Shortly afterwards she and her brother James moved into the Blunston mansion, where they remained many years. The house, called "Belmont," became the center of much activity in the affairs of Lancaster County. Many came to ask her advice, and many were the disputes she successfully arbitrated. She was often consulted over the settlement of estates and was even resorted to as a physician by the sick.

She took great delight in manufacturing articles required for domestic use, distilling simples and compounding medicinal herbs. She successfully raised flax and attended to the spinning and weaving of her own household linen. For many years she engaged in the rearing of silkworms. In 1752 Robert Proud, the historian, in writing of his visit to James Wright at Hempfield, said that he saw 1,500 worms at their labor under the charge of "the celebrated Susanna Wright." At one time she had sixty yards of silk mantua of her own production. She is credited with having made the first pair of silk stockings in the Province. Charles Norris tells how, in 1759, a pair of them was presented to General Amherst, who vowed that he would not wear them until "he had the pleasure of waiting on His Majesty on his return to England."

Susanna Wright was a champion for the welfare of the Indians and tried to bring them redress after the Paxton boys' outrage at Turkey Hill. She acted as prothonotary after Blunston's death. Another side of her nature was that of poetess. In some of the old magazines short verses may be found with her name attached.

The evening of her life was spent at Hempfield, surrounded by an affectionate group of nephews and nieces. There she died in her eighty-eighth year on December 1, 1784, and was buried in the old Quaker burying ground in Columbia. According to the Quaker custom her grave was not marked, "All lying equal in death."

Susanna Wright was a forerunner of the modern woman, taking a leading part in meeting the responsibilities of her time, and using every opportunity to the fullest advantage for service and helpfulness to her neighbors and friends. Her brilliant mind and executive ability made her a leading figure in the administration and affairs of that part of Pennsylvania.

MARGARET E. WRIGHT
ELIZABETH FITZGERALD HIESTAND

ANN EVE WEISER

about 1700–1781

⋈⋉

ANN EVE, the daughter of Mr. and Mrs. Peter Feg, was born in the Rhenish Palatinate about 1700 and died in Womelsdorf, Pennsylvania, on June 11, 1781.

She came to America with her parents in that flood of fugitive German immigrants whom Queen Anne of England befriended and, in 1710, sent to her colony of New York. They landed in New York harbor on June 13 of that year. There she shared the trials and hardships of that colony for ten years, both in the Hudson and Mohawk valleys. On November 22, 1720, she was married to Conrad Weiser.

In 1729 the family—she was now the mother of four children—moved to Tulpehocken, making their journey on a rude river raft down the Susquehanna and up the Swatara. There they settled on several hundred acres of land just east of the present borough of Womelsdorf, and erected a small stone house (still standing), in which they lived for twenty-seven years, when they took up residence in the new town of Reading. Ten more children were born to them, but only seven of their family reached maturity. It is as wife and mother, hostess and distinguished ancestress that Mrs. Weiser's claims deserve a place among Pennsylvania's notable women.

Conrad Weiser's public duties as official Indian interpreter in this formative period of the State's history, from 1731 to the time of his death on July 13, 1760, called for frequent, long absences from home. It was during these intervals of time that the burden of the management of the home, the farm, and later the store, rested upon his capable wife. That the training of her children was not neglected meanwhile is evidenced by their characters and the positions they came to fill in later life. In the French and Indian War, when the frenzied, death-dealing invasion of their frontier settlements by the Indians came near their neighborhood, four of her five sons old enough to bear arms sprang to the defense of their countryside. They remained in service until after the foe had been driven away and the eldest son had received a wound which shortened his years. Her two daughters were well fitted for responsible positions, the elder as the wife of the eminent Reverend Henry Melchior Muhlenberg, known as the organizer and patriarch of the Lutheran Church in America. The younger daughter was first married to a Mr. Heinzleman, and then to Mr. Anthony Fincker, both men of note in the history of Reading.

Mrs. Weiser survived her husband by twenty-one years, served as executrix of his will, disposed of his complicated estate, and exerted a strong personal influence upon her children and grandchildren. While her name is not recorded in volumes of great achievements, her influence was felt for many generations. Among her direct descendants may be counted one United States senator and six congressmen, of whom one, her grandson, Frederick A. C. Muhlenberg, was the Speaker of the First, Third and Fourth United States congresses. She had (for she was still living) another grandson as major general in the Revolutionary War, a friend of Washington, General Peter Muhlenberg, and at least a score of other grandsons fighting in the ranks or collecting or hauling food and clothing for Washington's suffering army at Valley Forge. John Andrew Schulze, one of Pennsylvania's most capable and popular governors, was her greatgrandson, as was also Henry A. Muhlenberg, United States Minister Plenipotentiary to Austria.

Her domestic virtues shine down during six generations. Her kitchen and connected bake-oven are fortunately preserved, and such household tools and implements as she used to serve her day and generation. There she baked and cooked; there she sewed and spun; there she entertained long lists of relatives and daily fed her numerous family. It was seldom that her board was not graced by some relative or noted guests. We know that she entertained Shekilammy and other Indian chiefs frequently between the years 1731 and 1749. In 1743 she entertained the young Lutheran missionary, the Reverend Henry M. Muhlenberg, sent from Halle to the scattered Lutherans of Pennsylvania, and during these visits he fell in love with her eldest daughter, Annie Marie, whom he married April 22, 1745.

During these years three Moravian ministers were guests in her home while learning from her husband the Indian dialect to fit them as missionaries. Among others whom she entertained at various times were the renowned Moravian divine, Count Zinzendorf, John Bartram, the noted botanist of Philadelphia, and Lewis Evans, geographer and famous map-maker of Pennsylvania. Others who were glad to take advantage of her hospitality included Robert Morris and James Logan, friends of her husband.

P. C. CROLL

ANNE SHIPPEN WILLING

1710–1790

🦋

ANNE SHIPPEN was born in Philadelphia in the early years of its founding. Her activities spanned the full Colonial period. She lived to see the city of her birth become the birthplace of a nation, and lived through the long years of war, the framing of the Constitution and its acceptance by the Thirteen Colonies, and the inauguration of Washington as first president of the new Republic. Ere she passed from this life, she saw her home city chosen capital of the United Colonies. To review the life of Anne Shippen Willing is to recall one of the most distinguished of Philadelphia's many honored matrons in that circle of men and women, whose position, education, literary tastes, scientific and philanthropic interest, gave Philadelphia a pre-eminent place in the early years of America's independence.

Edward Shippen, grandfather of Anne, of good Yorkshire family, immigrated to Boston when thirty years of age, in 1668. During a residence there of twenty-five years he prospered in business; Shippen's wharves and his home on the waterfront appear on the early maps of Boston. He married Elizabeth Lybrand, uniting as the generations grew two strong influences that have ever been distinctive characteristics in Philadelphia life and history. The persecutions of Old England, extending to Massachusetts Bay, were a principal cause for his seeking a home in a more congenial environment. In 1693–94 he sold his property and came to Philadelphia. There he soon became a leader, socially, politically, and intellectually.

Anne was the daughter of his son Joseph, who lived in Boston, and had married Abigail Grosse, a family name listed in the *Book of Possessions* of Boston's first settlers. In 1704 they moved to Philadelphia, with two children. Of this journey a friend wrote, "she came all the way from Boston on horseback. Nor is that all—she brought a baby with her safely, resting it all the way on her lap." Anne was the fifth child and the only daughter who reached maturity. Her mother died in 1716, leaving seven children. Little Anne was thus early able to show a loving motherhood to the two younger children. She had a stately beauty and a strong character.

At the age of twenty she married Charles Willing. He was comparatively a newcomer, from his home in Bristol, England, where he was born May 18, 1710, the son of Joseph Willing and his wife Ava Lowie. At eighteen he came to Philadelphia to assume charge of a mercantile business already established by his brother, Thomas, who returned to England. He prospered and speedily attained influence in business circles. His home, Third Street below Walnut, at the southwest corner of Willings Alley, stood for more than a century. Here he and his charming wife dispensed continuous and generous hospitality. He was a member of Associators in 1744, Dancing Assembly, 1748–49, one of the founders of the University in 1754, mayor of Philadelphia in 1748 and again in 1754. When he died in the latter year of "ship fever," he was "lamented by a whole community."

After twenty-four years of happy married life, we find Anne bravely meeting the responsibilities of life, widowed, with eleven children, five sons and six daughters, the eldest a son of twenty-three, the youngest a babe of one year. All but three married and left issue.

Thomas, the eldest, was educated in England by his paternal grandfather. He entered business with Robert Morris and became a leader in the mercantile world, holding high official positions. Nine years after the death of his father, he too became mayor, in 1763. He was also Associate Justice of the Supreme Court. Though bitterly opposed to British aggression, at the parting of the ways he cast his vote against separation, thus failing to become with his partner, Robert Morris, a signer of the immortal Declaration. He is best known today for his career as a banker.

James, the youngest son, was a captain in the Revolution, was captured by the British, confined on the prison ships, suffered incredible hardships and died unmarried, as did Richard, Speaker of the House, who is buried in Christ's Churchyard.

Such an attractive group of daughters must have brought many suitors to the home; to name their husbands is to emphasize the quality of Philadelphia society at that time. Anne was married to Tench

Francis; Dorothy married Sir Walter Stirling, captain in the Royal Navy, and went to England to live; Mary married Sir William Byrd, 3d, of Westover, Virginia; Elizabeth married Samuel Powel in 1769, the last mayor under the Charter of 1701 and the first mayor under the Charter of 1789; Margaret, the youngest, was married to Robert Hare.

LOUISE KENT KEAY

REBECCA LYON ARMSTRONG

1719–1797

REBECCA LYON, daughter of William Lyon, was born in Enniskillen, County Fermanagh, Province of Ulster, Ireland, on May 2, 1719. Her father was a large land proprietor, who gave all the advantages of a superior education to his children and at his death left them a competency.

At about the age of twenty, Rebecca Lyon married John Armstrong and came with him to America. During the period of the Provincial wars, and subsequently the Revolution, Mrs. Armstrong, then residing at Carlisle, became one of the most prominent women of the Cumberland Valley. Her husband, Colonel Armstrong, destroyed the Indian town of Kittanning, September 8, 1756. From this time he dated his friendship with General Washington. Armstrong also commanded the Pennsylvania troops at Fort Duquesne. He was later a brigadier general of the Continental Army and major general in the Pennsylvania Militia, and a member of the Continental Congress.

Apart from her husband's distinguished career, it was owing to her services during the Indian wars in caring for the settlers who fled to Carlisle from the distant frontiers that Rebecca became noted for her sympathy and great benevolence. In a copy of the Reading *Eagle,* taken from an editorial in the Altoona *Tribune,* Colonel Henry Shoemaker named Rebecca Armstrong among fifty of the most famous Pennsylvania women, because of her maintenance of an establishment, at her own expense, for wounded soldiers of the French and Indian War.

When the Revolution opened, she led the women of Carlisle into active preparation for assistance to patriots who had enlisted. Organizing a society, the first in Pennsylvania, she superintended the furnishing of many of the comforts required by the soldiers. She was willing to sacrifice everything for the welfare of her fellow countrymen.

At the time of her death, on November 16, 1797, the Carlisle *Gazette* said:

This excellent woman in her very advanced age continued to enjoy the free exercise of a well-cultivated understanding and of her every faculty with much liveliness and vigor. If a disposition, benevolent in a very high degree and ever ready to sympathize and relieve the suffering; if a heart framed to delight in all the characteristics of social life, all the various and important duties of the consort, the mother and the friend; if a constant attendant to the duties and the piety and the ordinances of that Divine Redeemer in whom she trusted for salvation, in perfect concert with the pious partner of her cares for the long period of half a century, can give ground for the most pleasant hopes, her surviving friends may solace themselves with this most important of considerations, that death is to her invaluable and eternal gain.

MARION LEINBACH ARMSTRONG
DOROTHY LEINBACH ARMSTRONG

MARGARET DUNCAN

1721–1802

"MARGARET DUNCAN, merchant, 1 South Water street," in a Philadelphia directory, proclaims the fact that women in business today are simply repeating history. One hundred and fifty years ago, when Clement Biddle was completing his 1791 directory, Margaret Duncan was approximately seventy years old, an alert, active business woman.

Records do not show just how long she carried on her trade; however, she must have been successful for she found time and money to care for her family, take a trip to her native land, Scotland, and when she died at the age of eighty years, she left behind a nice little sum of money. Her husband was Isaac Duncan by whom she had three children—a son, Matthew, and two daughters whose given names we have not been able to obtain; their married names were Mrs. William Bailey and Mrs. David Telfair.

On her voyage back to Philadelphia from Scotland, Mrs. Duncan was shipwrecked, the passengers and crew taking to small boats as the ship went down. In their haste to escape, they neglected to bring enough food to last until they reached land. This made their plight desperate. When they realized that it would not be possible to keep all alive with their scant supply, they decided to cast lots to see who should be sacrificed in order that the remainder of the group could be saved.

The lot fell on Mrs. Duncan and several others. She immediately fell on her knees and prayed that her life might be spared, and made a solemn vow to God that if she were saved her life would be dedicated to Him and that she would build a church in His honor. As if in answer to her prayers the capes of Delaware were soon sighted and the weary passengers safely landed.

When she died in 1802, she left money and instructions that a church should be built to honor God and commemorate her deliverance. This was completed in 1814 and was known as the "Vow Church." The first congregation, the Associate Reformed Presbyterian, entered the Presbyterian Church of the United States of America.

In 1855 the site and church building were sold and a new edifice, the Second United Presbyterian Church of Philadelphia, was built with the proceeds. This is located on Sixteenth Street near Race and is still known as the "Vow Church." On a marble tablet over the door of this church are engraved these words:

"The Second Associate Reformed Church of Philadelphia built in pursuance of the will of the late Margaret Duncan 1814. Rebuilt 1855."

                                                    Mrs. J. W. Happer

MARY KIRK

1722–1804

❧❦

AMONG the women of Northumberland County, Pennsylvania, who performed noble work for family and country during the Revolution, Mary Kirk stands as a woman of energy and resource.

Her father, Moses Kirk, owned a tract of land containing 320 acres called "Partnership," situated on a branch of Warrior Run.

Meginness in his *Otzinachson* states that the families of many settlers gathered in Fort Freeland in the fall of 1778 and lived there that winter for protection from the Indians, among them being the family of Moses Kirk. Moses died before 1779, leaving his widow, Mary, and her ten children in the fort. On July 28, 1779, the British and Indian forces attacked the fort. *Otzinachson* says:

The fort only contained twenty-one effective men and a large number of women and children. But there were brave women in the fort, and when apprised of the danger Mary Kirk and Phoebe Vincent commenced to run bullets for the rifles of the men, and continued at this work as long as they had a dish or spoon that would melt.

But the attackers far outnumbered the besieged, and after a stubborn fight were victorious.

The articles of capitulation, as given in *Otzinachson,* provided that

all men bearing arms are to surrender themselves prisoners of war, and to be sent to Niagara; the women and children are not to be stripped of their clothing, nor molested by Indians, and to be at liberty to move down the country where they please.

Otzinachson continues:

While the respective commanders were discussing the terms of surrender the women were not idle in the fort. Every one put on as much clothing as she could possibly wear, taking care also to fill her pockets with every little thing of value that could be secured in this way.

When Mrs. Kirk heard the terms on which they were set free she put female clothing on her son William, a lad of sixteen, and he escaped with the women.

Mrs. Kirk and her family reached Fort Augusta safely, and after peace was declared returned to the old home. There her children reconstructed the buildings and under her guidance cleared the land and improved it.

Mary Kirk died in 1804, and is buried in the cemetery adjoining the old Warrior Run Presbyterian Church, above McEwensville, near the site of Fort Freeland.

NORTHUMBERLAND COUNTY HISTORICAL SOCIETY

BENIGNA DE WATTEVILLE

1725-1789

ALTHOUGH she lived less than six years of her life in America, and only three years of that consecutively, Benigna de Watteville left in Pennsylvania a memorial of energy and service which endures to this day—the Moravian College for Women at Bethlehem.

Benigna was born on December 23, 1725, at Berthelsdorf, Saxony, as Countess von Zinzendorf, daughter of the Count Nicholas Ludwig von Zinzendorf, an attaché of the Court of Dresden. She was educated by the best tutors available to children of noble birth, by her father, and by the pastor of the Moravian Church, of which her parent was a devout member and ardent patron.

The Count was especially interested in mission work in the New World and in 1741, accompanied by his sixteen-year-old daughter, set sail for America to supervise personally the work of the church in Pennsylvania, particularly the evangelization of Indians. Soon after her arrival, however, Benigna noticed that the children of the colonists were as much in need of education as the Indians were of Christianity, and called her father's attention to the matter. He in turn talked to John Bechtel, of Germantown, and to other associates. The upshot was that on April 3, 1742, a little printed circular appeared inviting parents to meet on April 17 at the Bechtel home to discuss the welfare of their children. At this meeting a school was organized which opened on May 4 in Ashmead House in Germantown, with Benigna as head-mistress and with Magdalena Miller, Anna Desmond, Anton Seyffert, and Zander and George Neisser as her assistants. This was the beginning of what eventually has become the Moravian Seminary and College for Women at Bethlehem. Instruction was given in reading, writing, and "manual instruction," the latter better known now as vocational education.

After six weeks it was deemed advisable to move the school to Bethlehem, where it was temporarily established in the old log Gemein Haus. Later it was removed to Nazareth for a time, but in 1749 was definitely and finally located in Bethlehem.

However, the Zinzendorfs, father and daughter, had returned to Europe in 1743, and there in 1746 the young Countess married John, Baron de Watteville. In 1747 he was consecrated a bishop of the Moravian Church and in 1748 was sent to America. His bride accompanied him on the trip. They landed in New York in 1749, traveling at once by coach to Bethlehem, where Benigna was much gratified to note the progress of the school. They returned to Europe soon after and it was not until thirty-five years later that they came to America again—in 1784, after the Revolution.

On this trip their ship encountered storms and was blown off its course and finally wrecked on one of the islands of the West Indies. De Watteville and his wife were rescued, however, and managed to get another vessel for Philadelphia, where they arrived June 2, 1784. They immediately went on to Bethlehem, where Benigna found that "her" school had grown so much it had become highly necessary to change its administration and convert it into a regular boarding school. She supervised this change and was present at its reopening on October 2, 1785.

A few months later the De Wattevilles sailed for home. Benigna died there in 1789 and is buried in the Hutberg, ancient burial place of the Moravians in Saxony. Her portrait in oils hangs in the hall of the Moravian Seminary in Bethlehem.

ELIZABETH L. MYERS

LYDIA DARRAGH

1728–1789

⁂

RARELY has a house in the "City of Homes" been deserving of more distinction than the home of Benjamin Loxley, created a lieutenant of artillery in 1756, on the occasion of Braddock's defeat. The house was known as Loxley House and stood at the corner of Little Dock and Second streets, Philadelphia. It was the key to this house which Captain Loxley's friend, Benjamin Franklin, used in his famous kite experiment.

It is also memorable as affording from its gallery a preaching place for the great Whitefield, his audience occupying the street (then out of town) and Society Hill opposite, at the margin of Bethsheba's Bath and Bower. On Society Hill lived Lydia Darragh during the occupation of Philadelphia by the British in Revolutionary days.

Lydia Darragh was the daughter of John Barrington, of Dublin, Ireland. She married William Darragh in the Friends' Meeting House, Sycamore Alley, Dublin, in 1753. Shortly after their marriage they came to this country and lived for the remainder of their days in Philadelphia, becoming members of the Monthly Meeting of Friends in that city.

While the British held possession of Philadelphia the officers appropriated the most desirable dwellings in the city for their headquarters. General Harris was camped in the palatial home of General Cadwalader. A place being required for a Council Chamber made the roomy Loxley House most desirable. The Darraghs were asked to vacate, but at Lydia's earnest solicitation, because of her inability to domicile her family elsewhere, the British agreed to accept the use of two rooms only.

One day Lydia was notified that a meeting would be held that evening and the officer added significantly: "You need not await our departure. In fact, be sure to go to bed early, you and all your family. When we are ready to leave, I will knock at your door, that you may rise and close after us."

Wakeful and anxious on overhearing the words "Washington" and

"Whitemarsh," the quick-witted Quakeress realized that business of special importance was on foot, and fearing it meant disaster for the Continental Army she determined to hear the rest. She overheard the plan for the surprise attack on the Army at Whitemarsh. The meeting being ended, she feigned sleep and only after repeated knocking answered the call.

As two of her children were absent in the country she had in her possession a pass granted through the intercession of her relative, Captain William Barrington. She was determined to get through to the camp with the information she had gleaned. Pretending need of flour from the mill at Frankford, she left home and started on her journey, ostensibly to the mill. Once outside of the city, she made all haste toward the American camp. On her way she met Lieutenant Colonel Craig, an American officer of her acquaintance, and told him what she had heard, asking that the information be carried to Washington without revealing her identity. The reply was "You have saved the Army, and you will not be forgotten as long as liberty endures." Obtaining the sack of flour, she returned to her home. With an anxious heart she listened to the departure of the British forty-eight hours afterwards. While Howe advanced with surety Washington was making preparation to meet him.

The frustration of the plan is history. But Lydia had yet to face the foe. On the night after the return of the British troops, Adjutant General Howe sent for her. "What I wish to know," he said, "is whether any of your family was up after 8 o'clock on the night I conferred with the other officers in your sitting room." She shook her head. "Thee knows that we all went to bed at eight o'clock." "I know that you were asleep, for I had to knock at your chamber door three times before you were aroused. But I wondered if anyone else was about. Someone must have given Washington information concerning our march. I know you were in bed; you say the others were also. I can't imagine who gave us away unless the walls had ears."

Lydia's methods of communication with the Army read like fiction. Her husband being a skilled shorthand writer was able to help. The messages in cipher on small bits of paper were concealed under the covers of the buttons used as trimmings on coats, and her son Charles, a member of the Continental Army, was trained to decipher them.

Lydia Darragh died in Philadelphia, December 1789, in the sixty-first year of her age, and was laid to rest in the Friends' Burial Ground, at Fourth and Arch streets.

Mrs. Montrose Graham Tull

SUSANNA HUNTINGTON DANA

1730–?

Susanna Huntington, the daughter of Caleb and Lydia Griswold Huntington, was born June 23, 1730. On June 5, 1757 she was married to Anderson Dana, a French Protestant, who had settled at Brighton, Massachusetts, in 1740.

In the fall of 1772 they moved with their family to Wyoming Valley in Pennsylvania, on the Susquehanna River. This hazardous three-hundred-mile journey was made when the youngest of her seven children was but two months old. Her sixth was a little boy of three who held on behind her as her horse picked its way over the rough roads and trails. When this boy, who became the Reverend Sylvester Dana, died, the Reverend George D. Horton said at his funeral on June 11, 1849:

For six years the Dana family prospered. In 1778 the father represented the town of Westmoreland in the General Assembly of Connecticut. Returning home the morning of the Battle of Wyoming after an absence of eight weeks, he stopped at his home only long enough to tell his wife, Susanna, to care for his papers if she were obliged to flee to Connecticut with her children. He rode on and was an actor (and a victim) in that tragic scene which occurred in the beautiful Valley of Wyoming.

On the third day of July 1778, a band of British soldiers and Tories led by Colonel John Butler, together with seven hundred Indians, attacked and utterly destroyed the settlement. Susanna and her seven children fled with the rest in a state of utter destitution. Her husband and eldest daughter dead, her home destroyed, she was barely able to make good her escape. Before she set off through the wilderness she lowered her valuables down the well, gathered some provisions, and, mindful of her husband's instructions, and as if there were still something besides present salvation, she collected his papers and public documents and carried them off in a pillowcase. During their flight she and her children underwent the most fearful privations and hardships before they reached safety in Ashford.

When she returned to Wilkes-Barre seven years later she brought the papers with her and with them aided in establishing the claims of the settlers to the rich coal lands of the Wyoming Valley. Her descendants justly feel that she was indeed a heroine of the Revolution and are proud of her in her rôle of wife, mother, and benefactor of the settlers and their descendants.

Augusta Dana Chase

ANN WEST LOWREY

1730–1791

Ann West, daughter of Francis West, was born in 1730 and received her early education in Philadelphia. When Cumberland County was organized her father was appointed one of the first justices, a position which he held until his death in 1770. In 1765 Ann West became the wife of Hermann Alricks, who died in 1772 in Carlisle. The following year his widow married Alexander Lowrey, a wealthy Indian trader of Donegal.

When the war of the Revolution broke out Mr. Lowrey was outspoken for the cause of freedom. In 1774 he was placed on the Committee of Correspondence and later became a member of the Provincial Conference of July 1774. He also was a member of the conference which convened in Carpenter's Hall in 1776, and of the later Constitutional Convention. He was in active service in the Revolutionary Army as senior colonel of Lancaster County troops. When Congress was in session at York there was a constant stream of distinguished visitors who came to cross the Susquehanna at Anderson's Ferry near the home of Colonel Lowrey.

Ann West Lowrey was active from the first in collecting material for clothing for the army and in assisting in making up the material. She was a leader in her community in sewing for the soldiers of the

Colonies. In this she secured many helpers who met regularly in her spacious home to organize women's committees for the cause of the Revolution and to work day by day on material for the patriot troops.

No more hospitable home was known in the Colonies than that of Ann West Lowrey of Donegal. Her contribution to the cause of the Revolution was a woman's contribution, but a noteworthy one because she inspired many to contribute to the existing needs. With her death on November 21, 1791, passed away one of the most hospitable, generous, and active women of the Revolutionary period.

W. F. LUTZ

ANN GALBRAITH

before 1732–?

LANCASTER witnessed in 1732 a contest for the Assembly seat between John Wright, an English Quaker, and Andrew Galbraith, a representative of the Scotch-Irish group. With feeling running high the principal feature of the race occurred when Galbraith absolutely declined to do any campaigning. Then it was that Ann Galbraith, his wife, came upon the scene. She was a woman of singular strength of character and influence in the community, with a keen intelligence and complete independence of spirit. Not for a moment was she ruled by any subjection to conventions in a day when women were greatly restricted in any field of endeavor outside the home. When these came in conflict with the driving force of Ann Galbraith, they were brushed aside as though they did not exist.

Ann had no idea of passively allowing an English Quaker to be elected to the Assembly because her Scotch-Irish husband refused to make any personal effort. So at the psychological moment she saddled her favorite mare, Nelly, and "booted and spurred for action"—she certainly had a spur on her stirrup ankle—with her riding cape like a "red badge of courage" floating in the breeze, she started on her tour of Lancaster County. Her efforts rounded up a large following of mounted men whom, like the commander of a regiment, she led in a procession to the steps of the Lancaster Courthouse.

One can see the picture as she turned and addressed the group, with the scarlet cape making a vivid and imperial background for her intrepid figure. She had the assured confidence and impassioned eloquence of the born leader. These qualities, combined perhaps with that subtle, persuasive influence known as "the eternal feminine" stirred her cohorts to enthusiastic support. Ann's triumph was complete when Andrew Galbraith was elected to the Assembly, where he served for five years.

Undoubtedly this speech was the first of its kind made by a Pennsylvania woman, and its great interest for the women of this state lies in the fact that Ann Galbraith, by her brilliant entry into the arena of American politics, became a herald of the dawn of the emancipation of woman.

RUBY H. RUSSELL

ANNE WOOD HENRY

1732–1799

ANNE WOOD was born at Burlington, New Jersey, on January 21, 1732. Her father was Abraham Wood and her mother Ursula Taylor. Upon the death of Abraham, his wife moved to Burlington, where Anne was born. Some years later Anne's mother married Joseph Rose and moved to Lancaster. Here Anne married William Henry in January 1755. He had been a successful gunsmith in Lancaster for some years.

As her husband was away on military duties much of the time, she took over the management of his store. Shortly after her marriage her husband served as armorer with the Braddock expedition and later in the same capacity with the Forbes expedition.

Anne Wood Henry was a typical matron of the Revolution, a woman of great energy and fine character and in full sympathy with her husband's actively patriotic life. Their home was the rendezvous of many prominent patriots. While the English held Philadelphia, David Rittenhouse, the State Treasurer, had his office there. Thomas Paine spent much time in the Henry home and did some of his best writing there. The talented artist Benjamin West was a frequent guest, and it is reported that he started painting historical scenes at the suggestion of William Henry.

At the outbreak of the Revolution, Henry became an ardent patriot. He was early appointed assistant commissary for Pennsylvania and armorer-general for the Continental Army for the states of Pennsylvania, New Jersey, and Delaware. In 1777 he was appointed treasurer for Lancaster County. His military duties keeping him away from home most of the time, his wife acted as treasurer for him, and upon his death in 1786 she filled his unexpired term. After that she was appointed by the Supreme Executive Council of Pennsylvania to be treasurer for Lancaster County for four years, the only recorded instance of a woman holding such an office in the annals of this state.

Anne Wood Henry died March 8, 1799, and was buried by the side of her husband in the Moravian Cemetery in Lancaster.

MULFORD STOUGH

MARTHA IBBETSON GRAY

1734-1799

MISERIES endured by hundreds of captured soldiers in the old Walnut Street Prison while Philadelphia was in British hands during the Revolution would have been much worse had it not been for the ministrations of Martha Ibbetson Gray.

She was born in London on January 28, 1734. As a young woman she exhibited much interest in surgery and in the care of the sick, and studied both these arts under an able apothecary. She arrived in America about 1750 with her father, Robert Ibbetson. On November 25, 1752, she became the wife of George Gray, of Grays Ferry, her wedding ring being inscribed: "Let Love Abide and God Provide, 1752." Mr. Gray was an outstanding man of his community and, although born a member of the Society of Friends, became a member of the Council of Safety in the early days of the Revolution.

When the British occupied Philadelphia, they captured many Revolutionary soldiers and officers, whom they confined in prison, treating them as rebels under arrest rather than as prisoners of war. It was to these men that Mrs. Gray ministered food and medicine which she supplied at her own expense, while surgical and nursing services were administered by her own hands. This exasperated the British officers, who finally denounced her as a spy, ordering her to leave the city. But she appealed to Lord Howe who permitted her to remain and continue her labor of love; later, when the tables were turned and the prisons housed British troops instead of Revolutionary, it was the King's men who soon came to call her blessed.

Mrs. Gray was the great-grandmother of Dr. Elisha Kent Kane, the explorer and scientist. She died in 1799.

Mrs. J. J. Thompson
Elizabeth Leiper Holmes

RACHEL MARX GRAYDON

1734–1809

Rachel Marx was born on the island of Barbadoes, August 22, 1734. She was the eldest of four daughters. Her father, engaged in the West India trade, was of German birth; her mother a native of Glasgow. When she was seven years old her parents brought her to Philadelphia, where she was well educated.

About the year 1750 she married Alexander Graydon, a native of Langford, Ireland, who at that time was in business in Bucks County. According to William Henry Egle's *Some Pennsylvania Women in the Revolution,* he was a gentleman of considerable prominence, and thoroughly patriotic. In 1747, when a general Indian war was threatened, he was Colonel of the Associated Regiment of Bucks County.

When he died in March 1761, Rachel was left a widow with four children, the eldest scarcely nine years of age. She moved to Philadelphia the better to educate them and obtain a livelihood. With the habits of a lady who might have been bred at court she managed to bring up her family with distinguished manners. She lived in Philadelphia about fourteen years until just before the outbreak of the Revolution, when she moved to Reading.

Alexander, her oldest child, born April 10, 1752, was educated at an academy in Philadelphia and studied law. When the war of the Revolution broke out he accepted a commission as captain of the Third Pennsylvania Battalion, under Colonel John Shee, January 5, 1776. He served with distinction at the battle of Long Island, and was taken prisoner at the surrender of Fort Washington, November 16, 1776. His mother proceeded at once to secure his release. General Washington being unable to do anything for her, this splendid woman undertook a trip to New York, where General Howe made his headquarters.

From Philadelphia a cousin offered to drive her to New York, but in Princeton they were overtaken by a detachment of the American cavalry, which stopped them because her cousin was a Loyalist. Rachel, however, was permitted to go on and, after being detained several days at Brunswick, embarked in a small boat for New York. Although the vessel was fired on from the shore, it at last succeeded in reaching port safely and Rachel lost no time in getting to her son.

She was advised by a man named Calloway to apply to Sir William Howe, and Calloway offered to help her draw up an application in which he explained that Mrs. Graydon was a faithful subject of George III, and her son had been deluded by designing men. At this point Mrs. Graydon refused to go on with the application, and Calloway would give her no further help on any other terms. More determined than ever, Rachel went boldly and unannounced to General Howe, and through her persistence and maternal eloquence succeeded in winning the desired parole for her son.

After this adventure she returned to Reading and, when the war was over, moved to Harrisburg. She was a lady much devoted to her family and, in the early days of the capital city of the state, prominent in deeds of love and charity. She died at Harrisburg January 23, 1809, and is buried there.

MARGARET LITTELL

ELIZABETH WORRELL

1734–1809

꙳

WITH her husband and five sons all enlisted at one time in the Revolutionary Army, Elizabeth Worrell had need of a stern and unfaltering patriotism to contemplate the war for liberty with any degree of equanimity, especially as applied to the possible and ever probable fate in store for these loved ones. Yet, so one of her biographers says of her, she once remarked to a friend that she "wished she had more sons to give to the cause." As a matter of history, two of her sons were killed, two others and her husband wounded, and the fifth son held prisoner by the British for several months. A casualty list, to her, of one hundred per cent.

Elizabeth Worrell was born Elizabeth Harper, on October 8, 1734, daughter of Robert and Sarah Duzby Harper. Little is known of her father's ancestry, but her maternal grandfather was a son of John and Marie Buzby, who came to Pennsylvania in 1682 from Milton, in the parish of Shipton, England. When Elizabeth Harper was nineteen years old she married Isaiah Worrell, great-grandson of Richard and Sarah Worrell, who came from Oare, in Berkshire, England, in 1682. Richard had a large grant of land from William Penn and was among the "first purchasers" in Philadelphia. The Worrells had been among the organizers in 1682 of Oxford Friends' Meeting, and when Elizabeth married into the family she also became a member.

Isaiah and Elizabeth established their home in the house built by Isaiah's father, Isaac, which still stands at 4335 Frankford Avenue. The place now is marked by a bronze tablet commemorating the reception there for General Lafayette tendered by Major General Isaac Worrell in 1824.

Elizabeth Worrell died on April 23, 1809, and with her husband and three generations of Worrells is buried in Oxford Friends' burial ground at Unity and Walnut streets, Frankford.

HALLIE ISABEL DEXTER

ELIZABETH GRAEME (LADY) FERGUSSON

1739–1801

⁂

PERHAPS no other woman of the Provincial and early Revolutionary period in this country had a more distinguished and romantic career than Lady Fergusson. Her history begins with Sir William Keith, baronet of an ancient, rich, and powerful Scot family. When quite young he was appointed by Queen Anne "surveyor general of the royal customs in the American Colonies." The early years of this royal commission he spent in Virginia, "where the refinement and generous living of the wealthy planters and the beauty and intelligence of the Southern women were exceedingly to his taste."

In 1716, in a letter written by James Logan, signed by him and by seven other influential Pennsylvanians, Hannah Penn was urged to appoint Sir William Keith as Deputy Governor of the Province. This was done, and he and his family arrived from England, to which he had returned from Virginia, on May 31, 1717. He took up his residence in the Shippen Mansion, on Chestnut Street, his family consisting of his second wife, Lady Keith (widow of Robert Diggs) and the only daughter of her first marriage, the lovely Ann Diggs, who married Dr. Thomas Graeme on November 12, 1719, in Christ Church, Philadelphia. The young couple continued to reside in the Keith household. Of their large family of eleven children the youngest, Elizabeth, is the subject of this sketch.

Born in luxury, highly educated for her day, beautiful, courted, beloved, she had a vivid, romantic, eventful, and well-nigh tragic life.

On March 5, 1718, Governor Keith bought a tract of twelve hundred acres near what is now Horsham, in Montgomery County. He erected a country seat, which is still a splendid example of the early American manor house. In 1731 he conveyed the property to trustees for his wife's use, and Dr. Graeme bought the place. Henceforth it was called Graeme Park. A neighborhood legend persists that the so-called field daisy was introduced into this country at Graeme Park and was called by the farmers whose fields it invaded "park-weed." In its heyday Graeme Park was the scene of splendid hospitality.

In this brilliant atmosphere young Elizabeth grew up. Fair to look upon, with a gifted mind, she soon became the center of a charming society and at sixteen was the toast of Philadelphia. An unhappy love affair with Benjamin Franklin's son, William, so affected her spirits and health that her parents sent her to Europe under the care of the Rev. Dr. Peters, of Christ Church. While mending her broken heart, she entertained herself by translating Fénelon's *Télémaque* into English verse.

During her absence her mother died, so when she came home it was as mistress of Graeme Park, which now became more than ever a center for the cultivated minds of the Colony. She wrote original verse as well as translations. The manuscript of her paraphrases of the Book of Psalms is in the Historical Society of Pennsylvania's collection. At Dr. Graeme's town house in Philadelphia their Saturday evenings at home became a salon where one might meet everyone of importance in the community. To one of these evenings a young Scotchman, Henry Hugh Fergusson, brought letters of introduction. Although he was ten years younger than Elizabeth, they became engaged and, because of her father's objection to the difference in their ages, were secretly married in April 1772, in Old Swedes' Church. Henceforth she was known as Lady Fergusson. According to the custom of the times, after the death of her father, her husband became lord of the manor. In 1776 Elizabeth and her husband sold two hundred acres of the estate to John Penn.

Mr. Fergusson seems to have had Tory affiliations and, because Elizabeth was the bearer of a letter from the Rev. Jacob Duché to General Washington, urging him to return to his allegiance to the King, she also was suspected of being a Tory. As a result of this apparent disloyalty to the Revolutionary cause Graeme Park was confiscated. After long and troublous experiences it and some of the furnishings were returned, perhaps through the influence of General Washington, who had often been a guest there in the early days of its splendor.

The end of her life was sad. Ill and impoverished, she died on February 23, 1801, aged sixty-two years, in the home of a Quaker neighbor, and was buried in Christ Churchyard.

ISABEL MCILHENNY NICHOLS

CATHERINE SMITH

1740–1800

᪶ᚫᚫ

AMONG the pioneers of Pennsylvania who showed fortitude and courage during the state's bloody Indian wars, Catherine Smith looms as an outstanding figure. Her husband, Peter Smith, died in 1773, leaving her with ten children to support and with no estate except a location for three hundred acres of land. This was near the mouth of White Deer Creek, in the present Union County.

The "Widow Smith," according to Frederic A. Godcharles' *Daily Stories of Pennsylvania,* was "of the type who did not sit idly by and let her neighbors help support her family, but, realizing that a grist and saw mill were both much wanted in that new country at that time, and being urged to erect these mills, she set about the task." Borrowing a small sum of money, Catherine Smith had both mills in operation by June 1775. With fortitude and patience she built up her business among the other settlers in the wild section.

During the summer of 1776 there came a demand for many rifles for the Continental Army. This early female Krupp, an ardent patriot, installed a boring mill and turned out many musket barrels. Her oldest son was called to the service and was killed. With patience the Widow Smith took up the still heavier load and even managed to start a hemp mill in addition to the other works.

Her efforts, however, seemed ill fated, for in 1778, following the great Wyoming Massacre, the Indians made many raids on the border. With soldiers withdrawn after the Hartley expedition they became even bolder, and 1779 was one of the most terrible years along the Susquehanna valleys. John Sample and his wife were killed by a score of savages in White Deer. The inhabitants began a retreat, and the Widow Smith's mills became the frontier. The buildings, with Widow Smith's stone house (still standing) and Fort Meninger, provided a triangular strong point.

Forced to abandon the places she had built so patiently, Catherine Smith left them in the hands of the soldiers. On July 8, 1779, the Indian attack swept over the new frontier, and the mills were burned by the redskins.

In 1783 the patient woman returned to the ruined mills and after much difficulty rebuilt them. But fortune once more struck at this feminine pioneer. An ejectment suit was brought by Messrs. Claypoole and Morris. She had no money to fight the action at law. In desperation she petitioned the legislature for relief. Although her son had laid down his life, the plea was not entertained.

The Widow Smith never recovered the business that she had developed through those dangerous times. She died, however, bearing the good will of the most prominent citizens of Northumberland County, including General James Potter and Colonel John Kelly, who had petitioned the legislature on her behalf. She was buried near by in the old settler's graveyard.

How well she had built is testified by the fact that part of the foundation of the second mill she erected is to this day serving the same purpose for a modern mill. Testimony of her energy and courage is that this early Pennsylvania woman walked to Philadelphia and back to White Deer thirteen times during her vain petitions to the legislature, covering four thousand miles over forest trails and winding roads.

MARIAN MAUSER

HANNAH TIFFANY SWETLAND

1740–1809

SOMETIMES an old house or an old fireplace can have all the value of a portrait. But the portrait that seems to be a speaking likeness, which one can evolve out of the old Swetland house in the Wyoming Valley across the Susquehanna River from Wilkes-Barre, is not of its builder, Luke Swetland, whose adventures and captivity among the Indians belong to the traditions of Luzerne County, but of his wife, Hannah Tiffany, born in Warren Township, Litchfield County, Connecticut.

She married Luke, in April 1762, and after forty years of the vicissitudes, anxieties, and frustration of pioneer life which included a massacre, a war, the captivity of her husband, and the long and dangerous journey back to Connecticut with her children, she remained undaunted in her resolution to return to try once again, at her husband's desire, the fulfillment of his dreams. It is Hannah Tiffany Swetland, a woman of nearly fifty, who made that house a home, of whom the old fireplace and quaint hospitable doorway seem eloquent.

As one finds her story between the vivid pages of her husband's diary, the comments of her descendants and the records of her family's neighbors, one gathers that a few years after her marriage, she came out of the ordered life of the New England settlement, an arduous life, perhaps, but no longer a dangerous one, into the pioneer existence of the group of Connecticut settlers, who penetrated into the river valleys far to the west and south of their village under the belief that Connecticut holdings ran indefinitely beyond the borders later allocated to her.

The Wyoming Valley promised to make rich farmlands, and it was beautiful country. The great river was navigable to the north and to the distant south. It promised a goodly heritage for their children in crops and herds. It proved richer still in coal, generations later. So Luke Swetland and his wife bent their energies and skill to making a place worth while for their children.

When the American Revolution broke out, they had been married fourteen years and had four sons. The eldest, Belding, was just beginning to be of assistance to his mother, and the youngest, Artemus, a child of six beginning to be less care, for he could now take care of himself. Luke Swetland could therefore join the patriot army with a mind somewhat free. He saw service as early as September 1776 in New Jersey, his enlistment lasting through the battles around Bound Brook, the winter drilling at Valley Forge, and the near debacle of the Brandywine. In 1778 he got his discharge to go back to help defend Wyoming Valley, rumors of an impending British and Indian raid having grown serious.

Hannah Swetland could carry on a farm without her husband, but men were needed to build a fort. So she welcomed him home with a graver danger facing them than all of the perils of the Revolution.

On the third of July what is known in history as the Wyoming Massacre began. Four men were detailed to defend the fort, the rest marched out to meet the foe and death. As Luke Swetland was one of the four who held the fort, Hannah did not lose her husband on that bloody day. The massacre raged elsewhere. But the Indians hung

about in skulking bands, killing, burning, and capturing, in little attacks and sharp forays.

In August when the farm harvest was ready for the mill, Luke
Swetland and a neighbor were hardy enough to risk taking some
sacks in a canoe down the river to a great mill on Fishing Creek. They
were surprised and captured by six Senecas, and as few travelers returned from that bourne, they were given up for dead. For fourteen
months Hannah Swetland heard not one single thing of Luke beyond
the fact of his disappearance and probable death from Indians. This
was, indeed, scarcely a fact to her, but a logical guess drawn from the
cruelly frequent happenings all about her.

As the days passed and winter approached and the Indian raids
made work in the fields or life outside the fort a constant and bitter
danger, Hannah Swetland resolved to rid her neighbors of the responsibility of her unprotected family. With what desperate courage
one can only imagine, she traveled back to her old home at Kent,
Connecticut, over forest trails for the most part through unbroken
wilderness. There she found a welcome and safety, and started her
boys on the old lines which she and Luke had supposed they had
left behind them forever.

And then, suddenly, fourteen months after he had vanished, Luke
Swetland returned. He had been a captive among Indians for nearly a
year, then a prisoner suspected of being a Tory spy among the Americans. Later, he was recognized and retained as a scout for the army
under General Sullivan, and finally set at liberty to pick up the
traces of his family at Wyoming, whence he journeyed on horseback
along the trails to Litchfield County and Kent. That might have ended
his and Hannah Swetland's adventures since their sons in the next
ten years were marrying and times were more peaceful in Litchfield
County than down in Luzerne, for Connecticut and Pennsylvania
were fighting over land boundaries in and out of the courts. But Luke
Swetland was not satisfied to call it a day, nor Belding ready to forget
the valley of his childhood.

Apparently Luke's wife, Belding's mother, was as game as either
of them. At all events, sometime before 1800 they returned to the
Susquehanna. Eventually they went to Wyoming Valley, and, within
sight of the old fort, Luke, at seventy-one years of age, built the Swetland homestead. Belding and Luke cleared their land, planted or-

chards and helped start the church. But Hannah Swetland did even more. She made both farm and house the Swetland home for the new generation of Swetland grandchildren. Belding's wife, Sally Gay, of Sharon, did her share, for she was to bear him twelve children. The eldest of the grandchildren, William, who was to become the owner of the house when the two older generations that had made it what it was had passed away, could remember all of these things, some of them first-hand, some from his grandmother's telling.

This was why, perhaps, the changes and chances of this grandson's seventy-five years did not shift him from the Swetland homestead. Its comfortable simplicity met his larger needs. Great courage, great faith and unfaltering loyalty had made that hearth his home on the evening that Hannah Swetland had once again stooped to swing the great iron pot over the glowing embers for the family meal. Hannah and Luke Swetland's great-great-grandchildren still cherish this rare old home.

SARAH D. LOWRIE

SARAH SIMPSON COOKE

1742–1822

UNCOMMON courage and fortitude have been, almost invariably, the common traits of the women who lived in Pennsylvania in the days of the first frontier. They were not swayed by any dream or hope that later generations would find a saga in their lives. They simply saw their duty and did it in day-by-day and matter-of-course fashion, some a little better than others.

One of these women of extra-epic stature was Sarah Simpson Cooke, daughter of one frontiersman and wife of another.

She was born in Paxtang Township, Lancaster County, in 1742, her parents being Samuel and Rebecca Simpson. Her grandfather, Thomas Simpson, was one of the first settlers in that locality, his name appearing upon the assessment list of Conestoga Township, Chester County, afterward Donegal and then Paxtang.

Samuel Simpson was a well-to-do farmer, according to Dr. William

H. Egle's *Some Pennsylvania Women During the War of the Revolution*, but his farm was so remote from town that his children, including Sarah, received only a limited education and most of that at home, since the few months of winter school barely sufficed to instill the rudiments. But in household accomplishments Sarah Simpson excelled. Dr. Egle's record declares, "She could spin and weave and therefore was personally fit to become the wife of a frontiersman."

So in 1762 she married William Cooke, son of John Cooke, who emigrated into Pennsylvania from near Londonderry, Enniskillen, Ireland.

In 1767 Mr. Cooke removed his family to Fort Augusta, now Sunbury. Dr. Egle's narrative continues:

He was elected the first Sheriff of Northumberland County, October 1772, and at the opening of the struggle for Independence was one of its firmest supporters. He was a member of the Committee of Observation for the county, of the Provincial Conference of June 18, 1776, and of the Constitutional Convention in July following. On the last day of the session of the latter body he was chosen to be colonel of the battalion to be raised in the counties of Northumberland and Northampton. This became the Twelfth Regiment of the Pennsylvania Line. Being composed of riflemen, it was employed upon picket duty and covered the front of General Washington's army during the year 1777, while detachments were sent from it to General Gates, materially assisting in the capture of Burgoyne. The regiment was so badly cut up at the battles of Brandywine and Germantown that it was disbanded, and Colonel Cooke mustered out of service. He was appointed Deputy Quartermaster of Stores during the years 1778, 1779 and 1780. In 1781 and 1782 he was chosen to the General Assembly; commissioned one of the Justices, October 3, 1786, and in January 1796, an Associate Judge of Northumberland County. He died at the town of Northumberland, April 22, 1804.

It was during the year 1775 that the Rev. Philip Fithian in his journal, alludes to the invitation of Sheriff Cooke to stop with him, remarking that "Mrs. Cooke was certainly an agreeable woman, hospitable and kind in the extreme."

Dr. Egle's book refers to the wartime activity of Mrs. Cooke:

Her husband in the patriot army, many duties devolved upon her, apart from the care and education of her children. Amidst the gloom, her strong old Calvinist faith buoyed up her heart, and her firm reliance upon the

God of Battles nerved her for whatever might befall her. Finally her husband returned from the war, relieving her anxiety. During the summer of 1778 their house was a hospital, as well as an asylum where the wounded and sick, the helpless women and children received care and succor. Mrs. Cooke was never weary in well-doing.

When peace dawned, plenty was added to their stores, for in a long letter to a brother in London in 1789, Colonel Cooke writes: "You desire me to make out such a list of books as Johnny (a son) requires to complete his library, and you would send them in the spring and I thought that would be sufficient at present; and yet I would take it a kindness if you would pack up a piece of chintz along with Johnny's books, that would make each of the girls a pattern of a gown." [He also adds that he had] "just completed a grist mill two and a half miles from here, which goes very well."

The Johnny referred to was the second child of Colonel and Mrs. Cooke. In 1792 he was made a captain in the Fourth Sub-Legion of the United States Army, serving with a Northumberland company under General Wayne at the battle of the Miami, assisting in checking the power of the confederated Indians in the Northwest Territory.

Her other children were Mary and Jane, who married, respectively, Robert and William P. Brady, sons of Captain John Brady; Rebecca, who became the wife of William Stedman; Elizabeth, who married Thomas Martin, and Sarah, who became the wife of William McClelland, and later of Judge Samuel Harris, of Lycoming County. William Cooke, the other son, married Martha Lemmon, daughter of James Lemmon.

Sarah Simpson Cooke died in 1822 and is buried in the town of Northumberland.

ALICE SCHUYLER HEEBNER

ELIZABETH WILLING POWEL

1742–1830

ᕦᕤ

ELIZABETH WILLING was the daughter of Charles Willing and Anne Shippen, both prominent Philadelphians. Unfortunately Charles Willing died when only forty-four years of age, leaving his young wife with the care of eleven children, six daughters and five sons. Thomas, the eldest son, entered his father's counting house at the age of eighteen, so that upon the latter's death he was able to assume full charge of the business. Associated with him was Robert Morris. Thomas later became first president of the Bank of North America and then of the Bank of the United States. He is remembered as "the old Regulator of American Finance." In addition to his many business responsibilities, he was always interested in the care of his younger brothers and sisters, and helped his mother in every possible way.

His sister Elizabeth was the sixth child of Charles Willing and was born in 1742. In 1769 she married Samuel Powel, who was not only a man of large wealth, but was one of the foremost Philadelphians of a day when there were many great men among her patriotic citizens. He was the last mayor of Philadelphia under the Charter of 1701, holding this office during the earlier part of the Revolution. When the new Charter of 1789 came into effect, he was elected first mayor under the new Republic, also Speaker of the Senate. He gave liberally to provision the Continental Army, was associated with Franklin in the American Philosophical Society, and was interested in many other worthwhile affairs. Both he and his wife were noted for their generous hospitality, and, after the seat of the Federal Government had been transferred from New York to Philadelphia, the famous statesmen of that day, from Washington down, enjoyed the Powel home. We can picture Washington going up the steps of that dignified house and through its beautiful doorway, to drink tea, or to sit in the pretty garden which ran back to Fourth Street. From his diary, or letters, are found frequent entries, such as, "Drank tea and sat until ten o'clock," or "Dined at the Powels'." Lafayette and Franklin were frequent guests there.

In a letter which John Adams wrote his dear Abigail he says of a dinner which he attended at Mrs. Powel's, "Again a most sinful feast, curds and creams, jellies, sweetmeats of all sorts, twenty kinds of tarts, truffles, floating-island, sylabubs, etc., in fact everything that could delight the eye or allure the taste." Although her husband criticized Mrs. Powel's food as a sinful feast, Mrs. Adams, after meeting her, says, "She is the best informed, most affable, very friendly, and full of conversation, a woman of many charms." When Mrs. Washington arrived in Philadelphia to join her husband, many entertainments were given for her. Among the women who received at these gatherings, Mrs. Powel heads all the lists. In a letter written by Sarah Bache to her father, Benjamin Franklin (who was then in France), she says, "Have been to a ball at the Powels' and danced the minuet with General Washington."

Samuel and Elizabeth Powel had two sons, but both died in infancy. Consequently she was greatly interested in her many nephews and nieces. Her youngest sister, Margaret, married Robert Hare. John Powel, born in 1786, was their youngest son. When quite young he was adopted by his Aunt Elizabeth Powel. Upon the death of his adopted mother, he came into possession of all of her estate. In gratitude to her for her kindness to him he changed his name, by an act of Assembly, from John Powel Hare to John Hare Powel. Among the properties which he inherited from her was the famous estate called Powelton which Samuel Powel had purchased in 1775 from Thomas Willing.

MARY WARD MERCUR

MARY JEMISON

1743–1833

THE daughter of Thomas and Mary Jemison, Scotch-Irish emigrants who came from their home in Ulster, Ireland, to Philadelphia early in October 1743, Mary Jemison was born on the voyage. Thomas Jemison settled on a farm in the Buchanan Valley about ten miles northwest of Gettysburg.

The family was captured by the Indians on April 5, 1758. Mary's two brothers, who were working in the barn, escaped, however, and made their way to Virginia, but her mother, her father, a neighbor, and a sister-in-law with her three small children were all taken prisoners with herself and carried off. The route was westward, though its exact course has not been determined.

At the end of the second day's march, they reached a densely wooded swamp, supposedly near Fort McCord, where they camped for the night. After supper, one of the Indians directed Mary to remove her shoes and stockings and replace them with moccasins. Her mother realized from this that her daughter's life would be spared, but that she herself and the other captives would probably be murdered. This suspicion proved true, for the Indians saved Mary and a little boy, while the others were all murdered during the night. When the Indians who committed this deed rejoined the others, they brought with them the scalps of the victims. Mary recognized with horror those of her parents.

After some days' travel, the party arrived at a small Seneca village, about seventy-six miles by water below Pittsburgh, and here Mary was given in charge of two squaws, who dressed her in Indian garb for adoption. Three years later she married an Indian named Sheninjee who treated her kindly and to whom she bore a son. Planning to set out on a hunting trip, her husband allowed her to go with some others of the tribe to Genesee, a distance of five or six hundred miles, which she covered on foot, carrying her child on her back.

She never saw her husband again, as he fell ill and died on his trip. About this time a reward was offered by the British Government to anyone who would bring into military trading posts white captives for release. A Dutchman, John Van Sice, discovered Mary and determined to take her to Fort Niagara but she would not give her consent, and the plan was abandoned. About three years later she married a Seneca chief commonly called Gardow, to whom she bore four daughters and two sons.

At Gardow Flats, in Genesee County, New York, she lived until the time of her death. She was given a large tract of land on the Genesee River at a council meeting at Big Tree, near Genesee, in 1797. With her husband and children she led a contented and happy life; the former attaining the age of 103 years. She died on September 19, 1833, aged ninety, and was buried in the graveyard near the Seneca Mission House on the Buffalo Creek Reservation.

WILLIAM HOMER AMES

ELIZABETH DRINKER

1743?–1807

ELIZABETH DRINKER was the daughter of William Sandwith, who came from the County of Wexford, in Ireland, and was descended from a family formerly seated at Sandwith, near Whitehaven, in England. He was a merchant and ship owner of Philadelphia who sometimes captained his own vessels.

Elizabeth was born in the house of her maternal grandfather, Martyn Jervis, on the west side of Second Street at the corner of an alley leading to Strawberry Alley. She married Henry Drinker, a member of the shipping firm of James & Drinker, on January 13, 1761. Their summer home at Frankford, called Chalkley Hall, is the subject of a poem by John Greenleaf Whittier. Their city home for many years was on the northwest corner of Front Street and Drinker's Alley.

Elizabeth Drinker's famous diary gives a vivid and realistic idea of Philadelphia and its surroundings. Among its many interesting pictures are some strange weather contrasts. On February 28, 1779, she notes that, "it is many years since we have had a season so forward as this. We have had crocuses in our garden for a week past and this day Persian irises are also blown." On January 15, 1780 she says, "H. D. and all the children went across the Delaware on the ice and friends went to Haddonfield from Philadelphia in a sleigh across the river."

The diary, during the unhappy time of the Revolution when the Friends, with their peace principles and their conscientious objections to taking part in any war, were bitterly reviled and sometimes abused, is a model of restraint and ability to see the opposite point of view even under persecution and misunderstanding.

Her husband, taken prisoner by the Revolutionary forces, was banished to Winchester, where with other Friends he was kept confined for eight months with no provision for support. It was Elizabeth's task to gather food and clothing for him and get them to him amidst the greatest difficulties. At the end of the eight months they were set free by Washington, who wrote, "These Friends have been called Tories, but that appears to be an erroneous stigmatization. Adhering as they did to their conscientious convictions in regard to war and taking oaths, while suffering grievously for the same, they might more properly claim our respect and admiration."

The journal gives, in addition, a graphic picture of the yellow fever epidemics of 1793 and 1798.

Confined to her bed as an invalid for many years during the latter part of her life, she died November 24, 1807.

MRS. WILMER KRUSEN

SARAH FRANKLIN BACHE

1744-1808

ORGANIZATION of a band of 2,200 Pennsylvania women to collect money, buy cloth, and sew shirts and other clothing for the Revolutionary soldiers was the principal contribution to American independence of Sarah Franklin Bache, daughter of Benjamin Franklin. In addition, however, she bought and administered medicines to the sick, bandaged many wounds and generally took a prominent part in relieving pain and distress.

Born in Philadelphia on September 11, 1744, little is known of her early life, but from her father's appreciation of the importance of education it is surmised she enjoyed the fullest possible advantages of this sort. On October 29, 1767, she married Richard Bache, a Philadelphia merchant who was also engaged, in partnership with his brother, in the business of insuring lives. Bache, in 1776, succeeded Franklin as Postmaster-General, serving until 1782.

During the Revolution he was an ardent advocate of the cause of liberty, and encouraged his wife in all the war work she undertook. That her labors were of great importance is amply attested by a letter written to Franklin by the Marquis de Chastellux, who was then visiting in Philadelphia. Another friend, writing to Franklin of the services being rendered by Sarah, said:

If there are in Europe any women who need a model of attachment to domestic duties and love for their country, Mrs. Bache may be pointed out

to them as such. She passed a part of last year in exertions to rouse the zeal
of the Pennsylvania ladies, and she made on this occasion such happy use
of the eloquence which you know she possesses, that a large part of the
American army was provided with shirts bought with their money or made
by their hands. In her applications for this purpose, she showed the most
indefatigable zeal, the most unwearied perseverance, and a courage in asking which surpassed even the obstinate reluctance of the Quakers in refusing.

After the war, in 1792, Mr. and Mrs. Bache visited England for
a time but were prevented from extending their tour to France by
reason of the increasing troubles of the Revolution there. In 1794
Bache retired from business and they removed to a farm on the Delaware River. Here Sarah Bache spent the final years of her life until
the winter of 1807–08, when she was brought to Philadelphia to be
treated for cancer, but nothing could be done to alleviate her condition and she died there on October 5, 1808.

Eight children were born to Mr. and Mrs. Bache, and through these
and their progeny the blood of Franklin has been transmitted on the
"distaff line" to modern times.

MARY MORRIS DUANE

ANNE WEST GIBSON

1744–1809

IT is recognized that distinguished men usually have had superior
mothers. Anne West Gibson, the mother of Chief Justice Gibson, and
his three brothers, adds proof to the validity of that theory. She was
born at Clover Hill, near Sligo, in northwestern Ireland, in 1744.
Her father, Francis West, a graduate of Trinity College, Dublin, was
a cousin of the distinguished artist Benjamin West.

When she was eleven years old her parents, with their family, immigrated to this country and settled in either Lancaster or Chester
County, Pennsylvania, afterward removing to Cumberland County.
There her father became Colonial Judge and a pronounced Tory at
the beginning of the Revolution. Anne, who was sent to boarding

school in Philadelphia, possessed an excellent mind, attended by a natural love of reading, and developed into a well-educated woman. She became the wife of Captain (afterward Colonel) George Gibson, an ardent Federalist and an officer in the Continental Army, who was killed in an expedition against the Indians in 1791, leaving his widow with four young sons.

The home of the family, originally the property of Anne's father in Cumberland County, stood on the picturesque banks of Sherman's Creek, in that part of Cumberland out of which Perry County was later erected. Though the homestead gradually fell into a state of dilapidation and decay, the spot where it stood is still pointed out as the location of the Gibson Mansion; the mill remains intact and a "rifle's shot" beyond looms that huge pile of boulders widely known as Gibson's Rock.

The farm, which consisted of seventy-eight acres, and a small mill on the creek were the sole means of support for the family after the death of Colonel Gibson. As the stretches of country surrounding Mrs. Gibson's home were too sparsely populated to make the milling business remunerative and the work of her boys, under her management, on the beautiful but mountainous farm land did not realize a sufficient income, she was unable to send them away to school.

Her splendid courage, sustained by a fine ambition for her children, led her to build a schoolhouse adjoining the homestead, and there, in addition to the management of farm and mill, she assumed the duties of school mistress for her own children and for others from the locality. Francis, the eldest son, is described as growing into handsome, agreeable manhood, possessing musical talent and becoming a well-known violinist. He filled the office of recorder and register in Cumberland County.

When her son George was twenty years of age, she obtained for him a position in the counting-house of an old friend of her husband, Alexander McDonald, a well-known importer in Baltimore. He became an officer in the United States Army, and, says one authority, in writing of his later life, "none held a higher place in the estimation of his fellow officers than did General George Gibson." He was the oldest officer in the army at the time of his death, and a public funeral was held in his honor by order of the President.

John Bannister, her third son, was sent to Dickinson College, Carlisle, and is listed in the *United States Law Magazine* as a graduate of the class of 1800 and as its most celebrated member. Since he had been from childhood the most studious of her boys, Mrs. Gibson always hoped that he might become a lawyer. When this son had achieved the position of a distinguished jurist, in a letter to a friend he paid tender tribute to the devotion and ability of his mother, and added this striking sentence: "Having placed me at the bar, she died."

William, the youngest, had meanwhile adopted commercial pursuits, and became supercargo of a vessel in the foreign trade from Baltimore.

Mrs. Gibson was a devout member of the Church of England, and habitually attended the Sunday services at St. John's in Carlisle, fifteen miles distant from her home and only to be reached over a mountain road.

From the day of her husband's death to her own, eighteen years afterward, her life was attended by hardships and privations upheld only by her gallant spirit.

GERTRUDE BOSLER BIDDLE

MARIE THERESA SCHILLINGER HOMET

1749?–1823

MARIE THERESA SCHILLINGER was born in Strasbourg. She was the god-child of Maria Theresa, Empress of Austria, for whom she was named. Educated in Paris, she grew to graceful womanhood as the maid of honor of Marie Antoinette, to whom she was related.

The French, encouraged by the success of the American Revolution, soon set their country aflame with war, exposing the royalists to horrible indignities, and forcing them to flee. Thousands of the French nobility fled to Haiti and San Domingo, unknowingly going into still greater danger.

Many came to the United States, feeling secure of a welcome because of services rendered by Lafayette and other brave officers. So great became the number of refugees that it was deemed expedient to make some provision for their settlement as a colony. Money was set aside and a tract of land which comprised 2,400 acres on the east branch of the Susquehanna near Wyalusing was purchased and the French settlement of Asylum begun. Into this wilderness came our heroine.

In January 1793, the King was beheaded and Mlle Schillinger made her escape. What mixed feelings she must have had as she stepped safely upon the ship which was to take her from her family, her country, and her Queen into a strange land! The boat was anchored a little way out, waiting no doubt for a favorable wind to fill her sails. After nightfall there swam out to their ship one who was not unknown to her, as he too had been in the King's service.

This strong swimmer was Charles Homet, whom Marie Theresa married at the end of the three months' voyage. They lived one year at Bottle Hill, New Jersey, where Charles, Jr., was born. With the little baby they came over the Pocono Mountains to Wilkes-Barre, and up the river in a Durban boat to Asylum on the beautiful Susquehanna, where a city was laid out for the French refugees. There they found fellow countrymen with a common sorrow. No doubt they had been in communication with the Viscount de Noailles in Philadelphia, whose secret plan it was to build a hiding place of safety for the Queen, to whom his mother was chief lady in waiting. Charles Homet was put in charge of the building of this house for the Queen, and no one could have been more anxious than Marie Theresa, with her ties of blood and companionship, for the safety of Marie Antoinette.

The location for these buildings commanded a horizon of mountains so distant as to melt into the sky. This was the home of Marie Theresa for two years while bricks were made for the Queen's house, a bakery built, orchards planted and some of the forests cleared. Work was slow, as everything had to be trundled out by ox carts from Asylum. Still slower was the news from France. Finally rumors of the Queen's death were verified. The Homets returned to Asylum in 1796, the year of Louis Philippe's visit.

After so many shiftings of the scenes, they settled down to make their way in farming, a new and difficult industry. But with true French frugality they succeeded so that in Marie's old age she was able to contemplate broad acres bought from less successful neighbors, and to view with pride the prosperity of her sons.

MARY ALLEN CALEY
THERESA HOMET PATTERSON

SARAH EVE

middle 1700's–1774

❧❧

SARAH EVE was the daughter of Oswell Eve and Anna Moore. Her *Journal of 1773–74* has come down in history as an authoritative article on manners and customs of the pre-Revolutionary period. She was engaged to Dr. Benjamin Rush, but died December 4, 1774, three weeks before the marriage was to have taken place.

Her clever sketches of the life of the period make her one of the foremost early American writers. Watson in his famous *Annals* and Scharf and Westcott in a later history quoted extensively from her journal.

Esther Singleton in her book, *The Furniture of Our Forefathers,* also quotes from Sarah Eve, February 10, 1773:

We stept in to Mrs. Parish's for a moment and then went to Mrs. S—'s. We were much pleased with our visit and her new house; the neatness and proportions of the furniture corresponding so well with the size of the house, that here one may see elegance in miniature. I don't mean the elegance of a palace, but of simplicity, which is preferable. The one pleased the eye but flatters the vanity—the other pleases the judgment and cherishes nature. As I walked through this home I could not help saying this surely might be taken for the habitation of happiness.

It is interesting to note that 150 years ago William Penn belonged to ancient history in the eyes of Sarah Eve. On May 6, 1773, she wrote:

Mrs. Bunton that lives here showed us some furniture which might really be termed relicks of antiquity which belonged to William Penn; they purchased the clock which it was said struck one just before William Penn died which was remarkable since it had not struck for some years before.

Her pen pictures of Dr. William Shippen and of Jacob Duché give an interesting insight into the social life of her time, and one cannot help wishing that she had been spared to make further entries of the stirring days that were to come in 1776.

CAROLYN WOOD STRETCH

MARGARET FORSTER STUART

middle 1700's–?

MARGARET FORSTER STUART was of Colonial stock. She was the grand-daughter of Captain Moses Dickey, of the French and Indian War of 1717–18 and daughter of John Forster, an officer in Provincial service during the later French and Indian Wars, as well as the Revolution. She was born in historic Paxtang, about two miles from Harrisburg.

It was in a little log cabin on Fourth Street near French, at Erie, Pennsylvania, in the month of July just prior to the decisive battle of Lake Erie (September 10, 1813) that a little coterie of women met on the invitation of Margaret Forster Stuart, wife of Thomas Stuart, an officer in the Pennsylvania troops. Their purpose was to make the battle-flag for the staunch fleet just completed in the improvised navy yard at the snug little harbor of Presque Isle Bay. According to old records and letters, several of the officers from the fleet themselves came to the house and assisted the ladies in cutting out the materials for the banner, which was made of dark blue cotton cloth. It was about nine feet square with letters of white muslin about thirteen inches high.

What a thrill the officers and crew must have experienced when, on that fateful day of battle, the decks having been cleared for action, Commodore Perry appeared bearing the inspiring battle-flag. "My brave lads," said he, "this flag contains the last words of Captain Lawrence: shall I hoist it?" "Aye, aye, sir," was the prompt response.

The beautiful needlework of the zealous women of Erie was hoisted to the mast. White as the foam of the sea, the words DON'T GIVE UP THE SHIP stood out on the ocean of blue. Through the vicissitudes of

that famous battle they remained an inspiration, and were instrumental in gaining that victory which dislodged the British from the
region around the Great Lakes.

The famous banner is preserved in the United States Naval Academy at Annapolis.

EMILY SPRANKLE HERON
KATHARINE B. BLAKE

SUSANNE KEELY CHRISTMAN

1750–1823

SUSANNE KEELY CHRISTMAN was born February 25, 1750, in Frederick Township, Montgomery County. When seventeen years of age
she was married to Henry Christman in the Lutheran church at New
Hanover.

During the Revolutionary War period they lived in Vincent Township, Chester County, and suffered all the privations of pioneer life.
There they saw much of the suffering of the soldiers.

Susanne was a woman of sterling worth who labored long and
arduously in deeds of love and devotion to her home and country.
Her many acts of kindness established her reputation as a true patriot, for she gave her aid wherever she could help the American
cause. In the autumn of 1777, after the battle of Brandywine and the
massacre at Paoli, while the Colonial troops were retreating over the
Warwick hills, hungry, cold, sick and wounded, she devoted herself
to baking bread for them and caring for their wounds.

Henry and Susanne were the owners of a large tract of land on
French Creek, Chester County. This property was a part of the Callowhill Manor of one thousand acres, which was conveyed by the
proprietary under William Penn in 1686 to Robert Thompson. This
tract of 276 acres was purchased at judicial sale, in the settlement of
the Hazel Thomas Estate.

Susanne Christman died September 19, 1823, just three days after
her husband. She is buried in the family burial plot at Zion's Church

in East Pikeland Township, Chester County, on the Ridge Road, where are also buried three other generations of Christmans.

Mrs. H. P. Christman

MARGARET COCHRAN CORBIN

1751–about 1800

WILLIAM AND SAMUEL COCHRAN were, in 1751, taxables in old Lurgan Township, now Letterkenny. Robert Cochran, son of William, was killed by Indians in 1756 and his wife carried into captivity. Mrs. Cochran was seen in November 1758, a hundred miles southwest of the Ohio River, but nothing further was ever heard of her. They left a son John, who died in 1785, and a daughter Margaret, born in what is now Franklin County, November 12, 1751. She married John Corbin and became a heroine of the Revolution.

When John Corbin enlisted in Captain Francis Proctor's First Company of Pennsylvania Artillery, his wife accompanied him to the field. During the attack by the British on Fort Washington, New York, Corbin was killed, and as there was no one to take his place, the officer in command ordered the gun to be withdrawn. When the patriotic Margaret heard of it she volunteered to take the place of her dead husband and nobly did his former duty, helping to load and fire the gun until severely wounded. The Supreme Council of Pennsylvania recognized her services by awarding her a pension, and Congress, in July 1779, unanimously resolved "that Margaret Corbin, wounded and disabled at the battle of Fort Washington while she heroically filled the post of her husband, do receive one-half the monthly pay drawn by a soldier in the service of these States, and that she now receive, out of the public stores, one suit of clothes or value thereof in money."

The name of Margaret Corbin is found on the rolls of the Invalid Regiment in Pennsylvania, commanded by Colonel Lewis Nicola, and discharged in April 1783. She resided in Westmoreland County, and died about the year 1800.

After most exhaustive research by the Daughters of the American

Revolution of New York State, assisted by interested persons, her grave was found on land of J. Pierpont Morgan, near Highland Falls about three miles from West Point. Permission was obtained to have her remains reinterred in the United States Military Cemetery at West Point. A handsome granite memorial monument erected at her grave bears a suitable inscription on a bronze tablet showing the figure in relief of a woman firing a cannon.

John A. H. Keith

MARGARET MILLER FOERING

1752–1823

MARGARET MILLER, daughter of Sebastian Miller, merchant of Germantown, married Christian Frederic Foering who, about 1769, was minister of the German Reformed Church which stood on the present site of the Market Square Presbyterian Church in Germantown. In 1772 she moved with her husband to the German Reformed Church in New York, but returned a little over two years later to the church in Millstone, Pennsylvania.

In January 1777, Washington marched his forces through the township and the patriotic Foerings collecting all the stores of their house distributed them to the hungry, weary soldiers who encamped in the field south of the parsonage. Millstone was plundered by the British in June 1777, and the interior of the German Reformed Church destroyed, but religious meetings were held wherever possible. In the fall of 1778, after the battle of Freehold, when Washington again took up his winter quarters at Middlebrook, Mr. Foering preached a stirring sermon which, together with the staunch patriotic efforts of his wife, let to the formation of a company from his congregation.

So active were this loyal pair that the British sent a party to capture Mr. Foering. His wife received word of their intention, and, he being sick in bed, hastily dispatched some of the men servants to a safe place with a wagonload of goods. She then helped her husband prepare for flight. With the aid of a terrified maid she harnessed the horse and Mr. Foering started on his way, while she returned to defend her house and three children. The British soldiers soon arrived, and in their angry search thrust their swords through every bed in the house.

Millstone was again in the enemy lines during the winters of 1778 and 1779. Several British officers were quartered in the parsonage. With the exception of one petty subordinate, they treated their compulsory hostess with courtesy. Every day after dinner they gave her son a glass of wine to carry to his mother, bidding her "drink the health of General Washington." Day by day she received it but poured it into a demijohn, reserving it for her husband. On the departure of her unwelcome guests, and her husband's return, greatly enfeebled in health, she took down the demijohn and to her consternation found it empty. An Irishwoman in her employ had drunk it all.

An anecdote is preserved in the family of Mrs. Foering's courage and spirit. In the dark days of the occupancy of the British they made frequent levies on the parsonage for butter. This in spite of the fact that they had taken all the cows they could lay their hands on. One time Mrs. Foering told her maid to hide the butter when she knew of their approach, and when the British soldiers came with their usual demand she replied that she had no butter for them (her veracity depending on her emphasis). "A likely story indeed," they said, "that such a fine place should be without butter." "How can you expect butter," exclaimed she, "when you have taken my cows?" Just then the maid came into the room with a pewter tray of butter, and when she saw the soldiers, cried in terror, "Where shall I hide it? What shall I do with it?" "Do with it," exclaimed Mrs. Foering, "throw it to the pigs rather than let them have it." Seizing the butter from the maid she threw it across the room where it lodged behind the oven, out of sight of the men and, as they supposed, out of reach. Exasperated as they were they did not injure her and after they had retired it was recovered.

ELSIE M. JOHNSON

ELIZABETH PARKER PORTER

1752–1821

ᘏᘡ

ELIZABETH PARKER was the daughter of Alexander Parker, and the wife of Captain Andrew Porter. She was one of those many women of unusual culture and untiring industry who reared their children so excellently while their husbands were absent in the business of war.

Although Captain Porter's brother officers often appeared in ragged uniforms, the husband of Elizabeth Porter was invariably turned out in clothes carefully mended and kept spick and span under her relentless care. She found time to read as many books as came to hand, the Bible and *Paradise Lost* being her favorites. Her intelligence combined with her own zeal for knowledge made her an unusually capable teacher for her children.

One day while riding to Valley Forge with some gifts for her husband, the harness of her horse became loosened. Near the camp a stranger offered to help her in adjusting it, and, when it was in order, accompanied her into camp, asking many questions of her in regard to the attitude of her friends toward the war and the army. Upon seeing her husband, he pointed him out and continued on his way. When Elizabeth Porter rode to her husband's side there was a smile of surprised pleasure on his face. He explained to her, as he helped her to dismount, that she had been escorted by General Washington. This experience was one which she retold repeatedly during the course of her life, which terminated May 18, 1821.

MARGARET LITTELL

BETSY ROSS

1752–1836

❧❦

BETSY ROSS, of American flag fame, was born in Philadelphia, January 1, 1752. Her father, Samuel Griscom, helped build Independence Hall. Betsy was skilful with the needle and did embroidery and other delicate work in artistic fashion.

In 1773 she married John Ross, a young upholsterer who died in January 1776, from injuries received in guarding military stores in Philadelphia. His widow, Betsy Ross, continued the business.

The *National Cyclopedia of American Biography* says:

When Congress appointed a committee "authorized to design a suitable flag for the Nation" in June, 1776, the committee accompanied by George Washington, called upon her in her shop, at No. 239 Arch street, and engaged her to make a flag from a pencil drawing made by Washington. The drawing represented the outlines of a flag of thirteen stripes with a field dotted with thirteen stars.

The stars had six points, as Washington wished to avoid making a design for a flag that would be an exact copy of his coat-of-arms. Upon Mrs. Ross's suggestion, however, the star was changed to a five-pointed one and the sample flag made by her was accepted by the committee and adopted by Congress June 14, 1777.

The house in which this flag was made is now known as the American Flag House at 239 Arch Street, Philadelphia. It was purchased by the Betsy Ross Association, and is thus preserved to posterity as an American historic shrine.

Betsy Ross made the flag while she was a widow, after the death of her first husband, John Ross. She married twice afterward and continued flag-making until 1833, when she retired and went to live with her son-in-law, Edward Satterthwaite, in Abington, Montgomery County.

She returned to Philadelphia in 1835, where she lived with the family of her daughter, Jane Camby, until her death on January 30, 1836. Her remains lie buried in Mount Moriah Cemetery, Philadelphia.

JOHN A. H. KEITH

MOLLY PITCHER

1754-1832

In the original plotting of the settlement of Carlisle, Cumberland County, a certain piece of ground was dedicated by the Penn family to the perpetual service of the community as a place for the burial of its dead. The remains of many people, the record of whose lives lends distinction to the history of the nation, are interred in that ground, widely known and tenderly referred to as "The Old Graveyard at Carlisle."

In this historic place of interment was laid, in 1832, the body of a woman whose courageous conduct on the battlefield entitled her to recognition among the fearless patriots of her days, a woman who is known solely under her sobriquet of "Molly Pitcher." Her name was Mary Ludwig, and while many of the statements concerning her are based on tradition, current accounts indicate that she came from New Jersey to Carlisle in 1769, and lived there as a servant in the home of General William Irvine.

On July 24 of that year she married a young barber named Hays. On December 1, 1775, her husband enlisted as a gunner in Proctor's Artillery, and in 1777 reënlisted as a private in an infantry regiment commanded by Colonel, afterwards General, William Irvine, of Carlisle. This regiment was at Valley Forge during the memorable winter of 1777-78, and marched from there under General Washington to take part in the battle of Monmouth.

When and where "Molly" became associated with the troops is not known, but it is believed that she had returned to her home in New Jersey and from there went to join the battalion in which her husband was serving.

The battle of Monmouth was fought on June 28, 1778. The day was an extremely hot Sunday on which many of the soldiers of both armies perished from exhaustion and thirst. While the battle was in progress Molly diligently carried water from a well to the suffering Continental troops. Her constant passing to and from with a pitcher in her hand caused the men to hail her as "Molly Pitcher."

But the outstanding service for which her memory is honored was her unhesitating assumption of her husband's place when he fell wounded at the side of the cannon he had been serving. She at once, so the story goes, took his position at the gun and served as cannoneer.

It is known that after the end of the Revolution, Mr. and Mrs. Hays lived in Carlisle, where he died and where she later became the wife of John McCauley. It was under that name that she received the annuity that was granted her by a special act of the legislature of Pennsylvania on February 21, 1822, "for services during the Revolutionary War." Many women were awarded pensions as widows of soldiers, but Molly McCauley is one of the few women who were ever placed on the pension rolls of Pennsylvania because of her own services.

On June 28, 1916, the handsome monument which now marks her resting place was presented on behalf of the Commonwealth of Pennsylvania by Governor Martin G. Brumbaugh and was accepted on behalf of the borough of Carlisle by Hon. Edward W. Biddle, president of the Historical Association of Cumberland County. The address made upon that occasion by Judge Biddle was afterwards published in pamphlet form and has been used as the sole authority for this sketch. In this address he points out that the story of "Molly Pitcher's" life prior to the close of the Revolution rests alone on tradition and legend.

GERTRUDE BOSLER BIDDLE
JOHN A. H. KEITH

REBECCA CORNELL BIDDLE

1755–about 1834

LIFE in an armed camp during a war is difficult for a woman to bear, yet love of country and of husband impelled Rebecca Cornell Biddle to forsake the safety of home and the precepts of her religion to participate in the American Revolution, and render signal service to the cause of liberty.

She was born on February 17, 1755, near Newport, Rhode Island, the daughter of Gideon and Rebecca Vaughan Cornell. Her father at one time was Lieutenant-Governor of Rhode Island and later Chief

Justice for that colony. After enjoying what was for her time a conventional girlhood and education, she became the bride of Colonel Clement Biddle, of Philadelphia, in 1774.

Both were members of the Society of Friends, but when the Revolution was proclaimed they were among the first to volunteer for service. As an immediate result, Colonel Biddle was "read out of meeting" of the Society of Friends; and when his wife expressed approval of his course she was subjected to similar discipline. Undeterred by this, however, Colonel Biddle went into camp with his regiment, and Mrs. Biddle promptly joined him there.

Among the anecdotes of Mrs. Biddle's services in the field is one related by Mrs. E. P. Ellet in her *American Revolutionary Women*. When the American Army was encamped near Brandywine, Mrs. Biddle was informed by an aide of Washington that a large British foraging party was near and that orders had been issued for an American raiding party to attempt to cut off their retreat. Since an engagement was expected it was deemed best that the women leave camp.

Mrs. Biddle, unwilling to be included in the order, asked General Washington to permit her to remain, saying that the men involved in the raid would return hungry and fatigued and that she would make provision for their refreshment. She won her point and, although the British retreated without a fight, had in readiness for the expedition a bounteous feast which at least a hundred officers attended, including General Lafayette. "Madam, we heard that you feed the army today," was their favorite remark in presenting themselves.

After the war the friendships with Mrs. Greene and Mrs. Knox and with General and Mrs. Washington, which she had formed in camp endured. The Washingtons frequently entertained the Biddles, and it is worth noting that Lafayette, during his last visit to Philadelphia, did not fail to call at their home to pay his respects to Mrs. Biddle.

Mrs. Biddle survived her husband by many years. Her death terminated a residence in Philadelphia of over sixty years.

EVELINA HEAP GLEAVES

ANN HUPP

1757?–1823

꙰

ANN HUPP, the heroine of Miller's Blockhouse, was one of the most heroic women of pioneer Washington County. Miller's Blockhouse, on what is now the Clinton Miller farm, on the Dutch fork of Buffalo Creek, about five miles northwest of Claysville, was one of the strongest and most exposed on the western frontier. On Easter Sunday, March 31, 1782, Jacob Miller and John Hupp, husband of Ann, left the fort in search of a colt that had strayed away. As they neared a spring a short distance off they were both killed by Indians in ambush. A few minutes later the forest swarmed with Shawnee warriors, who expected to capture the blockhouse without resistance, for Captain Jacob Miller, Jr., had gone to Rice's Fort with his scouts.

In the blockhouse were Ann Hupp and her four children, several women of the Miller family, the family of Edward Gaither, Frederick Miller, a boy of eleven, and Mathias Ault, an aged man. As the Indians swarmed down upon them Ann Hupp dispatched young Miller to Rice's for help, but he was unable to get through the enemy lines and escaped back to the blockhouse only after a thrilling race for life.

With children screaming about her and the other women wringing their hands in despair, Ann Hupp never lost her head. Gathering all the guns in the blockhouse, she fired from one porthole after another, giving the impression that the place was well defended. Surprised, the Indians stopped their advance and sought shelter behind trees. This gave a breathing spell during which Ann rallied the frightened women until she got several to man the portholes. The others, with the help of Ault, kept the guns loaded. The firing was heard at Rice's Fort and half an hour later Captain Miller with Philip Hupp and Jacob Rowe, Ann's younger brother, dashed through the Indian lines to the blockhouse. After a parting volley the Shawnees withdrew, taking the scalps of Jacob Miller, Sr., and John Hupp as their only trophies. But for the heroism of Ann they would have had the scalps of every woman and child in the blockhouse.

Ann Hupp lies in an unmarked grave in the old private graveyard on the Miller farm, 150 feet from the spot where the blockhouse stood.

EARLE R. FORREST

ANN BIDDLE WILKINSON

1757–1807

⚛

ANN BIDDLE was born in Philadelphia in 1757, a daughter of John and Sarah Owen Biddle. Her father, a son of one of the earliest Quaker settlers of Burlington, New Jersey, had moved to Philadelphia before his marriage.

In Christ Church, Philadelphia, November 12, 1778, Ann was married to James Wilkinson, then a colonel in the Continental Army. After Wilkinson had been appointed brigadier general by the Congress in recognition of his services at Saratoga, and a member of the Board of War, he came to feel obliged to resign these honors because of involved circumstances. This left him his old rank of colonel but no command. At the time of his marriage his fortunes were at a low ebb, and he had need of all Ann's faith and loyalty. She did not fail him then or ever.

The first years of their married life were very trying. During this period they were living in Philadelphia. Colonel Wilkinson continued active in any capacity in which he could be useful. Loyally supported by his friends, he was finally appointed clothier general of the army. Afterward, resigning that office, he became brigadier and adjutant general of Pennsylvania. In the meantime two sons had been born to them.

With the coming of peace, the need of an opening induced him to journey to Kentucky, where many of the officers held grants of land. Favorably impressed, he returned for his wife and family, and Ann Biddle Wilkinson made the dangerous journey to the "dark and bloody ground," encumbered with the care of two small children. Her third son was born after she reached Kentucky. There her first years in the new settlement held much of illness. The birth of a fourth child, who lived but a short time, added sorrow to isolation and discomfort. During the latter days of their Kentucky residence her husband went out on those expeditions against the Indians in which he won the heart of the militia and the praise of Washington. They were seasons of great anxiety to her.

Wilkinson's appointment to the command of all the western Army followed. This necessitated her removal to Fort Washington (now Cincinnati), a far-flung outpost of the Indian country. Her two oldest boys were sent to Philadelphia for schooling, returning to the Ohio country through perils that might have daunted the strongest.

Just before the battle of Fallen Timbers ("Wayne's Victory") she went out with the last wagon-train from Fort Jefferson, an encampment to which she had gone to aid her husband's recovery from illness. She was at Fort Washington to comfort the wounded as they came in from battle.

Soon after came news of the death of her eldest son, at a time when she was particularly concerned over her husband's affairs. She was quite prostrated. But Wilkinson's triumphant emergence from the cloud; his reappointment as the commander of the army, and the respite of a short residence in the East contributed to her recovery. Before long she was following down the Ohio and Mississippi, wherever her husband's duty led him during those critical times: in Natchez, as commander; in New Orleans, to assist in taking over the Louisiana Territory; in St. Louis, as Governor of the Upper Louisiana (Missouri) Territory. Everywhere she was affectionately esteemed.

But the many years of travel and anxiety, as well as the trying climates she had encountered, took their toll. She died in New Orleans in 1807, amid the excitement incident to the suppression of the Burr expedition.

Ann Biddle Wilkinson was one of the leaders of that little band of pioneer women who took with them into the western wilds the refinement and standards of civilization that redeemed the wilderness into a land of promise.

Marion M. Davis

CHARLOTTE ESTE

1761–1801

>&<

A SERVICE to the Colonial cause so conspicuous in its gallantry that it won her the personal thanks of George Washington is but one of the reasons why the memory of Charlotte Este is revered as a Pennsylvania heroine of Revolutionary times.

She was born in Hesse, Germany, in the year 1761, and probably would have lived out her life and died there had her father not been a surgeon in one of the Hessian regiments which King George III sent to America in 1777. He acquiesced in her desire to make the voyage with him, being the more easily persuaded because, like so many other European soldiers, he considered the revolt in America to be more frolic than fight as the raw Colonials would be little more than cannon fodder to the seasoned veterans of Continental wars.

Dr. Este, with the Hessian levies and his daughter, arrived at Philadelphia in the autumn of 1777. With several other officers of the contingent he was quartered in a house on Second Street in Frankford. Here the sixteen-year-old Charlotte first learned the true motives for the revolt. Before long her sympathies were strongly with the Revolutionary cause.

Unaware of this new allegiance nurtured in secret by the pretty girl, Dr. Hesse and the Crown officers were not as careful in their conversation before her as they might otherwise have been. So it was that one night Charlotte overheard a discussion of a British plan for a surprise attack on the Americans designed to bring about the capture of General Washington. Charlotte listened diligently, memorized the details, and determined to warn the gallant Colonial commander of the enterprise.

Actually she headed straight for General Washington's headquarters at Carlton on Bowman's Lane (now Queen Lane), Germantown. Delivering her warning, she received his personal thanks. Then she returned to her father's quarters by way of Reading Road (now Wissahickon Avenue) and Nicetown Lane (now Hunting Park Avenue), stopping at the Frankford mill for flour, threading the Hessian lines again and arriving safely without arousing suspicion.

From this initial service to the Revolutionary cause, Charlotte proceeded to others which, while less spectacular, were of great value and consisted of dressing the wounds of innumerable soldiers as well as nursing hundreds of them through an epidemic of smallpox.

In 1779 she fell in love with and married an American soldier named George Wenzell. They established a home near Byberry where she lived until her death in 1801.

MRS. NELSON F. EBERBACH

SARAH EWING HALL

1761–1830

BESIDES being one of the first women in America to attain fame as a writer, Sarah Ewing Hall also endeared herself to later memory as a devoted mother and a brilliant conversationalist. She was born on October 30, 1761, the daughter of the Rev. John Ewing, an eminently learned and pious man, who presided for many years over the University of Pennsylvania. Her mother's maiden name was Hannah Sergeant.

Even as a girl, Sarah betrayed an ambition, rare among the women of her time, to achieve something extraordinary during her lifetime. By way of preparation, she devoted herself to study and soon attained great proficiency in the Latin and Greek languages, as well as acquiring a comprehensive knowledge of astronomy and the sciences. She studied all her life, in fact, undertaking to learn Hebrew when she was fifty.

Sarah married at an early age and became the mother of five children. Yet she found time among her housewifely duties to contribute many sprightly essays and spirited criticisms to Dennie's *Port Folio,* one of the most important magazines of the post-Revolutionary period. Later, in 1806, Mrs. Hall's eldest son, John Elihu, became editor of the *Port Folio;* and during the ten years of his regime she aided him materially in his work, both with advice and with the products of her pen.

Outstanding among Mrs. Hall's writings was her book *Conversa-*

tions on the Bible, which was popular in England as well as in America. Among her friends were numbered some of the most brilliant and erudite persons of her time, and she herself enjoyed considerable reputation as a humorous, witty, and scholarly conversationalist.

Her husband, John Hall, was secretary to the Land Office, and United States Marshal for the District of Pennsylvania. After his death she retired to a retreat on the Susquehanna River, where she remained eight years. She was quite happy there, except that she missed her friends and books, and so she finally returned to Philadelphia, where she died on April 8, 1830. She was buried in Pine Street Burying Ground beside her father and mother.

Lucy E. Lee Ewing

DEBORAH NORRIS LOGAN

1761–1839

Deborah Norris was the daughter of Charles Norris and his second wife, Mary Parker. She was born in the mansion built by her father at the corner of Fourth and Chestnut streets. Its beautiful garden stretched to Fifth Street, where it adjoined the new State House. It was from the top of the wall surrounding this garden that Deborah, at the age of fifteen, heard the first public reading of the Declaration of Independence.

"I distinctly heard the words of that instrument read to the people," she says in her memoirs. "It took place a little after 12 at noon. It was a time of fearful doubt and great anxiety with the people, many of whom were appalled at the boldness of the measure, and the first audience of the Declaration was neither very numerous nor confined to the most respectable class of citizens."

Deborah married Dr. George Logan, the grandson of James Logan, who was the intimate friend of William Penn, first Secretary of the Quaker Commonwealth, and always a leading figure in its government. In 1782, a year after their marriage, Dr. and Mrs. Logan left Philadelphia and made their permanent home in the village of Germantown at Stenton, the beautiful mansion built by James Logan in 1728.

Dr. Logan's hobby was agriculture, and he soon redeemed the Stenton estate from the ravages of war and made it a model of scientific farming. The records of Deborah Logan's life there reveal her orderly and scientific mind. She invariably began the day by overseeing the work of the maids and then visiting the kitchen, where she herself prepared the dishes especially liked by the different members of her family. "I have a great reputation in the neighborhood," she wrote, "for my cakes and mince pies."

She did her own clear-starching, for the fine linen of the Quaker caps and kerchiefs required as light a hand as lace, and some part of every day she devoted to her cherished garden. But these duties were only for the morning. With the "leisure and repose" that followed the noonday dinner came the thimble or the knitting needles or a book or the paying of neighborly visits. The book was often in evidence, for Deborah Logan kept fully abreast of the thought and literature of her time and was herself a poet of no small distinction.

Dr. Logan, as a public man and for a time United States Senator, was well acquainted with the statesmen of the day, and many distinguished guests, including visiting Europeans, were entertained at Stenton. No one of them was more interesting to Deborah Logan than Benjamin Franklin. "If you did not find you had acquired something by being with him," she wrote, "it must be placed to your own lack of attention." Her memoirs record with pride a visit from Washington, then in Philadelphia officially as president of the Federal Convention. He passed a day at Stenton "in the most social and friendly manner possible."

Jefferson was an intimate friend of Dr. Logan and visited him frequently. Of him Deborah wrote:

He had visited at the Court of France and upon his return appeared in somewhat of its costume and wore a suit of silk, ruffles and an elegant topaz ring, but he soon accustomed himself to a more republican garb and was reproached with going to the other extreme as a bait for popularity.

In her youth and blooming womanhood Deborah Logan charmed everyone with her beauty. Her friend and schoolmate, Susannah Dilwyn, wrote of her:

Debby Logan is acknowledged by every one who has seen her, whether they have been used only to the women of our land or to the more highly polished Europeans, to be one of the most completely beautiful women they have ever seen. I cannot find words to express the rapture with which I gaze upon her.

After the War of 1812 Dr. Logan retired from public life, and he and his beautiful wife lived at Stenton a life of placid enjoyment and domestic content. Mrs. Logan entertained herself with her memoirs and her verses, and she tells us that, though she was fond of the sonnet form of verse, it had always seemed to her like "putting the muse into corsets."

In one of the roomy attics of Stenton she found a mass of neglected papers relating to the early history of Pennsylvania, and she devoted many years of her life to the task of copying and collecting them. They were published later by the Historical Society of Pennsylvania under the name of the *Penn-Logan Correspondence*. This contribution to Pennsylvania's history is one that cannot be overestimated. Had it not been for her diligence all the valuable Penn-Logan papers would most probably have been destroyed.

Dr. Logan died in 1831 after a long illness. Deborah survived him eight years, but they were all years of mourning. She died in 1839 and was buried in the little burying ground on the Stenton estate beside her adored husband and the children.

Imogen B. Oakley

SALLY WISTER

1761–1804

The author of Sally Wister's *Journal,* a sixteen-year-old Quaker maiden, stands out from the pages of history with a clarity and humanness attained by few other characters of her period. Sally Wister painted for posterity a pen-picture of herself and the thrilling times through which she lived that is unique.

The journal covered a period of only nine months, but they were by far the most exciting months of the young diarist's life, as they were of all Philadelphians at that time. During those days occurred the British capture of the city, the battle of Germantown, the sur-

render of Burgoyne, the skirmishes before Washington's entrench-
ments at Whitemarsh, the winter encampment at Valley Forge, the
Conway cabal against Washington, the acknowledgment of American independence by France, and the final evacuation of Philadelphia
by the enemy.

Previous to the beginning of her journal, addressed by its author to
her intimate school friend, Deborah Norris, Sally Wister's life had
been no more unusual than that of any well-bred daughter of the
times. Born on July 20, 1761, in the home of her grandfather, John
Wister, at what is now 325 Market Street, Philadelphia, she came of
a distinguished ancestry. Her father, Daniel Wister, was of German
descent; her mother, Lowry Jones Wister, also a Philadelphian, of
Welsh stock, while her grandfather was a Palatine, hailing from the
village of Hilsbach in Baden, seventeen miles from Heidelberg.

Although little is known of Sally's school days, from what has been
learned it is assumed that she was sent to the Quaker philanthropist,
Anthony Benezet. Here, doubtless, she gained her knowledge of the
higher classic and literary studies and of French and Latin indicated
in her journal, as well as the "needle wisdom" and sampler stitchery
which caused the gallant Captain Dandridge, as related in the diary,
to draw comparisons to the detriment of the girls of his native Virginia. And here, too, was formed the friendship with Deborah Norris
which resulted in the writing of the journal when the frequent correspondence of the two girls was interrupted by the British occupation of Philadelphia.

The little book presents a thoroughly naïve and interesting picture
of the various Continental officers who were quartered at different
times in the farmhouse of the widow Hannah Foulke, at North
Wales, where Sally and her family were staying during the anxious
days of 1777 and 1778. Quite ingenuously it tells of her girlish palpi-
tations over the numerous gentlemen with whom she came in contact, with especial stress on a certain Major William Truman Stodard.
Her own account of one of her mischievous pranks is recorded in the
following quotations from the journal. She is writing about a conversation with Major Stodard:

I was darning an apron upon which he was pleased to compliment me.
"Well, Miss Sally," said he, "what would you do if the British were to
come here?"

"Do!" exclaimed I. "Be frightened just to death!"

He laughed and said we would escape their rage by getting behind the representative of a British grenadier that we had upstairs.

[This was a pasteboard model made by Major André as part of scenery in the old South Street Theatre.]

"Of all things," said he, "I should like to frighten Major Tilly with it. Pray, ladies, let's fix it in his chamber tonight."

"If thee will take all the blame, we will assist thee," said I.

"That I will," he replied, and this was the plan:

We had bought, some weeks before, the British grenadier from Uncle Miles on purpose to divert us. It is remarkably well executed, six feet high and makes a martial appearance. This we agreed to stand in the door that opens into the road with another figure that would add to the deceit. One of our servants was to stand behind them, others were to serve as occasion offered. In the beginning of the evening I went to Liddy [Foulke] and begged her to secure the swords and pistols which were in the parlor. Liddy went in and brought her apron full of swords and pistols. When this was done Stodard joined the officers. We girls went and stood at the first landing of the stairs.

The gentlemen were very merry and chatted on public affairs, when Seaton's Negro opened the door, candle in hand, and said: "There's somebody at the door that wishes to see you."

"Who, all of us?" said Tilly.

"Yes, sir," said the boy.

They all rose and walked into the entry, Tilly first, in full expectation of news. The first object that struck his view was a British soldier. In a moment his ears were saluted with: "Is there any rebel officers here?" in a thundering voice. Not waiting for a second word, he darted like lightning out one front door, through the yard, bolted over the fence. Swamps, fences, thornhedges and plowed fields in no way impeded his retreat. He was soon out of hearing. The woods echoed with: "Which way did he go?" "Stop him!" "Surround the house!"

We females rushed downstairs to join the general laugh. Figure to thyself this Tilly, of a snowy evening, no hat, shoes down at the heel, hair untied, flying across meadows, creeks, and mud holes. Flying from what? Why, a bit of painted wood. But he was entirely ignorant of what it was. The idea of being made a prisoner wholly engrossed his mind.

After the death of John Wister in 1798, Daniel Wister and his family took up their permanent residence in the Germantown house, and here Sally spent the remainder of her life. She was fond of writing poetry, and some of her verses, written over the nom de plume

"Laura," appeared in the Philadelphia *Port Folio*. During her later years she went little into society, lavishing most of her attention and affection on her mother, whose death, in February 1804, was such a blow to her that she survived only two months.

MARY ALLEN CALEY

MARGARET ARMSTRONG LYON

before 1763–1793

THE period of the French and Indian Wars, and notably the period from 1754 to 1763, with its horrors and suffering, is to us of the present generation a kind of saga, and one which is almost unbelievable to the average person. If the pioneer knew suffering, physical, mental and spiritual, in this era, how much did this same suffering reflect upon the wife and mother of the pioneer? Many women who came to America and settled the so-called "back counties" of Pennsylvania before this era were women gently bred, of Scotch birth or ancestry, who, by virtue of a hundred years or less spent by their families in the Province of Ulster in Ireland, came into the name Scotch-Irish by which they are generally known to us today. These women, the mothers of large families, bore the hardships of physical toil, of privation where neighbors were separated not only by wilderness with trails as communication links, but the solitude and danger that accompanied these wilderness stretches made them often a thing of dread and horror. Inhabited not only by wild beasts but the much more to be feared redskins, who came as spies from the dreaded Captain Jacobs or the Shingas in their Kittanning stronghold.

When Margaret Armstrong Lyon came with her husband John Lyon, to America with their family of children, settling in the county of Cumberland in the year 1763, Shingas and Captain Jacobs were no longer feared. Colonel John Armstrong, brother of Margaret Armstrong Lyon, in his celebrated raid upon Kittanning, in the decade preceding, had lessened the Indian danger. And from this exploit of Colonel Armstrong, then in command of every fortification in the back counties from the Susquehanna westward to Fort

Bedford's limits, dated his friendship with General Washington. When General John Armstrong and William Lyon, her eldest son, who had joined his uncle in Cumberland early in the 1750 decade, decided that the Lyon family should leave their home in Enniskillen, Ireland, they doubtless felt that the Indian menace was ended forever except for occasional forays. But they had not counted upon the great Delaware chieftain, Pontiac, whose strategy and magnificent ability made him fit for the councils of any race. In the same year, 1763, that the Lyons landed in Cumberland, Pontiac laid bare his well-planned conspiracy. The fury of its attack was spent, however, before Cumberland County was reached, and the settlers saw with relief that the frontier lines had advanced already beyond their confines.

The section which is now Juniata County near Miffintown, where the Lyons had a grant of land from the Proprietaries, lay in what was then Cumberland, which was cut off and made Miffin County in 1789, afterward Juniata. Famous for its scenic beauty, it teemed with game in greatest abundance and fish such as sportsmen could not dream of seeing in the streams of today. Here, after the Pontiac insurrection had been crushed and the Indian captives had been returned to Carlisle, dwelt Margaret Lyon with seven of her eight children; William, the eldest, having married his cousin, Alice Armstrong. She found much to do about her home, spinning and weaving, knitting and sewing: a capable housewife we may be certain, with her grown daughters about her, rapidly being married and making homes of their own. In 1773, John Lyon was granted twenty acres of land in the Tuscarora Valley for a church. This must have been a matter of much moment to the sturdy Scotch-Irish Presbyterian that she was. Churches and schools were synonymous, and the church thus erected occasioned much organization and planning. Here in the graveyard by the church her husband was buried in 1780, and here she followed him about 1793.

Most Scotch-Irish families carry a portrait, woven for them by the word of their mothers, of some ancestress who labored truly and well, who read her Bible and was beloved by all who knew her. More often the record comes of the paternal ancestor, his lands, his exploits, told to his children by his wife.

But the family of Margaret Armstrong Lyon had what today we might call the "mother complex." They describe her as a brilliant conversationalist, in a day when that accomplishment ranked as an art. She was, we are told by historians, "one of the most patriotic and prominent women of the Colonial and Revolutionary periods in Pennsylvania." Far from magazines and books, far from even the ordinary supplies for her household, she maintained a degree of culture and charm that remains a pleasing heritage and makes of her a personality for her descendants even today. Carlisle was a long journey away, fifty-some miles, across the mountains by the nearest route, not always the easiest to follow; and no store was nearer than Carlisle until about 1791, when John Patterson, who married her granddaughter, opened one in the Academia section. In the last decade of her life she perhaps read *Kline's Gazette,* published in Carlisle, and before that she had had newspapers brought by the post from Philadelphia to Carlisle which had been established by the far-seeing Franklin as Postmaster General of the Colonies. But newspapers were very old when they reached the Tuscarora Valley, and Margaret Armstrong must have drawn much on letters from home, visits of the few travelers like James Blaine from Carlisle, who had visited abroad, and the books that came slowly into the Province by way of Philadelphia. But the wealth of Margaret Armstrong Lyon lay within herself, and she had the power to create a kingdom from her own surroundings. However much she contributed through the power of her own personality she is best judged, as a mother must always be, by her children. They are the investment of a mother's life and are in turn changed into the currency of citizenship true or spurious as the case may be.

Margaret Armstrong Lyon's children were worthy of their mother. William, her eldest son, was active in the French and Indian Wars as ensign and lieutenant. Later he resigned his command to become a magistrate, in reality a Colonial judge. Still later he was Prothonotary, Register of Wills, Clerk of the Orphans Court and Recorder of Deeds of Cumberland County, where his easily read signatures and records are seen in the courthouse today at Carlisle. During the Revolutionary War he served with ability as a member of the Supreme Executive Council in Pennsylvania, a position of real importance. Other sons and daughters later pushed out to the western counties of Pennsylvania and still farther into the states opening to the westward.

This progenitor of the Lyon family in Pennsylvania together with her husband blazed the way for those who came after them and are blazing it still, as we consider the work they accomplished and the manner in which they went about their task. Overcoming obstacles, they carried with them high courage and met with inspiration, tasks that would seem to us almost too vast to undertake. Margaret Armstrong Lyon, the pioneer wife of a settler in one of Pennsylvania's back counties and the sister of one of Pennsylvania's intrepid soldiers and heroes, is not without a certain aureole of her own.

LENORE EMBICK FLOWER

RACHEL KIRK PRICE

1763–1847

RACHEL KIRK, who became the wife of Philip Price, was the sixth child of William Kirk and Sibilla Davis, his second wife, being born in East Nantmeal, Chester County. Her paternal grandfather came to America in 1688 from Ulster, Ireland. Her ancestry on her mother's side was Welsh.

Such records of her early life as have been preserved are very scant of detail until her marriage to Philip Price, on October 20, 1784. After that it is a story of ardent devotion both to her family as wife and mother and to the Society of Friends as a member and minister.

Philip Price was the third generation in direct line from the Philip Price who came to Pennsylvania with William Penn in 1682. He was born in Kingsessing, now part of Philadelphia, where he remained in residence with his father until his marriage and for three years thereafter. Then, with Rachel, he removed to a farm in East Nantmeal, remaining there until March 23, 1791, when he bought the farm two miles southwest of West Chester, which they occupied or owned throughout their lives.

It is worth noting, in passing, that the children of Philip and Rachel Price were among the first persons in America to be vaccinated against smallpox, the cowpox virus for the inoculation being especially imported from England only a few years after the discovery of the process by Dr. Jenner in 1796.

Rachel and her husband became members of Concord Monthly

Meeting on May 4, 1791, being admitted upon presentation of a certificate from Uwchlan Monthly Meeting, dated April 21. Philip became clerk of Concord Meeting in 1797; and on July 7, 1802, Rachel was recommended as minister, proceeding forthwith to assume her new duties, which entailed much traveling, some of it through wilderness regions.

In 1804, Rachel Price made a religious visitation to Societies of Friends in New Jersey and on the Eastern Shore. On this occasion she had her first sight of the sea. In 1807 her ministry required her to travel to the new country of Ohio, a mission she undertook in company with an Englishwoman. This journey was made upon horseback over mountains and rivers and often through regions so rough that the women were forced to dismount and walk, at times being slowed to a pace of less than two miles an hour. Nevertheless they accomplished their purpose and returned safely to Pennsylvania. Two years later, Rachel traveled extensively in Virginia and Maryland. In 1810 she visited the Western Quarter, and in 1812 called at Abington.

From 1818 to 1830 she and her husband, as its first supervisors, were in charge of the Westtown School, the grounds of which were laid out and planted under their direction.

Philip Price inaugurated scientific farming and ground fertilization, cattle and sheep breeding on his farm. He was one of the founders of the first agricultural society of Pennsylvania.

Their son Eli Kirk Price was the originator of the Greater Philadelphia project and of the larger Fairmount Park which their great-grandson, Eli Kirk Price, Jr. extended and embellished.

HELEN E. RHOADES

ANN WILLING BINGHAM

1764–1801

ESTABLISHMENT of American social prestige in the courts of the Old World was a matter of importance to the United States in the years immediately after the founding of the Republic when the very fate of democracy, dependent on friendships and financial help abroad, hung trembling in the balance. The political maneuvering and the diplomacy were, of course, formally delegated to men; but however great their ability and fitness for their tasks, success often hung on the charm and social tact of the women they sponsored.

Outstanding among the women entrusted, if unofficially, with the delicate task of creating and upholding America's social prestige both at home and abroad was Ann Willing Bingham, wife of William Bingham.

She was born in Philadelphia in 1764, daughter of Thomas Willing and Ann McCall, and was the eldest girl in a family of ten children. Her father was the son of Charles Willing and Anne Shippen, and therefore a scion of two of the leading families of Colonial Philadelphia. Thomas Willing was a wealthy merchant and shipowner, partner of Robert Morris; he was chairman of the meeting in State House Yard June 18, 1774; president of the First Provisional Congress in Carpenter's Hall, July 22, 1774, and delegate to the Federal Constitutional Convention, 1787–89. In 1781 he helped organize the Bank of North America, the first chartered institution of its kind in the United States, and was its president until 1791. He was later president of the Bank of the United States.

Her mother died while Ann was still in her early teens, but nevertheless the child was immediately installed as mistress of her father's house, presiding as hostess at innumerable entertainments for visiting notables. One notable dinner over which she presided is described by John Adams in his diary, which notes that others present included George Washington, John Jay, Philip Livingston, Patrick Henry, Peyton Randolph, William Paca, and Samuel Chase.

By the time she was seventeen, Ann Willing had established herself as one of the leaders of Philadelphia's society. That year, 1780, she married William Bingham, the wedding in Old Christ Church being one of the fashionable events of the season. William Bingham was a Philadelphian by birth, and after graduation from the College of Philadelphia was sent to the West Indies by the British as agent for the Crown. When the Revolution came, he remained as agent of the Continental Congress. He had inherited some money from his father, but amassed great wealth in the tropics. Soon he decided to return to his native place.

For several years the Binghams remained at the Willing home, where they entertained in a lavish manner, which was noticed by

Griswold in his *Republican Court* with: "Mrs. Bingham maintained a court all her own." In 1784 the Binghams traveled to England. One of the most marked honors accorded them was presentation, at a time when George III was not favorably disposed toward Americans. The Binghams also were presented at the Court of Louis XVI and Marie Antoinette of France.

Mrs. Bingham made a distinctly favorable impression in London, sufficient at least to cause Mrs. John Adams to write to friends in America: "Taken as a whole she is the finest woman I ever saw; her easy deportment that has all the pride and grace of high breeding, the intelligence of her countenance, and the entire affability of her attitude, disarmed every feeling of unfriendliness and converted every one into adoration." John Adams' daughter, also writing to friends in America, expressed the same thing differently: "Mrs. Bingham is quite the fashion here in London, and very much admired." And this: "The hairdresser who dresses our hair for us on court days, asked mamma if she knew the lady so much talked about from America."

In Paris the Binghams were dinner guests of Lafayette, as was Mrs. Adams who again wrote home, referring to Mrs. Bingham as "more beautiful and amiable than ever," and describing her gown as "of black velvet with pink satin sleeves and stomacher, a pink satin petticoat, and over it a skirt of white crepe spotted all over with gray fur. It was superb and the gracefulness of her person made it appear to peculiar advantage."

While they were still abroad Mr. Bingham was elected to Congress and they returned to Philadelphia. About 1790 they built their famous mansion on a three-acre lot on Third Street between Walnut and Spruce streets; it was considered the most splendid private residence in the country at that time, being modeled after the town house of the Duke of Manchester, in London. The gardens extended through to Fourth Street.

Upon opening this house, Mrs. Bingham introduced Philadelphia to four-tined eating forks, the first ever used here. Mr. Bingham, not to be outdone, appeared on the streets bearing an umbrella, the first man in town to carry that device. The Binghams, in addition to their city house, also had a palatial country home, originally built by John Penn, on what is now the site of Horticultural Hall, in Fairmount Park. This estate the Binghams named Lansdowne, after the Marquis of Lansdowne, who had been most friendly to them in England. For ten years these two homes were the center of social life in America, almost every notable American of the period and virtually all distinguished visitors from overseas being guests at one time or another.

In 1800 Mrs. Bingham's health failed and she was taken to Bermuda to recover. The trip was in vain, however, for she died there. In the old churchyard in St. George's, Bermuda there is a tomb with the inscription:

ANN WILLING

Daughter of Thomas Willing
of Philadelphia

1764–1801

Mr. Bingham, broken in health and spirit by the bereavement, took his family to Europe and never returned to America. He died at Bath, England, in 1804. He left two daughters and one son. Ann Louisa Bingham was married to Alexander Baring, a son of Sir Francis, the English banker. Alexander became a member of Parliament and was raised to the peerage as Lord Ashburton. When he was appointed a special minister to the United States he helped adjust the northeastern boundary contention in what became known as the Ashburton Treaty.

Gilbert Stuart painted more than one portrait of Ann Willing Bingham, and it was through her that George Washington was persuaded to sit for him.

Esther L. Little
Mary Ward Mercur

MARY (POLLY) ROBESON BENSELL

1764–1857

⚜

Mary Robeson, daughter of Jonathan, Jr., and Catherine Farmer Robeson, was born in February 1764, in Montgomery County. Her ancestors were among the early settlers of that part of the country, her grandmother being Catherine Farmer, whose parents gave the ground where now stands St. Thomas' Church, at Whitemarsh.

In 1795 she married Dr. George Bensell, grandson of Bishop Bensilius, of Upsala, Sweden. She survived her husband by thirty years, and died in 1857, at the age of ninety-three. Of her four children only one outlived her. Her youngest son died on the plains going to California in 1855. During her married life she lived on Germantown Avenue in Philadelphia, but spent a great deal of time on her brother Peter's property, known as Shoomac Park, bounded by the Schuylkill, the Wissahickon Creek and School and Gypsy lanes. His house is still standing on the corner of Ridge Road and Wissahickon Drive.

As may be seen from her portrait, a pen-and-ink drawing made in her later life, she was a woman of great integrity of character, and strong personality, full of spirit and patriotism. One of her descendants, living in Massachusetts, has a silver teapot which was presented to her by the First City Troop of Philadelphia whom she had entertained at Shoomac Park on their way to the "Westward in the year 1794" to help put down the Whisky Insurrection. It was in appreciation of her kindness that the teapot was presented to her.

Since she was twelve years of age at the time of the adoption of the Declaration of Independence, she must have seen and remembered much of the last days of the Revolutionary War. It is to such women as these that we are indebted for the stability of our institutions. She was known always in the family as "Polly." The stories about her which have been handed down leave the impression on her descendants that she must have been a woman of unusual character.

ANNA BAKER CARSON

MARY WELLS MORRIS

1764–1819

MARY WELLS, born in Philadelphia September 4, 1764, was married to Benjamin Wister Morris, son of Samuel Morris, merchant, Nov. 24, 1785. Benjamin Morris suffered financial reverses and turned over all his available property to his creditors, reserving only a tract of wild and apparently worthless land in Tioga Township, in what was then Lycoming County. There he went with his family in 1799 and built a log cabin on the site which seven years later was to be known as Wellsborough—now spelled Wellsboro—the present county seat of Tioga County, named in honor of his wife.

Devotedly Mary Wells chose to follow her husband, as a true settler's wife, into the wilderness. She who had been accustomed to comforts and luxuries and friends was now, in middle life, to adjust herself to a wholly different world, one of hardship, privation, and loneliness. With her were an unmarried daughter, Rebecca, and a son, Samuel.

They were all members of the Society of Friends, whose meeting place was their home, where religious services were held regularly for all comers. Mrs. Morris always wore the garb of her people.

In spite of the hardships of the Pine Creek Land Company, which Benjamin Morris represented as agent, the conditions of the Morris family improved. Mrs. Morris was beloved by all the early settlers, for she was the foremost woman in all the wilderness in acts of kindness, and always cheerful and unafraid in spite of threatened Indian attacks.

The children were reared in a devoted family life. Rebecca married William Cox Ellis, of Muncy, who became a member of the State Legislature and of Congress. Samuel attended Princeton College. At the age of twenty-six he was an associate judge of the new county. Later he was elected to the Legislature and to Congress. Of his children, Benjamin Wister became Protestant Episcopal Bishop of Oregon, and all the others had distinguished careers.

The devotion of Mary Wells, wife and mother, and her services as a leader in the wilderness had even in what appeared to be a misfortune prepared new ways to successful careers for her loved ones.

WILLIAM R. STRAUGHN

ELIZABETH SPEER BUCHANAN

1767–1833

THE tribute of a distinguished son drapes a mantle of greatness about the shoulders of this remarkable woman who might otherwise have remained unsung by fame, however much her indefatigable mother-liness entitled her to an extra meed of praise. The son was James Buchanan, Pennsylvania's only President of the United States, whose memoirs had this to say of his mother: "Under Providence, I attribute any little distinction which I may have acquired in the world to the blessing which He conferred upon me in granting me such a mother."

Elizabeth Speer was born on April 16, 1767, on a farm ten miles from Lancaster where her father, James Speer, of Scotch Presbyterian ancestry, settled soon after immigrating to Pennsylvania in 1756. Later he and his wife, who was Mary Patterson, with their only daughter, Elizabeth, removed to a parcel of ground at the foot of South Mountain between Chambersburg and Gettysburg. Elizabeth's opportunity for education was limited, but she made the most of what she had, enhancing it by a natural appreciation for poetry. So inherently sound was her taste that of her own accord and without ever having read a criticism of her favorite authors, she selected as worthy of memorizing the most acclaimed passages of Milton, Pope, Cowper, Young, and Thompson.

She was married on her twenty-first birthday to James Buchanan who, six years older than she, was the proprietor of a trading post for Indians and frontiersmen at Cove Gap, sometimes called Stony Batter, at the foot of North Mountain in what is now Franklin County. The wedding took place in Upper West Conococheague Church in Mercersburg. Of this marriage eleven children were born, James, who became fifteenth President of the United States, being the second.

Household tasks necessitated by such a large family, tasks which she would not delegate to servants despite her husband's pleas, consumed much of Mrs. Buchanan's time; but even so she managed to cultivate the friendship of her children as well as their love and affection, and instilled in them the elements of ambition, resourcefulness, patriotism, and proper living.

In 1796 the family moved into the village of Mercersburg, where Mr. Buchanan built a house and store. He was elected justice of the peace and was a generally recognized, solid citizen of the community until his death on June 11, 1821.

After her husband's death, Mrs. Buchanan was soon called upon to sustain new afflictions in the loss of two of her sons, William and George, and of a favorite daughter. But she was a woman of firm character and steadfast religiousness and so bore her grief with philosophy and reserve, although withdrawing more and more into a closer study of theology. She died on May 14, 1833, at Greensburg, and was buried beside her husband in the family plot in what is now Spring Grove Cemetery, near Mercersburg.

ETTA LONGSHORE WORRELL
MRS. C. P. FENDRICK

ANNE DUNLOP HARRIS

1767–1844

NESTLED among the foothills of the Allegheny Mountains in Centre County, Pennsylvania, and covering seven hills like Rome, is the town of Bellefonte. It has been called "the Home of Governors," as four of its sons have filled that high office at Harrisburg; among them the distinguished War Governor, Andrew Gregg Curtin. One wonders who had the vision to choose this site, surrounding a beautiful spring, in the midst of a wilderness, and give it its name.

In 1795 a caravan of horses and mules carried Anne Dunlop Harris, her husband, James Harris, their three children, and their servants over the seven mountains. They came to join Anne Harris' father, Colonel James Dunlop, who two years earlier had been drawn there by rich iron deposits. He purposed building an iron furnace along Spring Creek. Anne Harris' mind was one that was enthusiastic about building an ideal home in the wilderness, in helping to found a town and later in writing a book on metaphysics.

She was born at Shippensburg, March 14, 1767. On June 15, 1790, she married James Harris, son of Judge John Harris, Revolutionary patriot, member of the Provincial Conference of 1776, of the Constitutional Convention of 1776, and of the Pennsylvania Convention to ratify the Constitution of the United States. Her husband was a surveyor.

The site Anne and James selected for their home was at a beautiful spot on rising ground. The house, still standing, was built of native limestone with a Colonial pillared porch in front. The estate was christened "Marlbrook" by its mistress. Colonel Dunlop and James Harris laid out the town and, desiring a suitable name for it, consulted the fertile brain of Anne.

There is a legend in the family that Prince Talleyrand, passing through the forests of Pennsylvania, visited at Marlbrook and Mrs. Harris asked him to assist her in choosing a name. Standing before the Big Spring he said, "Call it for your spring." Anne Harris liked the idea and called it Bellefonte.

Colonel Dunlop and James Harris gave to the town, lots for an academy, a courthouse, and a Presbyterian church. They also gave lots to be sold, the money to be used for the buildings. They were built in the classical style of architecture and created an atmosphere of culture and beauty. It was in this environment that Anne Harris brought up her family of five sons and two daughters. One son was a physician, one an ironmaster. Three were civil engineers of reputation. One daughter married a minister, the other a physician.

ANNE HARRIS HOY
JOHN IRWIN BRIGHT

MASSA HARBISON

1770–1837

IN the early history of our western border are many records of the trials, privations, and heroic deeds of the pioneer men and women. Among these accounts of suffering and heroism, the capture of Massa Harbison by the Indians was one of the most memorable of any on the frontier.

Massa White was born in Amwell Township, Somerset County,

New Jersey, March 18, 1770. In 1783 her father, Edward White, a Revolutionary soldier, moved with his family to a place called Redstone Fox, now Brownsville, on the Monongahela River. In 1787 she married John Harbison, and at the time of her capture the family had their home on the Allegheny River, near Reed's Block House, about twenty-five miles from Pittsburgh.

Her husband was a soldier in General St. Clair's army, and having been wounded, was given lighter duty as an Indian scout serving on the Allegheny frontier. No danger was apprehended from the Indians at this time, as the frontier seemed quiet. But early on the morning of May 22, 1792, during the absence of her husband on duty, their home, which was about two hundred yards from the blockhouse, was entered by a party of Seneca and Munsee Indians.

She and her three children, two boys of three and five years of age, and a baby of one year, were dragged from their beds by their feet, the Indians refusing to allow them to put on any clothes. Some of the party then proceeded to plunder the house, while others made an attack on the blockhouse, killing one man and injuring others. Failing of success in this encounter they were forced to retreat, ordering their defenseless captives to accompany them.

On her refusal to go she was flogged, and her younger boy, who was standing by the fireplace crying, was grabbed by the feet, his head dashed against the threshold of the door, stabbed and scalped. At this inhuman act she attempted to scream to the blockhouse for help, but one Indian closed her mouth, another drew his tomahawk as if to kill her, while a third seized her and claimed her for his squaw.

The Indians then left, compelling her and her two remaining children to march along with them. During the journey that day her older boy, while lamenting the death of his brother, was also killed and scalped. At this barbaric cruelty she fell senseless, her captors carrying her to the river and holding her in the water until she recovered consciousness. Twice she tried to kill herself, but both times she was prevented by the Indians.

Pushing rapidly forward they reached the Indian camp that evening, near where Butler now stands. She and her child were then taken to a thicket about three hundred yards from the Indian camp. Her arms were so pinioned to her back that it was with difficulty that she was able to care for her child. A blanket thrown on the ground served as their bed. With a savage on each side of her as a guard, she passed the night here without wood or fire.

This unhappy mother spent two nights in the camp, two Indians guarding her through the night and one during the day, the other keeping watch on the trail to prevent any rescue. Her only food during this time was a piece of venison about the size of an egg, which she broke into small bits and fed to the child.

Early on the morning of the third day, May 25, stuffing the mouth of the her child with an old piece of cloth so that it could make no noise, she succeeded in escaping with him in her arms, while the Indian guard was sleeping. The North Star was her guide, but owing to her condition her progress was slow. Once during her escape she was almost recaptured by the Indians, and so forlorn and haggard was her appearance from her frightful sufferings during her captivity and escape that when she reached the cabin of John Crozier, a close neighbor, on May 27, he was unable to recognize her.

On May 28 she was carried to Pittsburgh, where before John Wilkins, a justice of the peace, she made an affidavit setting forth her terrible experiences. From there a scout went to Todd's Point the following morning and buried the body of her older son. She died in 1837, and is buried at Freeport.

EMILY SPRANKLE HERON

ELIZABETH FOX MEANS

1770–1851

SEVENTEEN days spent alone in a wilderness cabin, surrounded by scalp-hunting savages and ravenous wild beasts, constitute a severe test for a thirteen-year-old girl, yet it was a task cheerfully and voluntarily undertaken by Elizabeth Fox in 1783. Her fortitude in the pioneer life of the state now constitutes her claim to a place among Pennsylvania's notable women.

Elizabeth Fox was the first white child to be born in Bradford County, the event occurring in 1770; her advent being almost coincident with the capture of her father, Rudolf Fox, by marauding Indians who held him captive for nine months. Then he escaped and rejoined his family at Towanda; immediately removing with them to Sunbury, where they remained until after the Revolution.

He then moved to Wilkes-Barre and, a short time later, back to Towanda, where he found his old home in ashes. A bark cabin was hastily constructed, which Elizabeth, then thirteen years old, volunteered to occupy alone while the rest of the family returned to Wilkes-Barre for provisions. In Wilkes-Barre the mother was taken ill and the return was delayed more than two weeks.

In the meantime Elizabeth stuck to her post, although her food supply was running low and she was constantly menaced by wild beasts, among them one panther so bold that it actually entered the cabin and seized a haunch of venison from where it hung suspended over her bed. Finally after seventeen days, Elizabeth's food was exhausted and she set out to walk down the river, through an Indian-infested country, in search of help. Fortunately she encountered her family ascending the stream and they all returned to the cabin.

Five years later, in 1788, she married William Means. Her remarkable character is further revealed by the fact that when she was past seventy years old she learned to read and write. She died on July 21, 1851, at Towanda.

TOWANDA HISTORICAL CLUB

LUCRETIA MINER YORK

before 1772–1818

LUCRETIA MINER YORK was the wife of Amos York, pioneer settler of Mehoopany Township, now in Wyoming County, where he arrived in 1772. Here he built a log house and developed a considerable tract of land near the mouth of Meshoppen Creek. Subsequently, because of robbery and plundering by the Indians, the Yorks removed to Wyalusing, where they set up a new homestead on a grant conveyed to Mrs. York by her father, Manasseh Miner, one of the original proprietors in the Susquehanna Company.

At the outbreak of the Revolutionary War, York, being an ardent Whig and as such an object of enmity in his Tory neighborhood, considered removal of his family in the fall of 1777. Because of the early onset of winter, together with a belief that the enmity would not bring direct persecution before spring, he postponed flight.

That his idea was false became apparent on February 12, when a Negro from an old Indian town near by began calling at the York home and remaining on trifling excuses until late in the evenings. The climax came on February 14, when York was returned from a visit to a neighbor virtually in custody of Parshall Terry, Tom Green, and a party of Indians. Mrs. York's questioning elicited the fact from Terry and Green that York was indeed a prisoner, but that he would not be hurt, "only he must take an oath that he will be true to King George."

The Tories, then, according to York's daughter, Sarah, proceeded to rob the place;

They drove the cattle into the road, stripped the house of everything of value they could carry away, broke open the chests, tied up the plunder in sheets and blankets and put the bundles on the backs of the men. Father had to take a pack of his own goods. When they had got prepared to start, my father asked permission to speak to his wife—he took her by the hand, but did not speak. When the company started my father was compelled to walk, carry a bundle, and assist in driving his cattle, while his favorite riding mare carried Terry.

York's captivity extended to a period of nine months. He was finally released in New York and set out to find his family, but fell ill and died within eleven days.

In the interval, however, Mrs. York, Sarah, and eleven other children were forced to undergo a long series of hardships and precarious adventures, including a flight on foot and by canoe from Wyalusing to Wyoming with no track to follow save a dim trail blazed through the snow by three men who had come to offer succor. They finally took refuge in Forty Fort, where Mrs. York earned a living by cooking for the Revolutionary garrison.

Of her departure from this fort the morning after a battle in March 1778, her daughter wrote,

Colonel Denison said she must not go out. She declared she would; called her children to her, went to the gate and demanded a passage out. The sentry presented his bayonet to her breast and asked Colonel Denison if he should let her pass. The colonel said no. He then pushed the bayonet through her clothes so that it drew blood. She said to Colonel Denison: "I will go out with my children, or I will die here at the door." The Colonel said, "Let her pass."

Nothing daunted by this inauspicious start into a world made most unsafe by war-mad Indians, Mrs. York led her little flock down to the river. There they embarked in a large boat manned by a Mrs. Lock, a Dutch woman, whom they had to aid in poling the vessel downstream. That night they stopped at a house near the bank, where, next morning, they encountered a Lieutenant Forsman in charge of a boatload of wounded men. The Lieutenant detailed one of his men, Richard Fitzgerald, to aid the York family to the village of Paxton, where they stayed until October. At Paxton, Mrs. York buried her youngest child, a son, thirteen months old.

That October word was received that they might safely return to Wyoming, which they did, stopping over about two weeks at Wilkes-Barre. But depredations in the neighborhood were so frequent that Mrs. York decided to take flight again and make way on foot through Big Swamp to her father's home in Voluntown, Connecticut. After a torturing journey the family finally arrived at New Milford, where Mrs. York was taken sick and forced to rest for a fortnight. At North River, General Washington hearing that she was in distress near by had her brought to his tent, heard her story and gave her $50.

After the war, in 1786, the York family returned to their old home in Wyalusing where they found their old house still standing though in ruins, with the clearing greatly overgrown. However, Mrs. York's son pitched in and soon brought the farm back to abundant fertility. In a short time the family was in comfortable circumstances.

Mrs. York was a prominent woman in the little community until her death in Wysox on October 30, 1818. She was buried in Wyalusing.

LUTTA TUTHILL VAIL

FRANCES SLOCUM

about 1773–1847

᳇

FRANCES SLOCUM was born in Wilkes-Barre about 1773 and lived with her parents near the corner of Canal and North streets in that city.

On July 3, 1778, the Wyoming Massacre occurred in Wyoming Valley. For a few months after, the Indians frequently visited the scene of battle and continually wrought revenge on those whom they suspected of participating. Three Delaware Indians were seen near the home of Jacob Slocum on November 2, 1778, where the mother was at work inside and the children at play. Giles Slocum, a brother, suspected of taking part in the Wyoming Massacre, was shot, and Frances, about five years of age, carried away by the Indians. She was moved from camp to camp, and on March 2, 1780, was definitely known to be a prisoner at Niagara.

Although the family continued a diligent search, nothing was heard of her until 1835, when Colonel Ewing, connected with Indian trade, stopped at and found welcome in an Indian shelter in a remote section of Indiana. The venerable mistress of the lodge, rather light in color for an Indian, aroused his interest. She said there was something on her mind which she wished to tell him. She then confessed to her white blood, and said that she had been captured when a little girl and carried off by the Indians.

She was adopted into the Delawares and later married a member of the Miami tribe and had four children. Colonel Ewing wrote to Pennsylvania giving notice of the information. Frances Slocum's brothers, Joseph and Isaac, and her sister, Mary, who were still living, made arrangements to go to the Miami camp, near Logansport, Indiana. Isaac, who arrived first, was received by his sister at the lodge. She treated him with stoical indifference. Long years of Indian life and ways had practically changed her into an Indian herself.

Later, arrangements were made for a reunion in Peru, Indiana. This reunion was a notable event. The brothers and sisters tried to persuade Frances to return to their Wyoming Valley home, but she declined the invitation, stating that she had grown up as an Indian, that she had been treated well. It was too late to change her manner of life. She was too feeble to make the trip back home. The reunion revealed that she remembered her childhood days on the banks of the Susquehanna, the abduction, and the early kindness of her Indian captors.

She had forgotten her native tongue, remembering only the name Slocum. She had adopted Indian thoughts, customs, and beliefs, and preferred to die as she had lived from the time of her capture. The Government, when it removed the Indians from Indiana, granted Frances Slocum, her four children and her seventeen grandchildren, the concession of remaining at the old home. She died March 13, 1847, and lies on the little hilltop in Reserve, Indiana, where friends have erected a monument recording her story.

                                                        C. F. HOBAN

ELIZABETH GILMORE BERRY

before 1775–1824

IN the old Robinson Run Churchyard near McDonald, Washington County, is the grave of Elizabeth Gilmore Berry who as a nurse in the Continental forces and as an enlisted private in Pennsylvania's Rangers on the Frontier followed the fortunes of Washington's army for seven years. She spent the winter of 1777–78 at Valley Forge, and according to well-authenticated family tradition, she shouldered a musket and fought in the ranks at the side of her soldier lover, John Berry.

Sometime in 1775 Elizabeth Gilmore and her younger sister, Ann, left Ireland for America. On their ship was a young soldier named John Berry, who during the long voyage fell in love with Elizabeth.

As soon as the ship reached Philadelphia, Berry enlisted in Colonel Daniel Brodhead's Pennsylvania Regiment of Riflemen. The Gilmore sisters joined as nurses, although there is no official record of Ann's service. In 1778 John Berry was in Colonel Harman's Sixth Pennsylvania Regiment of the Continental Line, and in 1780 he was a member of the Commander-in-Chief's Guard. Then we find the official record of Elizabeth Gilmore's enlistment as a private from Northumberland County, in the Rangers of the Frontier, among the soldiers of the Revolution who received pay for their services.

John Berry and Elizabeth Gilmore were married in 1780 and continued in the army until the close of the war. Later they settled in Colerain Township, Lancaster County, but in 1794 they moved to Washington County. In 1796 John Berry purchased 251 acres from the George Washington land near McDonald, where he died June 7, 1809, and was buried in the Robinson Run Churchyard.

Elizabeth Gilmore Berry died at the old home, August 21, 1824, and was buried beside her husband. There was nothing on the sandstone markers at their graves to tell their story; but recognition came when the story of Elizabeth Gilmore, one of three women known to have fought in the ranks of the Continental Army, was found in family records and the Pennsylvania archives.

The Pennsylvania Society, Daughters of the American Revolution eventually paid honor to this heroic woman by erecting a granite boulder at her grave with a bronze tablet upon which her record appears. This was unveiled with appropriate ceremony November 12, 1932, and a marker was also placed at her husband's grave.

EARLE R. FORREST
EMILY SPRANKLE HERON

MARY MELCHER HASSENCLEVER

before 1776–?

MARY MELCHER HASSENCLEVER may be said to have belonged to a family of patriots since she was the wife of Francis Caspar Hassenclever who was commissioned Sept. 3, 1776 as one of the first justices to serve in Philadelphia after the signing of the Declaration of Independence; the sister of Colonel Isaac Melcher of General Washington's army and a sister-in-law of Jacob Shallus, commissioned officer of the Continental Army, who penned the original document of the Constitution of the United States which is preserved in Washington, D. C.

Mrs. Hassenclever was a member of the celebrated group of patriotic ladies of Philadelphia who in 1780 "during the darkest days of our War of American Independence when the army at Norristown was undergoing privations and sufferings equal to those at Valley Forge" formed a committee under whose direction contributions were obtained to supply destitute soldiers of the Continental Army with clothing.

This committee, of which Mrs. Esther de Berdt Reed, wife of General Joseph Reed, was "Chief Officer" until her death, raised $300,034.

These ladies, of whom Mrs. Hassenclever was one, must have done their canvassing thoroughly for not only did the Marquis de Lafayette contribute "a hundred guineas in specie" and the "Comtesse de Luzerne six thousand in Continental money and one hundred and fifty dollars in specie," but it is likewise recorded that "Phylis, a colored woman," contributed "seven shillings and sixpence."

Both Mrs. Hassenclever and her husband died young, leaving no descendants.

BEATRICE PASTORIUS TURNER

AMY DRAPER WILKINS

before 1776–?

WHILE the British Army under the command of General Howe invested Philadelphia, there was an American officer confined as a prisoner in the State House, which was then used as a prison by the British.

It was not long after his imprisonment that he succeeded one afternoon in making his escape unperceived, to the residence of a gentleman who favored the American cause. There he remained hidden until the following morning, when with the aid of two ladies, one of whom was Amy Draper Wilkins, a plan was formed to enable him to escape to the Continental Army then stationed at Frankford. Permits to pass the British line were obtained by the two women for themselves and another to go into the country to obtain a supply of provisions. Then, disguising the officer in a female dress, the three succeeded in passing to the Continental Army without the deception being discovered. The two ladies, after having performed this service in their country's cause, returned to the city.

A short time after this occurrence, an American private acquainted with the circumstances deserted from the American to the British army. While walking through the streets of Philadelphia one day he met and recognized Amy Wilkins as one who had assisted in the escape of the officer. Stopping her, he informed her that he would be under the necessity of taking her before General Howe to make known the part she had taken in assisting the American to escape. Without appearing in the least disconcerted she replied that she was willing to accompany him, but that she must change her dress for a better one before appearing in the presence of the General. She requested him to accompany her to her place of residence in order to make the change. To this he assented and both proceeded to the residence of her sister.

On entering the parlor he took a seat by a large fire which was blazing in the fireplace while she went up to her chamber to change her dress. Instead of proceeding to her chamber, however, she made her exit from the house by a back way to her mother's home, whence she was sent to the country.

The guard waited some time for his charge to make her appearance; a longer time, however, elapsed than he thought necessary for a woman to change her dress and he became suspicious that all was not right. On making a search he found, to his surprise and chagrin, that the bird had flown.

Quick wits and a cool courage in the face of danger were the attributes of this Revolutionary heroine.

INDEPENDENCE HALL CHAPTER, D.A.R.

MARY ISRAEL ELLET

1776?–1885

MARY ISRAEL was born in Philadelphia in the trying times when America was making her revolutionary struggle for freedom. Graduating in 1794 from the Philadelphia Academy, with a diploma announcing that she had "been admitted to the highest honors of the institution," she lived until 1885 and was the oldest woman graduate of any institution in America at the time of her death.

Through years and years as the brain of this child developed into that of a mature woman, the religion of freedom matured more and more completely. The Negro slaves she knew intimately through visits to her friends and family connections in Southern states. The rabid abolitionists she scorned, for she knew by actual contact and personal experience that many of the Negroes were better off on the plantations of their Southern master than were poor white laborers in the North. Irritation and counter-irritation over this vexing question of African slavery boiled and spluttered around her until it finally seethed over in the lurid flames of civil war.

What was Mary Israel Ellet, child of the early freedom of the Revolution, to do? When some of her family and friends adhered to the side of secession and some held firmly to the Union, the sands of life were running out for her, but that early inbred feeling of freedom demanded that she cast her influence with the Union. So it was that she sent several sons willingly to fight and die for its preservation and ordered that when she be called to the Great Beyond she be buried with the Union flag around her.

When she died, an obituary notice in one of the Philadelphia newspapers had this to say of her:

Her extraordinary mental and physical vigor up to the day of her death prove that she has come of stalwart stock. Her father was the stern old patriot Israel Israel, and her mother was possessed of the same patriotic zeal and determination.

Reared among the associations of the last century and with such a father and mother, Mary Israel had rare opportunities to know the men and to study the events of the Revolution, and it was her pleasure in her declining years to rehearse the stories of her early days and to narrate what she had seen and heard of the distinguished personages who lived more than eighty years ago. While a child she was remarkable for acuteness of intellect and great resolution of mind and perseverance in all she undertook. As a consequence she was successful in all her pursuits and received the best token of merit which the Academy could give at the time of her graduation.

In 1801 Mary Israel was married to Charles Ellet, of Salem County, New Jersey, a great-grandson of Samuel Carpenter, and a member of one of the most distinguished families in the United States. Mrs.

Ellet was the mother of fourteen children, of whom only three survived her.

Of her sons, Colonel Charles Ellet, the great engineer, was the most distinguished, and his death from a wound received while performing his duty sent a shock throughout the whole country. The son of Colonel Ellet, Charles Rives Ellet, also fell a victim to his conscientious devotion to the arduous labors of his position, and died in 1863, one year after his father. Mrs. Ellet received the news of the death of her son and grandson with the heroism of a truly patriotic woman. She remarked: "I do not regret the gift to my country. If I had twenty sons I would give them all. For the country must be preserved; and if I were twenty years younger I would go and fight myself to the last."

In 1869 her appearance is thus described by the editor of the *Press,* who was a neighbor of the venerable heroine and at that time, in the issue of January 11, devoted a page to her biography:

Her face reminded me, when I first beheld it, of the faces of the antique medallions—strongly marked with a prominent nose, clear, light eyes, and firm and almost masculine mouth. Her conversation is precise and rapid, showing rare command of language and her grace in receiving visitors and listening to them without unseemly interruptions shows equal refinement and culture.

S. HARBERT HAMILTON

EXPERIENCE BOZARTH

before 1779–?

THE hardy pioneers who lived in the vicinity of the chain of forts which stretched across Pennsylvania from southwest to northwest were peculiarly liable to attacks from neighboring Indians, who resented, more and more, encroachment upon their territory.

The home of Experience Bozarth became a place of refuge when attacks were imminent.

In March 1779, some children brought news of Indians in the vicinity. One of the men, going to the door to reconnoitre, was shot.

As he fell back, Indians rushed in. Another man threw one of the invaders on the bed and called for a knife. Unable to find one, Mrs. Bozarth seized an ax with which she killed the Indian.

A second appeared. She clove his head. Another Indian drew out the wounded savage. Then, with the assistance of the man the Indian had shot first, she closed and fastened the door and succeeded in keeping out the besiegers until a party of men arrived for their relief.

This adventure took place in the southwestern part of what is now Greene County, and while Indian attacks were common, it was unusual for a woman to be called upon to defend her home and herself by so violent a method and one which called for such great personal courage.

MARY ALLEN CALEY

LYDIA R. BAILEY

1779–1869

THOUGH the birthplace of Lydia R. Bailey is not definitely known, it is believed to have been in Lancaster County. The inscription on the stone at her grave in old Pine Street Churchyard, Philadelphia, states the date of her birth as 1779.

The service she rendered through a successful business career was a notable one and very unusual for a woman in the period in which she lived. At the age of nineteen she married Robert Bailey, the son and business associate of Francis Bailey, a well-known and highly respected printer and journalist of Lancaster County, who had become official printer for Congress and the State of Pennsylvania with headquarters in both Lancaster and Philadelphia.

The father gradually withdrew from the business in favor of his son. Robert, however, was not able to hold together his father's clientèle; and when he died ten years later, left his young wife and four children, the youngest four months old, with practically no income from the dwindling, debt-burdened trade. Lydia immediately made plans for the reëstablishment of the family business, and ultimately achieved what few women of her time would have attempted.

Philip Freneau, the patriot poet of the Revolution, hearing of her plight and her courageous undertaking, promptly entrusted to her the publication of a new edition of his poems to be issued in two volumes. They appeared in 1809. Through her ability, her integrity, and her painstaking care in the discharge of the obligations of her business she created widespread confidence in her work. During the old Whig administration she enjoyed a valuable patronage in Philadelphia from city councils and the various municipal departments, and for a long period, from about 1830 to 1850, she was officially designated the City Printer of Philadelphia, the first and only woman who ever filled that office.

Her son Robert, as soon as he was old enough to stand at a case and set type, was assigned to that task, and later became assistant to his mother, particularly in book work of which her office made a specialty. The death of this son in 1861 was a sad blow to her, and with the realization that she was no longer equal to the performance of the strenuous duties imposed on her, she soon retired.

She had lived a long, active, useful life, fruitful in good deeds. She brought up her children, paid off her husband's indebtedness, and was generous in her consideration of those less fortunate than herself. She provided opportunity for the training of printers, many of whom later became well-known and successful men in that important department of the world's work. It is said that the endowment fund of the Third Presbyterian Church, better known as the old Pine Street Church, where she is buried, received its initial gift through a bequest in her will.

GERTRUDE BOSLER BIDDLE

HANNAH MYTINGER BUCHER

1780–?

HANNAH MYTINGER was the eldest child of Captain Jacob Mytinger, a charter member of the Order of the Cincinnati, who had served throughout the Revolution. Hannah had many vivid memories of Washington and delighted to tell her children and grandchildren of his friendship for her father, of his visits to their home when he would take her on his knee and interest himself in her childish affairs.

Jacob Mytinger's parents were Bavarians who had adventured to America when he was an infant. They settled in Lancaster where they became members of Henry M. Muhlenberg's church. Jacob early cast his lot with the Revolutionary forces and was second in command of Von Heer's Dragoons, a battalion of tried and trusted men organized by the Commander-in-Chief for special duty. They served through the winter at Valley Forge, crossed the Delaware to Trenton, and were not mustered out until they had escorted General Washington back to Mount Vernon, after the close of the war.

Elizabeth Mattieu, Hannah's mother, was of a Huguenot family. Her forbears had been driven from France and had settled at Pottsgrove, Pennsylvania. During the encampment of the army at Valley Forge the young people met at one of the functions given by a local dignitary for the American officers. They were married in 1779 and, following the example of many of Jacob's companions in arms, removed to Philadelphia. Here Hannah was born in August 1780.

In the dread yellow fever scourge of 1793 both of her parents perished, leaving Hannah with the care of five younger children. This courageous and resourceful child tended and guarded the little family through perilous days and weeks until the authorities permitted their Uncle Lewis Mytinger to come to their rescue.

Hannah and the children were taken to Harrisburg where they lived with relatives until she was nineteen, when she married Conrad Bucher and took with her to her new home her only brother, George Washington Mytinger, and her sister, Catherine. Her husband was the son of Colonel Conrad Bucher who had served in three Colonial campaigns and the Revolution. Bounty lands for military service having been assigned the Revolutionary officers, the young couple decided to claim those due Captain Mytinger, and joined the many families migrating toward the western border line. An ancient mahogany secretary holds letters describing the then undeveloped condition of Beaver, Butler, and Mercer counties, where the grants were located.

After some years in the western counties, interest in iron ore developments and other industries brought them to Huntingdon County where they made their permanent home.

During her husband's terms in the Assembly, Hannah seems to

have assumed all family responsibilities, both domestic and financial. In 1824 a letter came announcing the death of an aunt, Countess Elizabeth von Pyriemhoff, Im Shaffhausen, Switzerland, and stating that her estate would revert to her two American nephews, Conrad and Jacob Bucher, should they come to claim it. Conrad decided to make the journey, and again Hannah was left in command of the large family and his very considerable business interests.

Conrad Bucher died in 1852, but Hannah lived on in her beautiful home surrounded by many descendants and loyal friends to the age of eighty-three. Her descendants have filled many positions of trust in Church and State.

SUSAN B. BRISBANE LOWRIE

AGNES NOBLE AGNEW

1781–1871

AGNES NOBLE was born January 30, 1781, at Nobleville, Lancaster County. She was the daughter of Margaret McWhorter and James Noble, an elder in the Associate Church of Octorara, and a granddaughter of William Noble, who was one of the founders of this church which, with the neighboring congregation of Oxford, formed the original seat of Associate Presbyterianism in America.

Agnes Noble was first married to the Rev. Ebenezer Henderson, whose father, the Rev. Matthew Henderson, was sent to this country by the Associate Synod of Edinburgh together with the Rev. John Mason; they being the fourth and fifth ministers of that church, in order of time, to enter upon the work in America. Ebenezer Henderson was first settled in Pittsburgh, which was at that time wild and uncivilized. In taking this journey it was necessary to make the trip over the Allegheny Mountains on horseback. Agnes Noble Henderson made this difficult journey, carrying her infant son upon a pillow on the saddle before her.

Upon their arrival in Pittsburgh Mr. Henderson entered upon his work with a real handicap—the absence of a church building. In later years Mrs. Henderson spoke of sitting, in those early difficult days, out in the open air in midwinter, the ground deeply covered with snow, during long Sabbath services. Not only did she care for her own family in those frontier days, but she also cared for the members of the congregation, bringing cheer and comfort to the suffering by her presence. It is small wonder that she was regarded as an angel of mercy.

When Mr. Henderson was appointed to succeed the Rev. William Marshall, the first pastor of the First Associate, now First United Presbyterian Church of Philadelphia, he was ordered to visit the scattered congregations in the South. This he did, taking his family with him; but through exposure from swimming rivers and other hardships, which he had to endure in fulfilling the duty assigned him, he contracted a violent fever and died at Stanton, Virginia.

Agnes Noble Henderson, in her sorrow, returned with her son, James Noble Henderson, and her daughter, Mary A. Henderson, to the home of her parents near Nobleville.

A few years later a new phase in her life began in Nobleville. This town was named in honor of the Noble family, the name being changed to Christiana in 1847, in honor of Christiana Noble, the wife of William Noble, a brother of Agnes. To this village came an eminent physician, Dr. Robert Agnew, the son of David and Mary Edwin Agnew, descended from a family also well known in the annals of American Presbyterianism. Having served as a surgeon in the United States Navy, which he had entered after completing his course in medicine following his graduation from Dickinson College, he had tendered his resignation and settled in Nobleville. Here he met Agnes Henderson, a "handsome widow"; a meeting which culminated in their marriage on August 1, 1815. Here also was born the only child of their marriage, a son, D. Hayes Agnew, who was later to achieve world renown in the field of surgery.

In 1840, Agnes Noble Agnew removed to Baltimore County, Maryland, where Dr. Robert Agnew had purchased a handsome country-seat called "Blenheim." There he died on October 10, 1858. His wife passed away on February 25, 1871, in the ninety-first year of her life. Her remains were laid to rest beside those of her husband and her ancestors in the old burying ground of Fagg's Manor in Chester County, Pennsylvania.

Agnes Noble Agnew was well qualified to occupy the places she held as the wife of a minister and the wife of a physician, for she was a woman of extraordinary force of character, possessing a powerful mind and inexhaustible energy. From her descent and associations she was of a deeply religious nature. As a young woman, possessing a magnificent physique, rare beauty, and charm of manner, combined with a tireless energy, she had lived a life of severest hardships in her rôle of a frontier minister's wife—hardships so severe that her husband succumbed to them while she endured and withstood the trials. As the wife of a prominent physician, she possessed those faculties suited to such a station. Always serene, contented, and cheerful, she met with ease the many trials and sudden emergencies confronting the wife of a practicing physician. Through her sympathetic understanding and her readiness to assist those in suffering, she endeared herself to her husband's patients and proved herself to be a woman of sterling qualities.

HELEN NOBLE WORST

REBECCA GRATZ

1781–1869

REBECCA GRATZ was born on March 4, 1781, in Philadelphia, one of a family of ten children, five boys and five girls. Her parents were people of considerable wealth and culture moving habitually in circles of influence. Among her more intimate acquaintances were included the Ogdens, the Gouverneurs, the Hoffmans, the Fennos, Washington Irving, James Paulding, and Sam Ewing, nearly all of whom were noted for their wit and intellectual attainments.

She was also a friend of Matilda Hoffman, to whom Washington Irving was engaged to be married. But before the date set for the wedding Miss Hoffman fell sick and, despite the tenderest care, died in Rebecca's arms. Irving was inconsolable; but the sad event served to cement the warm friendship already existing between him and Rebecca which endured as long as they lived.

Although she did not know Sir Walter Scott it transpired that he modeled the Rebecca in his *Ivanhoe* after her. For Irving happened to be a friend of Scott's, and during a visit to England was asked by the great novelist to describe some of his American friends. Irving's praise of Rebecca Gratz evidently fired Scott's imagination, for shortly after *Ivanhoe* was published Irving received an autographed copy together with a note from the author inquiring how he liked his Rebecca.

Rebecca Gratz, a woman of unusual beauty with many admirers, never married, although, according to Sara Hays Mordecai, her niece and biographer, she bestowed her affections upon one young man of her time and was loved by him in return. Later, at her mother's home in Kentucky, Henry Clay is said to have paid her marked attention, but Rebecca seems to have abandoned all thoughts of marriage and to have dedicated her energies to works of benevolence and philanthropy.

In Philadelphia she lived for many years on Chestnut Street near Twelfth in a house which was one of four forming what was known as "Boston Row." It was from here that she dispensed her charity, and it was remarked of her that "scarce a charitable institution of the day in her native city . . . did not have her name inscribed upon its records as an active officer or as an adviser and benefactress."

Among other things, she was one of the twenty-four women who founded the Asylum for Orphans in Philadelphia. For forty years she acted as its secretary and a member of its Purchasing Committee. The Hebrew Benevolent Society was the work of her hands, and the Sewing Society had its first impulse from her. The Fuel Society was encouraged and benefited by her substantial aid, and she wrote the constitution and by-laws for the Foster Home for Poor Hebrew Children.

Upon her death on August 27, 1869, all of these institutions and many others passed resolutions of regret and tribute. She now lies buried in the Jewish Cemetery at Ninth and Spruce streets.

EVELINA HEAP GLEAVES
EMILY SOLIS-COHEN

ELIZA LESLIE

1787–1858

ᕲᕽ

ELIZA LESLIE was born in Philadelphia on November 15, 1787. Her Scotch father was a watchmaker and especially fond of mathematics and natural philosophy, which led him into close association with Benjamin Franklin, Joseph Rittenhouse, Thomas Jefferson, and others of kindred taste living in Philadelphia at that time.

Eliza was the firstborn, and when she was six years old the family went to London where, during seven years, her father was engaged in the exportation of clocks to America and where Eliza was placed in school.

They returned to Philadelphia in 1800. Eliza passed the remaining portion of her life in that city. She was a pupil in private schools there and at an early age manifested a predilection for writing. Her pronounced devotion to reading and study led her naturally into authorship. She first essayed verse. Then followed the publication of a series of volumes for juvenile readers which became very popular.

The work, however, through which she first became known in the real literary world was *Pencil Sketches: Outlines of Character and Manners,* published in 1833. This was followed by a second and third series upon the same subject. In this work she proved herself an entertaining satirist, as well as a keen and kindly portrayer of the many angles that may enter into the character and manners of one's fellow beings. She became a popular contributor to magazines and continued to produce novels.

Her *Mrs. Washington Potts* was awarded a prize offered by *Godey's* in a story contest. She established a magazine of her own under the name of *Miss Leslie's Magazine.* Her stories, and especially her juveniles, proved her possession of a quiet humor, rich imagination, and facility of expression.

In all her writings she manifested the possession of marked talent and individuality which have established her place in American literature. Her indefatigable industry in the midst of her literary activities enabled her to render a service to housekeepers through a collection of carefully selected recipes which she published in 1837 under the title of

The Domestic Cookery Book, of which forty thousand copies were sold, a notable achievement for those days.

GERTRUDE BOSLER BIDDLE

SARA JOSEPHA HALE

1788–1879

SARAH JOSEPHA HALE was born in Newport, New Hampshire, October 24, 1788. While a New Englander by birth, her outstanding contributions to literature and social movements were made while a resident of Pennsylvania. When her lawyer husband, David Hale, died in 1822, she resorted to literature as a means of livelihood. In 1828 she became the editor of the Boston *Ladies' Magazine,* the first women's periodical published in America. In 1837 this magazine was merged with a Philadelphia publication and the name was changed to *Godey's Lady's Book.* Mrs. Hale moved to Philadelphia in 1841 where she served as editor of *Godey's Lady's Book* until 1877.

She was an enthusiastic advocate of the social and intellectual advancement of women, and urged the education of women for medical and missionary service. This movement was advanced through the Women's Union Missionary Association of which Mrs. Hale was the president for several years. It was she who urged the celebration of Thanksgiving Day uniformly throughout the United States, advocating this in her magazine for twenty years. Finally, in 1864, President Lincoln adopted her suggestion and the observance had its national inception.

Her chief claims to fame are her advocacy of the celebration of Thanksgiving Day, her efforts to advance women, her constructive editorship of *Godey's Lady's Book,* and her literary contributions. Among her important writings are the following: *A Dictionary of Poetical Quotations; The Ladies' Wreath; Sketches of Distinguished Women from Creation to 1853; The Judge, a Drama of American Life; Manners, or Happy Homes and Good Society; Love, or Women's Destiny, with Other Poems.*

JOHN A. H. KEITH

ANNA C. PEALE

1791–1878

≫≪

ANNA C. PEALE, born in Philadelphia in 1791, was the daughter of Captain James Peale, an eminent portrait painter, and Mary Clay-poole, his wife. Her maternal ancestors, the Claypooles, came to this country with William Penn and were among the earliest settlers in Philadelphia. Charles Wilson Peale was her uncle, and Rembrandt Peale her cousin.

As a member of a family distinguished in the world of art, Anna manifested from childhood an extraordinary talent. When she was but fourteen years of age she copied in oils two paintings by Vernet which, upon being offered at a public auction, were sold for thirty dollars. Stimulated by this recognition, she enthusiastically persevered in her study until finally her work commanded an independent income. This recognition was achieved, however, through miniature painting on ivory, to which she was urged by her father to devote herself "as being the medium most suitable for a lady."

She was assiduous in the study of her father's work, both in oil portraits and miniatures, and naturally he was a painstaking master for her. Her ambition and industry were constantly stimulated by the broadening recognition of her work. The copy made in her youth of a celebrated miniature of Napoleon was sold in Philadelphia for one hundred and fifty dollars. The first miniature portraits from life which she undertook were those of Dr. Spencer H. Cone and his mother. These were shown in the annual exhibition of the Academy of the Fine Arts in Philadelphia. She was later elected an honorary member of the Academy, whether as a tribute alone to the excellence of her work, or because of a chivalric recognition of a woman devoting her life to art is not known.

Her artistic career was accorded remarkable recognition, considering the period in which she lived and worked, and, since she was for years the only professional woman artist in Philadelphia, she occupied a unique position. Later on, her sister, Sarah, was added to the list of professionals as a portrait painter in oil. The brushes of these two gifted women have preserved for the country the portraits of many distinguished men of their day. They painted General Lafayette, General Jackson, President Monroe, Henry Clay, John Randolph, and many others. Daniel Webster sat to Anna Peale twice for miniature portraits.

She abandoned professional portraiture upon her marriage to General William Duncan.

GERTRUDE BOSLER BIDDLE

LUCRETIA MOTT

1793–1880

FAR-SEEING, courageous, and gentle, Lucretia Mott stands in the history of Pennsylvania and of the United States as one of those figures who lived a hundred years before their time.

With an enlightenment greater than that of the day in which she lived, she dared to appear as the friend of the Negro slave. Flying brickbats and rioters never swerved her from her belief. In the days before the Civil War, when the cause of woman suffrage was considered by a man-ruled world as something sublimely ridiculous, she helped call the first Woman's Rights Convention. She lived to see slavery abolished. Her charm and wit and courage paved the way for the recognition of woman's rights, which came long after she was dead.

Lucretia Mott was born on the island of Nantucket, January 3, 1793. She was a descendant of the oldest settlers, Thomas Macy and James Coffin, who sought refuge there in 1659, when the government of Massachusetts Bay was persecuting the Quakers. Her father, Thomas Coffin, a sea captain, moved to Boston when she was eleven years old. After attending public schools there she was sent to a Friends' boarding school in Dutchess County, New York, and there she met James Mott, the teacher who later became her husband.

At fifteen she was an assistant teacher, and at eighteen she married and moved to Philadelphia. The War of 1812 brought financial troubles but, turning to the cotton business, the Motts began to swell the family income. It was then that Lucretia Mott made her first bold step.

Believing that the slave system was unjust, she resolved to abstain from all slave-grown products. Their business faded, difficulties increased again, and Mrs. Mott opened a private school. Later she turned to the study of theology and engaged in the ministry of the Friends until the separation in 1827. The meetinghouse was closed against her but she continued her almost solitary path on behalf of the Hicksite Quakers. Of distinguished appearance, with singularly beautiful features and a nobility of expression, she began to win recognition as an intellectual leader.

At the convention in Philadelphia in 1833, which formed the American Anti-Slavery Society, she was one of four women in the United States who dared appear as a friend of the slave. She became president of the Female Anti-Slavery Society, founded in that city the same year. At their meetings rioters surrounded the hall; and brickbats, those pieces of repartee so popular in that less gallant age, flew about her head. Calm and undaunted by persecution, she traveled thousands of miles preaching deliverance of the slave. Her home became a famous station in the Underground Railway, which aided escaped slaves to the border.

Little by little her charm, her wit, her sparkling answers to hecklers, and her rare personality, brought a kindlier reception. She was appointed as delegate to the world's antislavery convention in London in 1840. There she was refused admission as a delegate on the ground that no woman could ascend the platform. She went to a seat in the gallery, and Mr. Garrison, another American delegate, gallantly left his seat of honor and took his place in the gallery beside her.

This occurrence, the rudeness that had been inflicted upon her, drew the attention of Britain to her. Her calm bearing, her wit, her great mind did the rest. She was lionized by people of rank and letters and stayed for some months in England preaching antislavery.

The London incident also focused her attention more keenly upon the "woman question." She had long resented the injustice worked upon women teachers, and pondered upon the vast differences in salary between men and women educators. With Mrs. Stanton and others she sent out the call for the first Woman's Rights Convention held in Seneca Falls, New York, in 1848. Her fight for woman's rights was a repetition of her long combat against slavery. She was ridiculed, heckled, and interrupted. But Lucretia Mott was now a more accomplished speaker. Her gentleness and wit were always with her. Her antagonists invariably found the laugh turned against them. And in this way she accomplished as much as any other woman toward disarming the critics of woman's rights.

In 1856, after forty years of arduous labor, she moved into the country outside Philadelphia. Her last public appearance was made in her eighty-sixth year at the Suffrage Convention held in New York in 1878. Though feeble, her eyes sparkled as she told of happenings in the early days of the contest. An earnest audience tearfully rose as she left the hall.

On November 11, 1880, she died. The goal of woman's suffrage had not been reached during her life, but she had lived to see woman's position more improved than anyone would have dreamed in the days of her youth. And it was her balance of high intellectual and moral qualities, her vigor and faith and courage, her firm belief that reason is greater than custom, that achieved much of the work.

LUCRETIA L. BLANKENBURG

REBECCA WEBB PENNOCK LUKENS

1794-1854

THE following words, unless otherwise identified, would appear to be those of a business man versed in the technique of iron mills:

In the winter of 1821 or 1822 (I am not certain as to the exact date) the whole mill was carried away in a freshet. This we rebuilt and about or near that time we put in a new large water wheel and a new head—new pinion housings and other new castings in the mill.

As a matter of fact, they are taken from a statement written by a woman, Rebecca Webb Lukens. What an interesting commentary they form on the idea that the business woman is a social and economic phenomenon peculiar to these modern days! Rebecca Webb Lukens, daughter of adventurous colonials, whose ancestors left comfortable and cultured surroundings to cross the Atlantic and make a new home, was born at Rokeby, south of Chester, in Chester County, January 1794.

Her father, Isaac Pennock, was a grandson of Joseph Pennock, who in Colonial days built in Chester County the mansion known as Primitive Hall for which every pane of window-glass was imported from England. Rebecca was to become, by the time she reached thirty, the peer of man as a business executor as well as the foremost, if not the only, business woman of her day.

At the age of twelve Rebecca was sent to boarding school at Wilmington, Delaware, where, except for vacations, she remained until she was eighteen. Other than the usual studies she devoted herself particularly to French and chemistry. The fact that she studied chemistry was not only indicative of her trend of mind and of her character but was also prophetic of the events to come, for she was to become the director of an iron mill. While on a visit to Philadelphia she met Dr. Charles Lukens, a descendant of one of the thirteen heads of families who arrived in Philadelphia on the ship *Concord* from Amsterdam in 1683. Upon their marriage in 1813, her father invited Dr. Lukens to enter partnership with him in the conduct of the Federal Slitting Mill at Rokeby. This type of mill converted charcoal slabs into plates which were slit into rods for blacksmith use. After four years Dr. Lukens rented the Brandywine Mill property which his father-in-law owned. This was the first mill for rolling boiler plates in the United States. Against very great odds, Dr. Lukens managed to operate it for twelve years; the mill was in constant need of repair and was occasionally so damaged by freshets that when he died in 1825 his estate was practically bankrupt. On his deathbed, knowing the ability and character of his wife, he asked her to take charge of the business as his successor. In those days it was almost an unheard-of thing for a woman to head a business establishment, especially such a business as that of a rolling mill.

Mrs. Lukens proved to have unusual business abilities. In nine years she had paid off all Dr. Lukens' debts, including the balance due the Pennock estate on the mill and the farm, and had virtually reconstructed the old mill, as she herself wrote. While operating it she also conducted a farm, which made it possible for her to give employment to the men at the mill when the water that supplied the power ran low. The farm also enabled her to pay her workmen in its products at times when currency was scarce.

Rebecca Webb Lukens' iron mill is today (1930) the Lukens Iron and Steel Company of Coatesville, and although she died in 1854 control of the mill still remains in the hands of her descendants.

MARTHA G. THOMAS

HANNAH COX

1795–1876

⊱⊰

LONGWOOD, the home of John and Hannah Peirce Cox, in East Marlborough Township, Chester County, was one of the chief Pennsylvania centers of activity in the abolitionist movement for many years. Of Quaker stock, Hannah was the fifth generation in direct line of descent from George Peirce, who came from England in 1684. He purchased land in Chester County in 1731, and there seven generations of his family lived.

Hannah's father, Jacob Peirce, built a brick house for his family home and also erected the first schoolhouse in that neighborhood. It was in this home that his daughter was born, lived, and died. In 1823 she married John Cox, also a Quaker, a man of high character and fine public spirit.

The Liberator, a weekly paper edited by William Lloyd Garrison, and Whittier's poems awakened the interest of Mr. and Mrs. Cox in the antislavery movement, and for years Hannah labored unceasingly in its furtherance, being regarded as one of its ablest leaders. She and her husband conducted in the farmhouse at Longwood a station of the Underground Railroad where fugitive slaves were received, fed, clothed, and assisted northward in their flight. This was the most important Pennsylvania branch of the Underground Railroad which Thomas Garrett conducted in Wilmington.

Longwood gradually became a center for the assembly of leaders in reform movements from points as far distant as Boston. The antislavery interest finally expanded to a point that warranted the organization and establishment of a liberal group under the name of The Progressive Friends of Longwood. Lucretia Mott, an intimate friend and counselor of Hannah Cox, and Whittier were frequent visitors at Longwood.

In addition to her activity in the antislavery movement, Hannah Cox's interests were many and widespread, and her public spirit unflagging. She devoted years of her life to the broadening of public interest in the causes of temperance, peace, and the abolition of capital punishment. When in 1873 Mr. and Mrs. Cox celebrated their golden wedding, a felicitous greeting was sent them by Bayard Taylor from Germany, and Whittier wrote in their honor "The Golden Wedding at Longwood." Letters from many distinguished people were read to the guests by Judge William Darrah Kelly, among them being a charming expression of high regard from William Lloyd Garrison.

Hannah Cox was an honored, beloved, and intelligent woman. She was regarded with a feeling of tender reverence and affection by all her close friends, and all those who had enjoyed her distinguished hospitality or open-handed charity. Her long and active life came to its close in 1876.

GERTRUDE BOSLER BIDDLE

DEBORAH FISHER WHARTON

1795–1888

DEBORAH FISHER was born October 24, 1795, in Philadelphia. Her father, Samuel Rowland Fisher, owner of a large importing and exporting business, had married rather late in life Hannah Rodman, a charming young Quakeress of Newport, Rhode Island. Their wedding journey was unique, for they traveled from Newport to Philadelphia on horseback, the young wife riding on a pillion behind her husband.

Their second daughter, Deborah, was reared in comfort but without luxury, as her father approved of plain living. At the age of seventeen, when a young girl's life is usually given over to worldly interests, Deborah decided to adopt the plain dress of the Quaker costume, which she wore during her entire life. At about this time she became interested in William Wharton, also a member of the Society of Friends. Their marriage was opposed by Deborah's father for the reason—an unusual one in this age—that both families were wealthy, and he believed each young person should marry one less fortunate, thus distributing the wealth in a more even manner.

After a year of waiting, Deborah spoke seriously to her father on the subject of her marriage, telling him that she would never marry without his consent, but would remain single unless permitted to wed the man of her affections. Her firm attitude had the desired effect and the young couple were married June 4, 1817.

Their first and only city home, at 336 Spruce Street, is still standing. In it were reared their ten children, five sons and five daughters and, until her death in 1888, Mrs. Wharton occupied this city home during the winter months. A country home, Bellevue, one mile from the Schuylkill, was the meeting place of family and friends during the summer months.

After raising nine of the ten children, and at an age when most women incline to ease, Deborah Fisher Wharton found time for much outside work. Her interest in the Negroes and the Indians was always keen. She served as clerk for the Yearly Meeting, and in addition to such public interests, she was always helpful to the needy and unhappy. In the years of her widowhood she became deeply stirred by the pitiful condition of the American Indians. She often visited Washington to petition Congress in their behalf, and when nearly eighty years old undertook a venturesome journey to see the tribes themselves. She persisted until she had inspected every Indian reservation in Kansas and Nebraska, among the tribes of the Iowas and Otoes.

The Indians were much impressed by her earnestness, and affectionately and reverently called her "Grandmother." Before she returned homeward, one big chief came to her saying, "Grandmother, I have something for you."

"Something for me?" she said, in gratified surprise. But when she opened his package and discovered a pair of earrings, she exclaimed in consternation, "Oh, I never wear ornaments of any sort."

He was greatly disturbed, saying, "But Grandmother, I made them on purpose for you!" So of course she accepted them and brought them home—large hoops of hand-wrought silver. These mementoes of her travels are still carefully preserved by her descendants.

In a letter written during the summer of 1873, she says, "We found our Iowas greatly improved by the four years of care and teaching, and much interested in their new life—living in houses, quite comfortably, much more so than some poor abodes of our white population. The men ploughing their beautiful corn fields, which were as fine as any we saw on our trip, and perfectly clear of weeds. Potatoes and other vegetables also fine. The soil very rich and I felt it was no marvel that those who do not obey the command 'Thou shalt not covet' should desire to possess themselves even of the small remnant of our land which we boastingly call 'Our Country.' We found that this whole tribe had adopted citizens' dress, men and women. The latter able to make their own dresses, etc.

"But of the poor Otoes we cannot speak so encouragingly. They are still unsettled. The railroad having passed through their reservation and a treaty pending for the sale of their lands, their efforts for improvement are for the present paralyzed. But we hope this fall, when Congress meets, to be able to secure part of them and, with proceeds of what is sold, to help them in carrying on the work of civilization."

During the latter years of her life Deborah Wharton spent each summer at the home of her daughter, Mrs. Benjamin R. Smith, in Newport, where she died in her ninety-third year on August 16, 1888.

JOANNA WHARTON LIPPINCOTT

SARAH WILSON

1795–1871

IT was the year 1868 that witnessed the initial steps of a group of Presbyterians in Franklin County, Pennsylvania, which successfully led to the establishment of a College for Women at Chambersburg.

The raising of the necessary funds for even a modest foundation was a difficult task in those days, and the encouragement given to the project by Miss Sallie Wilson through contributions totaling $30,000 served so to stimulate the movement that in January 1869 Wilson College was incorporated.

Though Mary Lyon founded the pioneer institution for the higher education of women at Mount Holyoke, it did not become a college until 1893. Elmira Female College was opened in 1855, preceding Wilson by fourteen years, and to it later went Matthew Vassar in quest of information.

Miss Sallie Wilson, who was born in 1795, was not what the world calls an educated woman. Her father and brothers were unusually successful agriculturists, and when Mr. Wilson died his estate comprised twenty-four fine farms and in addition a large amount of timber land. The timber and farms together aggregated several thousand acres, which enormous holdings became eventually, after the death of her brothers, the inherited property of Miss Sallie.

She chose from among her tenants two in whom she had confidence and to them she gave a power of attorney to manage her estate.

Not only did the fund for the proposed college receive her munificent aid, but on the same day upon which that institution was incorporated there was also incorporated in Chambersburg the Central Presbyterian Congregation. That, too, was made possible through the generosity of Sarah Wilson. Her deep interest in her church; her devotion to the study of her Bible; her willing spirit; her sense of personal responsibility, had made practicable without delay the realization of the dream of the founders of Wilson College. It has become one of the outstanding colleges for women in the country, with a high academic standing that is maintained under the guidance of a distinguished president and an able faculty. For long the attendance of students has been about four hundred.

Sallie Wilson's portrait hangs in the reception room of the main building in greeting to its students and its friends. She died in 1871.

GERTRUDE BOSLER BIDDLE
CORINNE RAMSEY HUMER

MIRA SHARPLESS TOWNSEND

1798–1859

❧

MIRA SHARPLESS was born in Philadelphia on September 26, 1798, the daughter of Jesse Sharpless and Joanna Townsend Sharpless. She was a direct descendant of Richard Townsend, who came to America with William Penn on the ship *Welcome*. She attended the Select School, where, according to many certificates presented to her and signed by her teacher, William J. Bedlock, from 1811 to 1813, "she excelled all the members of her class in the grammar exercises, and her deportment was such as to secure the approbation and esteem of her teacher and the friendship of her companions."

A decided talent which she enjoyed was the ability to write. Her letters written when she was in her early twenties to her cousin, Edward Darlington, the son of Dr. William Darlington of Chester County, have been preserved for their interesting and amusing accounts of her life and travels in this country before her marriage in 1828 to Samuel Townsend. By this marriage she had six children, only two of whom lived to maturity, Emily Sharpless Townsend (Mrs. Powell Stackhouse, Jr.) and Clara Gordon Townsend (Mrs. William Penn Troth).

Although always a Friend, she did not wear the plain dress, but was very fond of the handsomest of silks and the finest of real lace. During Yearly Meeting week it was her custom to entertain as many as fifty persons at her home on Franklin Square. She writes that as she grew older she came to feel that she

. . . by birth and circumstances had been placed among the princes of the land, while others had been left in the hand of the spoiler, and therefore it was her duty, having been given the health and ability, to help the friendless and the unfortunate, to give them the power as far as she could to make for themselves a name, a position and a respectable living.

In 1847 at a meeting for the abolition of capital punishment she made known her desire to have formed "a society to open a house for the reformation and employment and instruction of unfortunate women who had led immoral lives." The result was the Rosina Home, which was first on the west side of Eighth Street above Wood, and later removed to Germantown Avenue and Westmoreland Street. The Rosina Home was the first of its kind to be established and carried on entirely by women. It became the inspiration for similar institutions in Baltimore, New Orleans, Providence, and Cincinnati. Mira Townsend was treasurer of the home and on the Board of Managers until her death.

She felt that having received women from every part of the Commonwealth and from every part of the world, it was not merely a local charity. In 1854, she and Mrs. Sophia Lewis went to Harrisburg to present a petition to the Legislature for a yearly appropriation of $3,000. Through Eli K. Price they met almost all of the members of the Legislature, and so impressed them with their charm, their sincerity, and their bravery at appearing and speaking before so many men, an almost unheard-of proceeding at that time, that the bill was overwhelmingly passed.

In 1855 Mira Townsend wrote a book, *Reports and Realities from the Sketch Book of a Manager,* which she published almost entirely at her own expense to further the interests of the Rosina Home. In it are a few of her poems, beautifully sincere and exquisitely expressed.

In 1849 Mira Townsend, with her sister, Eliza Parker, founded the Temporary Home (of which she was secretary and a manager), which is still on Sixth Street near Buttonwood,

. . . a transient boarding house for respectable women out of employment, where those with funds can be accommodated at a moderate board, and those without be received until suitable situations can be procured for them; and where also destitute children can be taken care of until suitable homes can be procured; and to secure from fraud and imposition a class of persons whose homeless situation exposes them to the arts of the vicious and designing, and to provide a safe shelter.

It was through the influence of Mira Townsend that the House of the Good Shepherd was started in Philadelphia.

Mrs. Townsend died in 1859.

EMILIE S. TROTH
MRS. EDWARD D. LORIMER

ANN RIDGWAY RUSH

1799–1857

DURING the greater part of the first half of the nineteenth century the most brilliant and dominant figure in the social life of Pennsylvania was the distinguished "Madam Rush," as everyone called her. Born Phoebe Ann Ridgway, she was the daughter of Jacob Ridgway, shipper and merchant, who, next to Stephen Girard, was the wealthiest man of his time in America.

Jacob Ridgway established a branch of his business in London and later in Antwerp. His children were thus enabled to have the advantages of a European education and culture. Phoebe Ann lived in Paris during the time of Madame Récamier and of Madame de Staël, by the latter of whom she was undoubtedly much influenced.

At the age of twenty she married Dr. James Rush, the scholarly son of the famous Dr. Benjamin Rush, a signer of the Declaration of Independence. Upon her father's death she inherited one-third of his wealth, estimated at more than three millions of dollars, and she and her husband built the great mansion on Chestnut Street, near Twentieth, which afterward became the Aldine Hotel.

Here they maintained a lavish hospitality, the great dining room having twenty-five tables which could be placed in rows to seat all her numerous guests. At her large parties six thousand candles lighted the festivities. She entertained at her famous levees not only all the most noted of her own countrymen but also many distinguished visitors from abroad, among them being the great singers, Mario and Grisi, and numerous members of the nobility of Europe.

Mrs. Rush improved her mind by constant study. She read and spoke several of the modern languages and discussed their writers with a clearness of analysis and beauty of conception that made her society charming to intelligent and cultivated men in all walks of life. Her powers of conversation were great and she was able to create an intellectual fascination that made her the center of a brilliant circle. To her own sex she was not so attractive because it was with men that her mind had most sympathy, but with a few women, whenever she cared to be, she was as popular as with men.

There is a charming miniature of her at the Ridgway Branch of the Philadelphia Library. This shows her as a most attractive young woman. In later life she grew excessively corpulent and perhaps for that reason, feeling the need of exercise, she inaugurated the custom which she maintained for many years of taking long daily walks in rain or shine and of holding an outdoor reception for all her friends and acquaintances during her progress. She was usually attended by two of her admirers among her host of gentlemen friends, and on one occasion, in 1853, received thus the President of the United States, Franklin Pierce, who had been told that his visit to Philadelphia would be incomplete unless he attended one of Madam Rush's outdoor levees.

The entrée to her friendship was through the possession of unusual talent or genius, to which she gave liberal encouragement. She was known for her lofty scorn of the little cliques that so often disfigure the world of fashion, and her guests were selected for their wit or intellect rather than for their wealth or birth.

In a letter written to her husband in 1845, she perhaps unconsciously embodied something of her philosophy of life. She writes, "Amuse yourself, pleasure is the greatest specific against the moral and physical ills of life."

Madam Rush died at Saratoga, in October 1857, aged fifty-eight years, leaving her great wealth to her husband, who survived until 1869, when he willed his fortune to found a branch of the Philadelphia Library at the site of a farm which he had bought at Broad and Carpenter streets. This was to be a library for scholars and was to contain no fiction. Neither was it to have newspapers, which he considered ephemeral and biased. It was to be known as the Ridgway Branch of the Philadelphia Library in honor of his wife's family. This beautiful classical building still remains as a fitting monument to these two scholarly and interesting Philadelphians. Madame Rush lies buried within its halls.

MRS. WILMER KRUSEN

SARAH WORTHINGTON PETER

1800–1877

SARAH WORTHINGTON was born in Chillicothe, Ohio, May 10, 1800. She inherited an artistic background from a talented mother, a scholarly father, and the atmosphere of a cultured home. Her mother, Eleanor Van Swearingen, was a highly educated woman of refined tastes. Her father, Thomas Worthington, was once United States Senator and afterward Governor of Ohio.

At the early age of sixteen she married Edward King and after his death first came to Philadelphia in 1840 from Cambridge, Massachusetts where she had been supervising the education of her sons at Harvard. Shortly after taking up her residence in the Quaker City, she met Mr. William Peter, the British Consul in Philadelphia, a cultured gentleman and fine scholar. In October 1844 they were married and took up residence in one of those fine, ample old houses well adapted to the social activities for which it served as a center for ten years. Her home was characterized as a charming abode of good taste and refinement. In it she had rare opportunities to give expression to her quaint tastes.

Her contacts included the artists, musicians, writers and brilliant lights of that period. Margaret R. King in her *Memories of the Life of Mrs. Sarah Peter* says:

At the Peters' dinner table, were to be met such men as Horace Binney, John Sergeant, Mr. Duponceau, the brothers Henry and William B. Reed, Clement Biddle, Ingersoll, Tilghman, Wharton, the brilliant young Wallace, so soon to pass away—a circle too large to enumerate, often called together to meet strangers of note. The famous Mrs. Rush and her sister, Mrs. Barton; the lovely Mrs. Willing, the cultivated Misses Tilghman, beautiful Mary Wharton and the graceful Mrs. Montgomery, with many others, were bright stars in this galaxy.

Mrs. King continues:

In all this time of brilliant society life Mrs. Peter did not silence those inner suggestions which were ever present in her nature urging her to the mission of mercy. She seemed to have always sounding in her ears, "the still sad music of humanity." We find her already interested in carrying out the plan always nearest her heart for the help and elevation of her own sex. With a number of earnest women, a majority of them belonging to the Friends or Quakers, a society was formed to build up and put into active operation an asylum for degraded women. This was the Rosina House of Magdalens, which is still actively and efficiently working in the good cause for which it was founded.

Another and still greater work in its results was then commenced by this untiring lady. In her own house she appropriated a room and engaged a teacher of drawing to begin the initial steps of a school of design for women. This was carried on with great vigor during all her years of residence in Philadelphia, and the work grew into vast proportions. It was not long after the beginning that advance enough was made to authorize a systematic arrangement of the school in its different practical workings.

Teachers in the several departments were secured, and orders were obtained for patterns in iron work, for paperhanging, for calico prints, etc. No industry but might now be supplied by this valuable school.

After Mrs. Peter's removal from Philadelphia, this school still continued to grow in size and usefulness and . . . after passing through forty years, still grows in magnitude and is carrying out the good work designed by its charitable foundress.

While Mrs. Peter can be credited with many contributions to the advancement of Pennsylvania, her greatest and perhaps most enduring is the founding of the Philadelphia School of Design for Women. It was the first of its kind to be established in America, and has grown in influence, continuing to make valuable contributions to the training of American women.

Mrs. Peter died at her Long Island home on February 6, 1877. Her remains repose near by in the Mortuary Chapel in St. Joseph's Cemetery.

JOHN A. H. KEITH

DEBORAH MOULSON

1801–1839

❧

DEBORAH MOULSON was born at Paradise Creek, Virginia, in 1801, and died in Philadelphia in 1839. Descended from a long line of Quakers, both Welsh and English, her claim to distinction was her interest in the education of girls, as the quaint circular, quoted below, bears witness.

TO PARENTS AND GUARDIANS

DEBORAH MOULSON believes it is her duty to relinquish the school she is at this time engaged in, and to open one for the education of Girls, according to moral discipline in simplicity of speech, behaviour, and apparel; endeavoring to unite with an useful literary education that tuition of the understanding, which will induce them, on reasoning principles, to depart from that kind of dress and address which leads the youthful mind so far from the path of propriety. It is not intended to confine the pupils to one form of dress—but to that which is useful, and to endeavour so to engage their attention, that their ornaments may consist in the fruits of a well regulated mind. But knowing from experience, that it is necessary Parents and Guardians should coöperate with the Teacher in suitable restrictions, it is desirable that all persons who make application, may be satisfied that they are willing their children should be educated agreeably to this system.

The course of study will include the following branches of English Education:—Orthography, Reading, Writing, Arithmetic, Grammar, Geography, with the use of Maps and Globes, the Elements of Astronomy, Natural Philosophy and Chemistry, History and Composition.

The proposed new school was evidently located at Hamilton Village, on the outskirts of Philadelphia, now a part of West Philadelphia. The terms were moderate, $125 per annum for board and tuition.

Susan B. Anthony entered this school at the age of seventeen in the winter of 1837–38, and, in a letter written to her father from the school, she described a meeting which she attended with Lucretia Mott, a friend of Deborah Moulson's and a recognized minister of the Society of Friends. The question under discussion was the education of poor children and the proper use of money that had been collected for that purpose.

The majority were in favor of appropriating it to the paying of higher salaries to teachers in neighborhoods where the circumstances of friends were too limited to offer a remuneration that would induce well qualified teachers to settle among them, but although a majority were in favor of such an appropriation, yet there were some of the committee who were of the opinion that the great desideration of well qualified teachers was a rare phenomenon and for that reason the money would be extensively useful if applied to assist in the education of those who had fine talents, but whose means were inadequate to the expenditure attendant on a liberal education.

This coincided with Deborah's ideas, for Susan goes on to say:

It is her [Deborah's] sentiment that we much need qualified teachers, for, although there are many professing to teach, yet she is of the opinion that there are a very few who know how to impart knowledge understandingly. Hence the preference that Deborah gives to pupils of this class—and it is for the sake of these that she has made the terms so moderate.

Deborah Moulson was a talented artist and left many beautiful water-color paintings, principally of flowers, but she gave up painting soon after she was thirty years of age, considering it too frivolous an occupation. She was a cultured and estimable woman, deeply religious, and one of the prominent Quaker preachers of the day.

Mrs. Edward Ellwanger

MOTHER CONNELLY

1809–1879

One of Philadelphia's most distinguished educators, whose schools are established today all over the world, was Cornelia Augusta Peacock Connelly, foundress of the Society of the Holy Child Jesus, an outstanding teaching order in the Catholic Church. Her aim in life was the spread of learning, virtue, and noble living.

This remarkable woman, whose views on education, far in advance of her times, are embodied in her *Book of the Order of Studies* published in 1863, was born at No. 1 Filbert Street, Philadelphia, the daughter of Ralph Peacock, merchant of Philadelphia, and Mary Swope Bowen, widow of John Bowen, of the island of Jamaica.

She is described as a woman of beauty with a brilliant mind and a sweet, gracious manner. In 1831 she was married, by Bishop White in Christ's Church, to a young, learned Episcopal clergyman, the Reverend Pierce Connelly. The following year he was made rector of the Episcopal Church at Natchez, Mississippi. After four years he resigned and went to New Orleans. Here his wife entered the Catholic Church. A few years later, in 1840, he announced to his wife that he wished to become a priest and asked her to make the sacrifice necessary for him to take the step, to give up their children and enter a convent.

Together they went to Rome to consult with Pope Gregory XVI who was deeply impressed with her charm and learning and advised her to found a society of her own instead of becoming a member of an established order. Provision being made for the care and maintenance of the children, she made her novitiate at the Convent of the Religious of the Sacred Heart in Rome. Her desire was to return and found her first school in Philadelphia, but on the advice of the Pope she went instead to England.

While in London she met another American, the Duchess of Leeds, one of the Caton sisters of Catonsville, Maryland and a granddaughter of Charles Carroll of Carrollton, who gave her a tract of two thousand acres which she owned near Towanda, in Pennsylvania. To this place Mother Connelly in 1862 sent seven sisters to establish her first American school, but it proved an inconvenient locality. In the meantime, several of the sisters came to Philadelphia where, with the assistance and guidance of Archbishop Wood and the Reverend Charles Carter, they established the first house of the order in 1863 at the Convent of the Assumption, Twelfth and Spring Garden streets.

In 1864 a boarding school was established at Sharon Hill, which today is the Motherhouse of the Order in the American Province. While visiting her convents in America in 1867, Mother Connelly purchased the property for St. Leonard's Academy which was opened at Thirty-ninth and Chestnut streets. In 1921 Rosemont College was established for the higher education of women, and today has students from twenty-five states, Canada, and Poland.

The Motherhouse of the Order is in Rome with schools all over Europe and in the United States from Melrose, Massachusetts, to Portland, Oregon.

MARGARET WALTON

MARY ANNA LONGSTRETH

1811–1884

MARY ANNA LONGSTRETH was born in Philadelphia, February 9, 1811, and was educated according to the strictest traditions of the Society of Friends, following the custom of her ancestors. Her school life began when she was two and a half years old, and at thirteen she gave Latin lessons to her younger sisters. Her early training made work the habit of her life, and later, when she had made herself independent, it was still her pleasure to work with warm-hearted sympathy for others.

In 1829 Miss Longstreth opened a private school for girls at 3 North Eleventh Street, assisted by her two sisters. French teachers were their only outside help until, in 1830, Elizabeth was married to Israel Morris, and in the late forties Susan stayed home to care for an invalid mother and aunt.

Meanwhile the school, successful from the beginning, was moved in 1836 to a house on Cherry Street between Tenth and Eleventh that had been built for that purpose and had a larger garden. Miss Longstreth remained there twenty-one years. Needing a larger building, for now the younger sisters and even the children of her first pupils were coming to her, in 1857 she moved to the corner of Filbert and Juniper streets, and was there ten years until the property was bought for the Masonic Temple.

Her last move was to Merrick Street, West Penn Square below Filbert, where the Broad Street Station now is, into a broad-front, three-story brick house with high marble steps, typical of old Philadelphia dwellings.

Miss Longstreth was very advanced in the curriculum for her scholars. Her generous liberality and boundless interest in them made her give them the latest and best in books on history and science. She had the authors of these books come to the school and give lectures. Besides her regular corps, she had many visiting teachers for special branches, the best authorities in their respective lines, which gave the students a broad cultural outlook. She studied the disposition of each child and held monthly teachers' meetings to talk them over and point out where their characters needed strengthening. Thus her vision for them made its impress on their lives, and there were, and still are, many outstanding women who look back on their school days with "Miss Mary Anna" with affection and thankfulness for the integrity with which she inspired them.

In the spring of 1877 Miss Longstreth decided to close her school, having taught for fifty years. More than a thousand pupils had been enrolled, and at the last she was teaching the grandchildren of her first scholars. It was a great trial for her to stop her work. The guidance of youth was to her a work of love, but her strength was no longer equal to the strain and on June 20 the closing exercises were held. They were, as she expressed it, "like a golden wedding anniversary."

The few remaining years of Miss Longstreth's life were, like all that had gone before, filled with loving service to others, her special interest being General Armstrong's school at Hampton, Virginia, for the freedmen and Indians. She continued to be a generous and a faithful friend to that institution, and her portrait still hangs in one of its rooms.

The Mary Anna Longstreth Alumnae Association was formed in 1898, its object being to carry on some charitable work in her memory and to revive recollections of former schooldays. This association has been most successful. Scholarships have been established at Hampton Institute and Bryn Mawr College in her name, and each year between $200 and $300 is given to objects recommended by the Appropriation Committee of the Association. Many schools for both white and Negro children in this city and in the South, hospitals, homes, Bible societies and many other worthy institutions are among the beneficiaries; and though the members necessarily decrease, the enthusiasm inspired by such a teacher, leader, guide, and friend is still great and helpful to others.

Miss Longstreth died August 15, 1884, seventy-three years old, and was buried in South Laurel Hill Cemetery.

A. Margaretta Archambault

MARY GREW

1813–1896

Mary Grew was born September 1, 1813, in Hartford, Connecticut. In 1834 her family moved to Philadelphia, where they made their permanent home. She was interested in the antislavery movement and joined the Female Anti-Slavery Society of Philadelphia soon after her arrival. Appointed secretary, she wrote the annual reports for thirty-four years, until the Society's labors ceased on March 4, 1870.

In 1840 Mary Grew and her father, Henry Grew, were delegates to the London Anti-Slavery Convention, where the women delegates were rejected because of their sex. Antislavery fairs became a yearly feature of the Society. At first small with few in attendance, they later grew popular, netting thousands of dollars for the advancement of the cause. Miss Grew was an ardent and enthusiastic worker. She lectured and wrote articles for publication, advocating the liberation of the African slaves held in bondage in the United States. As a lecturer, she was acute, forcible, and above all a most earnest speaker; many were the converts she made to her cause.

She later turned her attention to woman suffrage. As early as 1869 a plan was suggested and formulated by John K. Wildman for forming the Pennsylvania Woman Suffrage Association, the object of which was to secure for women the same political rights that were granted to men. The first meeting to organize was held in December of 1869. Miss Grew, elected president, threw herself heart and soul into the movement; she wrote and spoke year after year, inspiring all around her with hope and energy. In the eastern part of the state a number of local societies were formed. In the western part, Matilda Hindman, a retired school teacher, took up the suffrage cause and together they planted enough seed to bring forth a harvest of success. For twenty-three years she continued as president, retiring from office in 1892 because of age and infirmity.

Mary Grew always took an interest in local affairs connected with the woman's movement. She helped organize the New Century Club of Philadelphia in 1877, later serving as a vice-president. She was prominent in efforts to secure police matrons in the station houses and represented the New Century Club on the Police Matron Committee for several years.

LUCRETIA L. BLANKENBURG

ANN PRESTON

1813–1872

ANN PRESTON was the daughter of Amos and Margaret Preston. She was born in West Grove, Chester County, December 1813. She went to an excellent neighborhood school and spent a short time at a boarding school in West Chester. She did a great deal of reading and, being convinced of the value and necessity of a classical education, mastered Latin.

As the years went on she became more and more aware of the significant social and political currents running through the public opinion of the country. This phase of her life is reflected in an address in her memory delivered by Dr. Eliza E. Judson on March 11, 1873, from which we quote:

Prior to the convention which organized the American Anti-Slavery Society, she had become a member of the Clarkson Anti-Slavery Society, formed in the neighborhood of her home. As this was one of the first and most active of such associations, its meetings called together much of the talent of the anti-slavery cause; and those were the days when the eloquence of Garrison and Phillips and Giddings roused all lovers of liberty to action and struck fear to hearts made callous by long indulgence in injustice.

Miss Preston enlisted in the work with all the ardor of a warm, sympathetic nature, and soon becoming known as a forcible writer, it devolved on her to write reports, addresses and petitions of the society, some of which are still extant, and are models of clearness, strength and simplicity.

Although not on the direct line of the underground railroad, she did much for the relief and protection of those who were fleeing from bondage. An interesting incident is related of her in this connection.

During the absence of her father and mother, who were attending a Friends meeting at some distance from home, a fugitive slave woman was forwarded to their house. Miss Preston concealed her in a closet in the garret, fed and made her comfortable and waited, we may imagine, with no small degree of interest the time of her removal to the next station.

One morning a man came running with the information that slave-catchers were in the neighborhood. His house, the point at which the woman was last concealed, was being searched and they would be there next. To Miss Preston's question as to what she should do, he replied that she must devise her own expedients, as he could not remain to advise or assist but must hasten on and arouse the neighborhood to assist in the rescue.

Miss Preston was alone, but with great coolness and forethought she locked the woman in the closet, went to the pasture, caught a horse, harnessed him to the carriage, then hastily dressing the woman in her mother's plain shawl and Quaker bonnet, carefully adding the two veils often worn by plain Friends when riding, she started with her in the direction from which the slave-catchers were expected, with the ostensible purpose of attending meeting, it being Sunday morning.

Soon the slave-hunters came in view, riding rapidly toward them, came close to the side of the carriage and peered curiously in; but seeing only a young girl and an apparently elderly woman, in the dress of a plain Friend, leisurely going to meeting, they rode rapidly on, to continue their search elsewhere. The great danger was past; Miss Preston carried the woman to the house which had been recently searched, where she was comparatively secure. She eventually reached Canada in safety.

As a writer of prose and poetry Ann Preston had a rare charm, and in 1848 published a small book of poems for children. When family responsibilities began to grow lighter her thoughts turned toward her future career. She learned of the proposed opening of the Woman's Medical College of Pennsylvania, in the fall of 1850 in Philadelphia. This aroused her interest and she was one of the first to apply for admission to the institution, a move which, in those days, was a brave challenge to ancient customs.

As she was one of the first students of the college she was also one of the first graduates, and so successful were her studies that she was urged to accept the chair of physiology and hygiene. Thus at thirty-nine she entered upon her career as a professor of medicine. She realized the necessity for clinical as well as didactic instruction, and after great difficulties funds were raised and in the first year of the Civil War a hospital was founded. Dr. Preston was appointed a member of the Board of Managers, corresponding secretary and consulting physician, holding these offices until her death. In 1866 she was elected dean of the college and the following year was elected a member of the Board of Corporators. For nineteen years she was professor of physiology and hygiene; for six years, dean of the college, and for four years a member of the Board of Corporators. Historians do not ignore the importance of the fact that Dr. Preston was blazing a trail for women at the very time that the country was passing decisively from the Colonial-seaboard period to the expanding empire which was to become a world power.

She died on April 18, 1872. In her will, which carried on her life work, she provided that the interest of $4,000 be used annually to assist in the medical education of one good, capable woman, who might not otherwise possess sufficient means to pursue a medical education.

SARAH LOGAN WISTER STARR

JANE GREY SWISSHELM

1815–1884

ONE of those rare women who braved the pillory of public opinion in the middle years of the nineteenth century was Jane Grey Swisshelm. She was short of stature, slender, and weighed less than one hundred pounds; but she dared to fight with voice, pen, and printer's ink for the causes she believed in; notably abolition and women's rights.

Jane Grey Cannon was born December 6, 1815. Her father was Thomas Cannon, a merchant of Pittsburgh, and her mother, Mary

Scott. The family home was on Water Street in Pittsburgh, and in it she had learned to read and write by the time she was three years old. Her more formal education was received in a subscription school and in a girls' seminary at Braddocks Field, at both of which she displayed distinct talents for writing and painting. She was married at twenty-one to James Swisshelm and went to live in the old homestead of the Swisshelm family at Swissdale.

She became an ardent abolitionist and soon began writing for various short-lived abolition papers. Her first article, appearing in the Pittsburgh *Spirit of Liberty,* was attacked by the secular press both on account of her views and because as a woman she dared express opinions on public affairs. Later she wrote for the Pittsburgh *Commercial Journal,* and soon joined with Lucretia Mott and Mary A. Grew in an endeavor to obtain passage by the Pennsylvania Legislature of a woman's rights bill. Part of the program was enacted in 1847–48, when a law was passed permitting a married woman to own property.

On January 20, 1848, Mrs. Swisshelm began publishing on her own account, issuing an organ called *The Saturday Visiter,* which featured news, politics, antislavery propaganda, and women's rights. In 1849 she added a department then new in journalism, a series of "Weekly Letters to Country Girls."

Mrs. Swisshelm moved to Minnesota in 1857, establishing in the town of St. Cloud another newspaper, *The Visiter,* which she conducted on lines similar to those she had followed in Pittsburgh, except she added an espousal of fair treatment for the Indians to her other causes. Finally her newspaper plant was mobbed and wrecked; but she continued her battling from the vantage point of lecture platforms. In January 1863 she was commissioned to go to Washington on behalf of the Indians, and was cordially received by President and Mrs. Lincoln.

During the Civil War she undertook relief work for the Federal soldiers, her first task being to distribute supplies she personally had solicited through the New York *Tribune.* Later she worked as a nurse in various army hospitals, finally going to Fredericksburg, where she aided in combating hospital gangrene and other terrible conditions, until she herself became too ill to continue the fight.

After Lee's surrender Mrs. Swisshelm, through the aid of Secretary of State Stanton, regained the old homestead at Swissdale, where she spent the remainder of her life, writing and working for greater recognition for women. She died on July 25, 1884, and is buried in Allegheny Cemetery, at Pittsburgh.

WILLIAM H. STEVENSON

MARIA JANE BIGLER

1816–1884?

MARIA JANE REED, the eldest daughter of Alexander B. and Rachel Reed was born in Pike Township, Clearfield County, on July 7, 1816. She was of Scotch descent and her ancestors were American citizens long prior to the Revolutionary War. Two of her maternal great-uncles were members of the convention which assembled at Mecklenburg, North Carolina, on May 9, 1775, to protest against England's oppression. Her maternal grandfather, Alexander Reed, was a Revolutionary soldier. Two others of her ancestry lost their lives in the struggle for American independence.

Her parents migrated to the section which afterward became Clearfield County, in 1803, to make for themselves a home in that mountain wilderness. In 1825, with her parents, she moved to the town of Clearfield, which then consisted of eleven houses. There was no school in the town at that time, and she attended school in a small log structure across the river. Her father having previously been elected county treasurer, and being the agent and representative of many of the land companies which had extensive holdings in Clearfield County, had become a man of large business affairs, which required his absence from home much of the time. His daughter served as his clerk and assisted him with his books and accounts, looking after his business during his absences.

On March 24, 1836, Maria Jane Reed and William Bigler were united in marriage by Richard Shaw, justice of the peace. Her husband was at this time engaged in the publication of the Clearfield *Democrat,* a Jacksonian newspaper. For a period of forty-four years her life was part and parcel of her distinguished husband's.

Mr. Bigler became a member of the state Senate, Speaker of the

Senate and Governor of Pennsylvania from 1851 to 1854. Later he was United States Senator and afterward State Supervisor and member of the Committee of Finance for the Centennial Exposition of 1876. Throughout all these years of public office, and especially during the critical period of our history just before the Civil War, she was his constant adviser and counselor.

During the administration of President Buchanan her husband represented Pennsylvania in the United States Senate, and, since both men were from the same state and of the same political party and had much the same views on political questions, there was naturally an intimacy between them. Mrs. Bigler was a familiar figure at the White House in those days and was as much at home in her surroundings at Washington as she was in the pine wilderness of Clearfield County.

For her generation she was quite a traveler; one most unusual trip with her husband took them around Cape Horn in a sailing vessel, on their way to visit his brother, the Governor of California. They returned after a lengthy visit by way of the Isthmus of Panama. Quiet and unobtrusive in her manner, she was yet a woman actively energetic and of great moral courage and force of character. Possessed of a remarkably clear judgment and great common sense, her advice was often sought by neighbors and friends in matters pertaining to the church and home.

CLEARFIELD WOMAN'S CLUB

MARY NEVLING BOYNTON

1816–1906

MARY NEVLING, the daughter of John Adam and Edith Vaughn Nevling, was brought up in Huntingdon County, and it was there that she met and married Jonathan Boynton, a descendant of John Boynton, who with his brother William emigrated from Yorkshire, England, in 1637, and settled at Rowley, Massachusetts.

Mary Nevling Boynton was a woman of unusual character and ability whose entire life was spent in acts of generosity and kindness to others. When her husband traveled the river with his men from the lumber camps, she attended to his business, taking care of a cash payroll of several thousand dollars. She was instrumental in building the Methodist Church in Clearfield, where her home was the headquarters for all visiting preachers and their families, and assisted her husband in bringing the railroad to that town in 1868.

Twice a year in those early days they drove to Lewistown and took a train from there to Philadelphia, bringing back supplies which were sent from Lewistown by wagon. In Philadelphia they used to stay at the Merchants Hotel on Second Street and did their shopping on High (now Market) Street. Mary Nevling Boynton's influence among the needy, with her outstanding character for loyalty, truth, and sincerity, made her well beloved in her community where her name is a memory not to be forgotten.

MARY DILL PATTON

HANNAH E. LONGSHORE

1819–1902

PENNSYLVANIA women have won high places in the history of state and nation, but it is not too much to say that Dr. Hannah E. Longshore wrote her name in blazing letters on the history of civilization. She was the most famous of the first eight women graduated from the Woman's Medical College of Pennsylvania, then known as the Female Medical College.

To understand Dr. Longshore's contribution to womanhood and to civilization, it must be remembered that the Woman's Medical College of Pennsylvania, as it is now known, upon its founding in 1850 was the first institution of the kind in the world. Today it is the only medical college exclusively for women in the Western Hemisphere. Until the first class was graduated in 1852, there had never been in all history a woman trained like a man for the profession of medicine. There had been other women who had exercised rare talents in the art of healing and of caring for the sick and wounded, but Dr. Longshore and the seven other women who were graduated with her were the first women who could be described as educated and licensed practitioners. In the middle of the last century, women students and physicians were derided and scorned, and it is to the bravery and the skill and the patience of Dr. Longshore that the women physicians of today owe much of their present distinction. What may be called the woman's movement in general owed much to Dr. Longshore.

When she had finished her college training, she at once opened an office and hung out her shingle. She was the first woman to do so in Philadelphia. Crowds gathered outside her office to ridicule her. Druggists refused at first to fill her prescriptions. Many men physicians would have nothing to do with her. She stood virtually alone, but before long, after a heroic fight, her place was secured because of her achievements. The reception of Hannah E. Longshore as a physician, and of that band of courageous spirits who worked with her, is reminiscent of the rioting and of the ostracism with which men physicians were greeted in the seventeenth century when they began to experiment with anesthetics for the relief of pain.

Hannah, the daughter of Samuel and Paulina Myers, was born in Montgomery County, Maryland, on May 30, 1819. As a child the future woman physician clearly foreshadowed her career in her deep interest in her studies and her taste for scientific pursuits. At twenty-two, Hannah Myers was married to Thomas E. Longshore, whose home was near Philadelphia. Her brother-in-law, Professor Joseph S. Longshore, who was later to be one of the founders of the Female Medical College, assisted her throughout her career by allowing her to use his library, where under his tuition she prepared for college. It is interesting to observe, as indicative of her originality and initiative, that she began to solve the problem of building up a practice in those difficult days by delivering a popular lecture on the Medical Education of Women. Lucretia Mott, a leading figure in the Society of Friends and a pioneer suffragist, presided at the lecture. In these days we can hardly appreciate the novelty of such a talk, and as such it was largely attended. Thereafter she gave courses of lectures on physiology and hygiene. Meanwhile her practice was growing. Her reputation was made when a patient, far advanced in dropsy, whose case had been abandoned as hopeless by other physicians, recovered under her care. For more than forty years she was a busy and successful practitioner.

Unlike other early women graduates of the College, she confined herself almost wholly to the practice of medicine. For a short time she served as a demonstrator of anatomy in the college. Her fame, however, rests upon her ability as a physician and her commanding place in the history of women in medicine.

She had two children, Channing Longshore, who became a practicing physician, and Lucretia L. Blankenburg, whose husband was mayor of Philadelphia from 1911 to 1916.

Mrs. Henry D. Jump
Mrs. L. P. Smook

LAURA GOODWIN SANFORD

1819–1907

Laura Goodwin Sanford was born November 11, 1819, in Erie, Pennsylvania. Her father, Giles Sanford, had come from Connecticut in 1810, and was a prominent merchant. Miss Sanford's family on her father's side can be traced as far back as John Sanford, President of Rhode Island in 1655.

Laura was educated in the accomplishments of the day to which young ladies devoted their time; embroidering, music, drawing, and painting. She was always willing to share with others anything she might have to impart. In a little note, written in her neat and precise handwriting and style, she commends a niece, in 1845, for her progress in music and ends by signing it her "aunt and instructor, L. G. Sanford."

In later years, she taught nephews and nieces how to play chess, and one of the memories connected with her is of the quaint little old lady courteously complying with a request to contribute to the entertainment of a family gathering by "performing upon the piano." The manner in which she did it was quaint, as was the old instrument upon which she played, now preserved in the Erie Museum.

Of a deeply religious nature, she felt "called" to be a missionary, and so was in Spain and Italy in 1870 and 1872. She wrote from Madrid in 1870, "I bought myself a Spanish Bible and mean to read it through this year aloud, both to learn the language and to get at the meaning of the Bible."

In local affairs she was interested and active, having been instrumental in organizing the Woman's Christian Temperance Union, of which she was the first president. She also helped to start the Home for the Friendless, and was one of its first incorporators.

Generous in her contributions to worthy causes, among many other gifts she and her sister-in-law, Mrs. Susan Sanford, gave the ground for the Erie Boys' Club, also the property on which the Sarah Hearn Memorial Presbyterian Church now stands.

That for which Miss Sanford especially deserves to be remembered is her *History of Erie County,* first published in 1861, with a supplementary edition in 1894, which has been the nucleus of all subsequent histories of Erie County, Pennsylvania. One writer says of it, "It evinces a vast amount of industry and research."

Miss Sanford died, after a life of varied activities and experiences, in Erie, August 16, 1907.

EMILY SPRANKLE HERON

MATILDA SAMUEL COHEN

1820–1888

MATILDA SAMUEL was born in Liverpool, England, in 1820. In that city she was married to Henry Cohen in 1844. He had been in America since 1837, and after his marriage took his bride to Philadelphia, where they lived at 1828 Rittenhouse Square for nearly forty years.

Mrs. Cohen was a generous supporter of music and a lover of literature. She participated actively in community affairs, both religious and social. When, therefore, the Women's Committee for the Centennial Exposition in Philadelphia was formed with Mrs. E. D. Gillespie as its chairman, Mrs. Cohen became one of her most valued co-workers as a member of the Executive Committee of Thirteen. To have been an active member of that committee is sufficient proof of the education, efficiency, and patriotism of any woman who was willing to engage in so unusual a movement. It offered an outstanding opportunity for American women to prove their possession of executive ability and public spirit.

Near the center of the Women's Building at the Centennial was a small office in which women compositors were engaged in setting up the type of a popular journal called *The New Century for Women*. Shortly after the close of the Exposition the first women's club in Philadelphia, known thereafter as the New Century Club, was organized. Mrs. Cohen was one of the charter members of the new organization. In 1887 she was made a director and in 1880 she became its vice-president, in which office she served the club until her death in 1888.

EVELINA HEAP GLEAVES

JANE CRAWFORD

1820–1889

⚜

JANE WILSON, the daughter of James Wilson, Chief Justice of the Isle of France, was born in Edinburgh in 1820. She was educated by governesses and finishing schools in Edinburgh and Paris, where she became proficient in French, Italian, literature, history, music, and mathematics up to long division, which latter was considered by the educators of the day entirely adequate for a lady's needs in checking her household accounts. Of far greater importance in her education was her acquisition of the arts of the drawing room, grace, accomplishments, and the ability to entertain.

At eighteen she was married to Stephen Rowan Crawford, son of a shipbuilder of Glasgow. Since the match was not altogether pleasing to the families in Scotland, Mr. and Mrs. Crawford gathered together their possessions, chartered a sailing vessel, and joined Mr. Crawford's brother, Joseph Tucker Crawford, the British consul at Havana. The climate of Havana proving unsatisfactory, Mr. Crawford brought his family to Philadelphia to be near his old friends: the Hutchinsons of Sunny Side; the Joshua Fishers of Alverthorne;

and the Outerbridges of Echo Hill. He purchased for his summer home Ury, the old Miers Fisher estate of one hundred acres near Fox Chase.

Stephen Crawford established a banking business in Philadelphia, and became president of the St. Andrew's Society. His town house was in fashionable old Girard Street. Here frequently of a warm evening in early spring when the drawing-room windows were open, the street outside would be filled with people listening as Mrs. Crawford sang Scotch ballads and arias from French and Italian opera.

They had thirteen children. Six sons grew to manhood. Much of Mr. Crawford's fortune had been invested in the South. This vanished during the early years of the Civil War, and Mr. Crawford did not long survive the shock and disappointment. Mrs. Crawford withdrew with her family to Ury, and friends sent their sons to her to share the tutors who had provided for the education of her younger boys. From this nucleus developed the Ury House Boarding School for Boys, which was famous for twenty-one years during the sixties, seventies, and early eighties. After Mrs. Crawford retired as principal in 1885, the school continued for forty years longer under Charles H. Strout, as the St. Luke's School, first at Bustleton and later at Wayne.

Perhaps the most notable service Mrs. Crawford rendered the boys in her school was her personal influence over them and her unfailing ability to guide them into the paths of virtue. She had great dignity of bearing and such distinction that she was known among the village people in her neighborhood as "Lady Crawford." Happy are the old boys when they return to Ury House, still extant in the country north of Fox Chase, and relate memories of the story hour, when old and young, equally entranced, gathered about the open fire of an evening in the old parlor to be thrilled by Mrs. Crawford's tales of adventure and past times.

Bronze tablets in memory of Jane Crawford, founder of Ury House School, are on the walls of the Old Trinity Oxford Church, and also in the St. Luke's Church, at Bustleton, placed there with affectionate care years ago by the Ury-St. Luke's Alumni Association.

H. JEAN CRAWFORD

MARY MORRIS HUSBAND

1820–1894

᧞

"THE lady with the apron!" Watch her as she goes from cot to cot in a hospital of Civil War times. She takes from the various pockets of that capacious apron an apple for one soldier, a newspaper for another, a Testament for one, a pair of stockings for another, and one lucky fellow gets a letter from home. Smiles and good cheer for all. The eyes of the boys follow her retreating figure, for there is healing in the shadow of Mary Morris Husband.

Her grandfather was the great financier of the Revolution, Robert Morris. Philadelphian by birth and patriot by blood, the first years of the Civil War found Mrs. Husband in the hospital work of her native city. The second summer of the war, when hope of easy victory had given place to dark foreboding, found her on the battle-field, in tent and in hospital, "a cup of strength" to hundreds whose love of country was costing them dear.

When malignant disease added its horrors to those of war she never quailed. A patient thus suffering, especially if removed far from ready help, was the very one she chose for her own. Little enough was known of dietetics in those days. But Mrs. Husband was a born dietician. She knew that a cup of tea cannot be boiled in an iron kettle that has just accommodated meat and vegetables, and many a sick or wounded soldier returned to his musket more quickly because of her milk punches, eggnogs, and simple but nutritious desserts.

Her motherly heart was also shown in her understanding of the need of amusement for the soldier-convalescent, not yet ready to return to the front. Her tent or office, provided with books, pictures, and games, was his rendezvous, and hours that otherwise would have been "tedious and tasteless" became happy memories. In her care for the physical needs of her patients Mrs. Husband was singularly fortunate in her home support. From the Ladies' Aid Society of Philadelphia she received constant supplies for the need and comfort of her patients. So great was the faith of her friends in her integrity and wisdom that wherever her word was "give" a hundred purses were open to her.

An outstanding work done by Mrs. Husband was that in behalf of soldiers unjustly sent to the guardhouse. In this it is said she had no equal among volunteer army workers. Her discerning mind saw that sentence passed upon offenders was often too swift to be just. Repeatedly the iron severity of martial law yielded to her persuasions. Her fine presence and legal knowledge, rare in her day for those of her sex, gave her many a victory. If unsuccessful with the various commanders, she took her case to the Secretary of War and, failing here, she repeatedly appealed to the gentle spirit in the White House. Many a life that otherwise would have been unjustly sacrificed was saved by her unflagging zeal and a persistency that would not know defeat.

FLORENCE P. McINTYRE

MARGARET JUNKIN PRESTON

1820–1897

"POETESS Laureate of the South" is a strange title to be conferred upon a Pennsylvania-born woman, yet it was freely bestowed on Margaret Junkin Preston. The honor is more remarkable in that it was awarded by general acclaim during those years immediately subsequent to the War between the States when sectionalism was bitterest.

Margaret Junkin was born on May 19, 1820, child of the marriage of George Junkin, of the Cumberland Valley, and Julia Rush Miller, of Philadelphia. Religion and education were the two great absorbing passions of her father's life. When Margaret was ten years old, her father moved his family to Germantown where he became head of the Manual Labor Academy of Pennsylvania. Two years later he moved to Easton to assume the presidency of Lafayette College, remaining there for nine years. It was during this period, spent on the beautiful forks of the Delaware, that Margaret was inspired to pen her first verses. When she was twenty-one, her parent accepted a call to Miami University in Ohio where the family stayed three years; after that back to Easton and Lafayette College for four years more.

Then came the move, in Margaret's twenty-eighth year, which

sharply divides her life, and which cast her lot with the people of the South. Until this time her education had been administered by her father and broadened by acquaintance with and study under the many professors she met in the universities he had headed. In 1840, she and her sister Eleanor (who later became the wife of General "Stonewall" Jackson) joined the First Presbyterian Church in Easton. It was during the period between 1840 and 1848 that her verses were first published, mostly in the columns of the local newspaper, including "Childhood," "The Forest Grave," "Where Dwelleth the Scent of the Rose," and others.

In 1848 her father received and accepted a call to Lexington, Virginia, to be president of Washington College, now Washington and Lee University. There she met a Major John T. L. Preston, professor of Latin at Virginia Military Institute. Romance entered her life notwithstanding the fact that he was a widower with seven children ranging in age from five years to twenty-one.

They were married on August 3, 1857, and for a short time the poet was submerged in the rôle of wife, homemaker and ideal stepmother. Her house became well known for its orderly arrangements and for a hospitality whose added attraction was an especially delicious brand of waffles with spicy apple butter. This, too, was a period of great readjustment while she accustomed herself to the new life in which slaves did the work while the whites devoted themselves to the graces of entertainment and social intercourse. Her verses again began to appear in the religious and secular journals and her only novel, *Silverwood,* portraying the characters of her mother, sister, and brother, was published anonymously about this time.

Then came the great conflict between the States, and the Junkin family became divided. Margaret, of course, elected to remain with her husband. Her father, an ardent abolitionist, resigned the presidency of Washington College and returned to Philadelphia, where he remained until his death. Her brother William espoused the cause of the Confederacy and became a captain of infantry; her other brother, John, cast his lot with the North and served as a surgeon in the Federal Army. The Preston children naturally served with the Gray.

Margaret herself heard the sound of cannon and the rattle of musketry as the armies fought, marching and countermarching, in the Valley of the Shenandoah. She saw the burning of Virginia Military

Academy and the denuding of Washington College. Her diaries are crammed with references to such events.

Following Lee's surrender at Appomattox, Mrs. Preston, aside from her household duties, devoted much time to reviewing books for various publishers and in arranging her own compositions, both prose and verse. The latter work resulted in the publication in 1866 of *Beechenbrook,* a book of verse voicing the sorrow and patriotism of the Southern people. This was followed by *Old Songs and New.* Then in 1880, or thereabouts, she contributed to the *Century Magazine* some reminiscences of General Robert E. Lee, who came to Lexington as president of Washington College after the war, and some recollections of General "Stonewall" Jackson, her sister's husband.

Margaret Junkin Preston died March 29, 1897, at her son's home in Baltimore. She is buried under a giant oak tree in the cemetery at Lexington.

Mrs. Lynwood R. Holmes
Marian Mauser

MARY ANN RAYMOND BLISS

1821–1912

Mary Ann Raymond Bliss, being a small woman and retiring, did not impress one as a person of much force, but when opportunity came for her to express her opinion, she was ever ready. In 1844 she married George R. Bliss, a man of brilliant intellect, professor of Greek at the University of Lewisburg, now Bucknell. In Lewisburg Mrs. Bliss's life was a help and inspiration to many of the young people with whom she came in contact.

Her brother was Dr. Raymond, the first president of Vassar College. He made a wonderful impression on the country in the early history of higher education for women.

Twelve children were born to Dr. and Mrs. Bliss, some of whom were endowed with marked ability. Among the sons was Tasker H. Bliss, military member of the American Commission to the Peace Conference at Versailles. Several lawyers, men of distinction in Chicago and Washington, were also sons of this noble woman. Lucy Bliss, a daughter, was for many years the head of a private school in Brooklyn. Another daughter, Frances Bliss, married a missionary and did notable service in Burma.

When Dr. Bliss was called to Crozier Theological Seminary at Chester, to take charge of the Greek department, the children had grown to manhood and womanhood, and Mrs. Bliss gave her time to wider interests. In her home on the campus many young men sought her advice in the matter of training for their life work.

MARGARET TUSTIN O'HARA

CATHARINE IRVINE WILSON CURTIN

1821–1903

CATHARINE IRVINE WILSON was born the daughter of a country doctor, Hugh Irvine Wilson, on January 17, 1821, at Earlystown, Center County. She spent her girlhood in her father's house in the country near Potter's Mills, known to Revolutionary fame because one of her ancestors, a Potter, made history for himself and his country as a notable officer in the war.

The Wilsons were hospitable country folk. A love of horses and of sport, agreeable manners, handsome looks, and a capacity for friendship made them well liked among their Center County neighbors and remembered traditionally to this day. One of Catharine's brothers who served in the Civil War was Colonel William Potter Wilson of General Hancock's staff.

Catharine married, May 29, 1844, a not-distant neighbor, Andrew Gregg Curtin, of Bellefonte, a lawyer of promise, on whose family land iron ore was discovered early in the settlement of the county and was smelted by furnaces burning charcoal long after coal was available. Mr. Curtin practiced law in Bellefonte, became Secretary of the Commonwealth in 1855; Governor of the State in 1861 for two terms; Minister to Russia, 1869–72; delegate-at-large for the Constitutional Convention, 1872–74; and member of Congress, 1881–87. He died in 1894. Mrs. Curtin survived him nine years, dying December 7, 1903.

As wife of the Governor of Pennsylvania during the war—in Harrisburg during the anxiety from threatening dangers of the Gettysburg campaign, in Washington in behalf of the wounded Pennsylvanians transferred to army hospitals there, and with the presidential party when Lincoln dedicated the field of battle as a national cemetery for the dead at Gettysburg—her place was conspicuous both for its power of service and for its nearness to the chief actors in the events of those years. She had a certain detachment of vision and candor of mind which made her a spectator as well as a gravely courteous participant on those occasions when the public had to be influenced and reassured by men whose minds were burdened with anxious decisions.

In the years after the war, when our trade with Russia was being established, the Curtins, residents in that country, gained not only the friendship of the Czar, but very important concessions for American manufacturers. Mrs. Curtin's beauty and charm as well as her good sense were notable factors in this delicate interchange of international courtesies.

Europe in the early seventies was as remote in its court conventions from Bellefonte as one could conceive possible. But it was an experience which Mrs. Curtin enjoyed with the same composed intelligence that she had enjoyed her American social and political contacts in which her husband's positions involved her. She was equal to her occasions without haste and without waste. At a period of our history when women had no political standing and very little intellectual recognition, she accepted the hardships and laurels of public life with quiet dignity.

And she served her generation none the less by consistently, and through an innate fineness of soul and manner, gracing any company she entered. As a representative of America by fate rather than by official training, she was worthy of a great opportunity.

SARAH D. LOWRIE

ELIZABETH DUANE GILLESPIE

1821–1901

ᴁᴕᴁ

ELIZABETH DUANE was born in Philadelphia in 1821. Her father, William Duane, in 1805 had married Deborah Bache, one of the children of Benjamin Franklin's only daughter, Sarah. This, of course, placed Elizabeth three generations away from Benjamin Franklin and Deborah, his wife, but she cherished many intimate recollections of the ancestor of whom she was most articulately proud. Her mother remembered Franklin very well in those last sunny years of his life, in his house and garden just off High Street, for Mrs. Duane's mother had kept house for him after his final return from France, and the Bache children were happily welcomed by their grandfather in their play and study about the house and garden.

Mrs. Gillespie's father, William Duane, was a man of parts and fine inheritable traits himself. He had left his publishing and printing business to study law after his marriage, and entered politics through the door of a cabinet position under Jackson. Later he had a difference with the President about the great bank question of the day, resigned, and took up his legal profession once more in Philadelphia. He lived in a house near Fifth and Walnut streets and opposite what was then called, phonetically, "State'us Yard." As Stephen Girard's lawyer and agent, William Duane wrote the great merchant's will with his own hand, and bought and transacted the business of his coal lands in the wilds of Pennsylvania.

Following Franklin's habit of travel, Europe was an adventure taken for granted by each generation of his descendants. Very early in her married life Mrs. Gillespie ventured on journeys in which she had an extraordinary number of interesting encounters. But what actually developed her masterful mind along the line of public service in which she eventually won such deserved credit was the military hospital service in Philadelphia during the Civil War.

The Sanitary Commission was the Red Cross of those days and inaugurated hospitals not only far behind the lines but also near the front. It was into one of the Philadelphia hospitals, under Dr. John Neil, that Mrs. Gillespie and many other women enlisted for the war.

Her position was that of matron. By her enthusiasm she stimulated the whole city to hold a great fair at Logan Square, the most elaborate and successful that had ever been assembled by amateurs for a philanthropic cause. Her three years in the hospitals, first on Reed Street and then on Cherry, gave her a grounding in public affairs; her organization of the Women's Committee of the Centennial ten years later was a natural result. Curiously enough her plan for the Centennial Committee, then unique, would now be but a matter of course. Its development from a small group to a larger one and from that to state and then to national groups had already been worked out in her mind on the basis of an organization of the wards of the city. She had originally meant to use such a representative body for working up enthusiasm for cleaning the streets. As a matter of fact it was now turned to account for a money drive for the Centennial. The astonished and congratulatory men's committee after this successful drive put one problem after another before Mrs. Gillespie and her cohorts to solve. Moving public opinion to force councils to vote money, moving statewide feeling to influence Congress, moving the country at large to demand an international celebration, climaxed by a personal approach to the doors of Congress for the national loan that would make the Centennial possible formed the backbone of her great services.

Then the committee having collected the money, built their own building, gathered in their exhibits from the women of the world and so helped start a new era for women all over the world. They did more than that for they brought from Europe the first kindergarten in America, built a schoolhouse for it next to their building, and ran it with real children for the Centennial season. This last venture started a whole new department of education and of child care in the United States. Finally they helped by their influence and their personal gifts the inauguration of the Pennsylvania Museum and of the School of Industrial Art as their appreciative gesture of farewell to the Centennial organization as a whole.

Mrs. Gillespie in later years was to inaugurate orchestra concerts under Theodore Thomas for Philadelphia and was to add other opportunities of culture and civic betterment to her native city, but the whole of her gifted and executive self went into the creativeness of that Centennial period.

Her husband was an officer in the United States Marines, and her only child, Ellen, married Dr. Edward Davies. In 1901 she published her reminiscences under the title of *A Book of Remembrance*.

SARAH D. LOWRIE
MARY MORRIS DUANE

GRACEANNA LEWIS

1821–after 1907

GRACEANNA LEWIS was born near Kimberton, Chester County, August 3, 1821. The daughter of John and Esther Fussell Lewis, she was a lover of nature, and the study which she first gave to it for pleasure became to her a support and consolation.

In 1869 she printed a pamphlet showing the relation of birds to the animal kingdom. Her classification was based on her own outdoor study and the use of the library and specimens of the Academy of Natural Sciences, Philadelphia, under the direction of John Cassin, one of the leading ornithologists in the world. Other works soon followed. She prepared a number of important charts, among which were "Chart of the Animal Kingdom" and "Chart of Geology, with a Special Reference to Paleontology." She also prepared *Microscopic Studies, Water Color Painting of Wild Flowers,* and *Studies in Forestry.*

At the fourth congress of the Association for Advancement of Women, she read a paper on "The Development of the Animal Kingdom," which was later printed in pamphlet form. In 1876 at the Centennial in Philadelphia she exhibited a wax model in connection with the chart of the animal kingdom, which was commended by Professor Huxley and other naturalists of prominence.

Among her other works are "Chart of the Vegetable Kingdom" and "Chart of True Fishes." She was an artist of note and executed many pictures of wild flowers, plant forms, and forest branches. At the request of the Commissioners of Forestry of Pennsylvania she made fifty paintings of forest trees in flower, fruitage, and autumnal coloring for the Chicago Fair in 1893. They were also exhibited at the St. Louis Fair in 1904, being awarded a diploma and gold medal. These paintings were purchased by the state.

In 1907 she was elected a member of the Academy of Natural Sciences. She was an honorary member of the Rochester Academy of Science, the American Philosophical Society, and the Women's Anthropological Society, as well as a life member of the Delaware County Institute of Science in which she was much interested. On numerous occasions she spoke at institute meetings. She was an active temperance worker and a member of the Media Woman's Christian Temperance Union and in many other ways advanced reform and philanthropy. She was an honorary member of the New Century Club of Philadelphia and secretary at one time of a suffrage association in Media. In addition she was chief of the cultural department of the Media Flower Mission and secretary of the Delaware County Forestry Association.

With two of her sisters, Mariann and Elizabeth R., she was one of the prime workers for abolition. The three sisters made the Lewis house, near Kimberton, the center for the Underground Railroad, by which fugitive slaves made good their escape.

LUCRETIA L. BLANKENBURG

ELIZABETH E. HUTTER

1822–1895

ELIZABETH, the daughter of Colonel Jacob Shindel of Lebanon, a veteran of the War of 1812, and Elizabeth Leisenring of Sunbury, was born November 18, 1822. She was a granddaughter of John Peter Shindel, who served in the Revolution and later represented his district in the Legislature of Pennsylvania. Her early education was received in the schools of her home town and in the Moravian Seminary at Bethlehem. At the age of seventeen she married Dr. Edwin Wilson Hutter, who was at the time editor and publisher of newspapers in Harrisburg, Allentown, Lancaster, and Richmond, Virginia.

It was while living in Lancaster that Dr. and Mrs. Hutter became the intimate friends of James Buchanan and his niece, Harriet Lane. Through President Buchanan Dr. Hutter was persuaded to enter political life, and held several appointive offices. One of them was Assistant Secretary of State under Buchanan in the Polk administration. Life in Washington proved Mrs. Hutter to be an attractive social star, figuring very prominently because of her beauty, culture, tact, and charming personality. Her home was the center where mingled men and women who were leaders in the affairs of the nation, such as Henry Clay, Daniel Webster, Jefferson Davis, John Calhoun, Chief Justice Taney, Generals Zachary Taylor and Winfield Scott, Susan B. Anthony and Harriet Beecher Stowe. On several occasions Mrs. Hutter and Harriet Lane were called upon to entertain foreign dignitaries; there was scarcely any type of official life with which she was not familiar.

Just at this period a transforming influence, the death by scarlet fever of their two sons, turned her husband's career from politics into the religious field, although as an inducement to keep him in political life President Polk offered him the post of Minister to Italy. They left Washington for a permanent home in Philadelphia, where Dr. Hutter became the pastor of St. Matthew's Lutheran Church at Broad and Mount Vernon streets. At this time Mrs. Hutter became deeply interested in works of philanthropy, one of which resulted in the founding of the Northern Home for Friendless Children at Twenty-third and Brown streets, Philadelphia, in 1853. She was chosen the first president of the Board of Managers, a position which she held until the end of her life forty-two years later.

During the Civil War a large building was added to this home devoted to the care and to the education of soldiers' and sailors' orphans. This was formally dedicated March 16, 1865. In her interest in these two institutions Mrs. Hutter closely followed the careers of the boys and girls, after they were graduated, often helping them to secure positions. In the spring of 1867 Mrs. Hutter was appointed by Governor Geary "Lady Inspector of the Department of Soldiers' Orphans," being then the only woman in the history of the Commonwealth to whom a Governor's Commission had been granted.

When the memorable Sanitary Fair was held in Logan Square, Philadelphia, in 1864, Mrs. Hutter was placed at the head of the Department of Labor, Income, and Revenue, and to her extraordinary ability and zeal were largely credited the success of that committee, which raised $250,000 for the relief and comfort of the soldiers on the field and in the hospitals. During the entire period of the war Mrs. Hutter and her husband did much to relieve the sick and wounded soldiers, laboring on many of the battlefields, including Gettysburg, where they ministered alike to the men of the Union and of the Confederacy.

After the battle of Bull Run, President Lincoln telegraphed for Dr. and Mrs. Hutter, so that they were the first civilians to pass through the Union lines. They enjoyed the confidence and the respect of the President, who on a number of occasions summoned them to the White House for consultation. One of Mrs. Hutter's most highly prized mementoes of Civil War days was a visiting card bearing the President's own handwriting, addressed to Secretary of War Stanton, which reads:

I really wish Mrs. Hutter to be obliged in this case. She is one of the very best friends of the soldiers. Hon. Secretary of War, please see her. Nov. 4th, 1864.

A. LINCOLN

Upon the occasion of the twenty-fifth anniversary of the founding of the Northern Home for Friendless Children and the Soldiers and Sailors Orphans Institute held in the Academy of Music in May, 1878, she was presented with a massive silver service by a committee of Philadelphia's prominent citizens. George W. Childs, in his speech of presentation, paid a glowing and beautiful tribute to her worth, her kindness, her thoughtfulness, and her broad sympathies.

After the great Chicago fire in 1871, and again after the terrible Johnstown flood of 1889, she was most active in collecting and forwarding aid. During the Centennial Exposition in 1876 she was at the head of the executive committee in charge of the State Educational Department. In 1879 she became the president of the Newsboys Aid Association of Philadelphia. There were indeed but few philanthropic or civic affairs organized in Philadelphia with which she was not connected. Her activities ended only with her death, which occurred after a brief illness on June 18, 1895.

MRS. ALEXANDER M. FOX
MRS. HENRY GORDON THUNDER

GRACE GREENWOOD

1823–1904

ON September 23, 1823, Sarah Jane Clarke was born at Pompey, in Onandaga County, New York. Although the years of her childhood and early girlhood were passed in Rochester her adult life belonged to Pennsylvania. It was to that state that her father moved when she was nineteen years old to settle at New Brighton, near Pittsburgh.

Sarah began to write at an early age using the pen name of Grace Greenwood. Her first prose publications to attract attention appeared in the New York *Mirror,* of which N. P. Willis was then editor. Of her poems, "Ariadne" is perhaps the best known.

In 1853 she became the wife of Leander K. Lippincott, of Philadelphia. Her literary activity covered a period of about twenty-five years and included the following books: *Greenwood Leaves; Haps and Mishaps of a Tour in Europe; A Forest Tragedy and Other Tales; Records of Five Years; Recollections of My Childhood; New Life in New Lands; Stories and Legends of Travel and History; The Life of Queen Victoria;* and a volume of poems. Her facile pen gave evidence of admirable descriptive power, as well as vivid imagination. Her literary work brought her into prominence in a period when Pennsylvania women writers were but few.

That she was a lover of nature and of child life and an interested student of animal life was made manifest in the monthly magazine for juvenile readers, *Little Pilgrim,* which she edited for several years in Philadelphia with marked success. As a student of history and an intelligent traveler she covered a wide range in the development of her literary work. Perhaps her most widely spread popularity was enjoyed through a number of years as a correspondent of the New York *Tribune* and the New York *Times* in Europe and Washington.

The movement for the abolition of slavery attracted her active sympathy and to it she gave the support of her pen in her most vigorous years. Other progressive measures attracted her later attention. On April 20, 1904, she died in New Rochelle, New York.

GERTRUDE BOSLER BIDDLE

ANNA MORRIS HOLSTEIN

1824–1900

ANNA MORRIS ELLIS, the daughter of Rebecca Morris and William Cox Ellis, was born in Muncy, Lycoming County, April 9, 1824, and died at her home near Bridgeport, Pennsylvania, December 31, 1900. She was married to Major William H. Holstein in 1848. They made their home on the farm which was part of the original tract of land purchased in 1705 by Matthias Holstein, ancestor of the Major, and lived there until their death. This land was located in Upper Merion.

Anna's ancestors had served their country with distinction. Captain Samuel Morris, commanding the First City Troop of Philadelphia, performed nobly at the battles of Trenton and Princeton during the Revolution, and Thomas Ellis, another ancestor, was Registrar General of the Province of Pennsylvania and a friend of William Penn. Mrs. Holstein's lovely, serene countenance indicated power as well as piety. She had high patriotic ideals and was an interested worker in all projects to perpetuate the memory of historic spots and places.

In 1862, during the Civil War, she offered her services to the Government as an army nurse and was recommended by General Hancock. Her capability and Christian spirit particularly fitted her for this work, to which she and her husband felt that they were called. She gave three years of untiring service, experiencing severe hardships, but at all times comforted with the assurance that she was alleviating the pain and bringing cheer and sympathy to the sick and dying soldiers. After the battle of Gettysburg, Camp Letterman, with three thousand seriously wounded men, was placed in her charge.

A book by Mrs. Holstein, *Three Years in Field Hospitals in the Army of the Potomac,* was published in 1866. It contains many pathetic and some amusing incidents. This work was compiled from notes hastily written by candlelight, with no idea of publication, but "to preserve some slight memento of the events of war for friends at home."

Mrs. Holstein was untiring in her effort to arouse public sentiment and appreciation for the great historical importance of the hills of Valley Forge, where Washington's army was encamped during that terrible winter of 1777–78. She was made regent of the Valley Forge Centennial and Memorial Association at its organization and held this office until her death. She labored untiringly that the association might purchase Washington's headquarters at Valley Forge and restore it "as a memorial for all time to come," and rejoiced when the camps of the Patriotic Order, Sons of America removed the final indebtedness from the property.

Mrs. Holstein was a member of the Historical Society of Montgomery County. Among the papers she contributed to the archives of the Society was "Women in Montgomery County in War Time."

The first effort to form a chapter of the Daughters of the American Revolution in Norristown was made in 1893. Mrs. Holstein was appointed regent by the National Society. When in May 1894, a meeting was held to decide on a chapter name, Mrs. Holstein advocated the name of Valley Forge as the most fitting, and it was adopted. Valley Forge Chapter was regularly organized December 17, 1894, and she was elected the first regent.

As a memorial to her memory, a beautifully carved prayer desk was presented to the Washington Memorial Chapel at Valley Forge by the Valley Forge Chapter, Daughters of the American Revolution, and dedicated June 19, 1916.

ANNA SCHALL FISHER
MRS. JOHN REX

ANNE E. McDOWELL

1826–1901

ANNE E. McDOWELL, born in Smyrna, Delaware, June 23, 1826, died in Philadelphia September 30, 1901. Her life was dedicated to the task of helping women.

She started the *Woman's Advocate* in 1855. This is said to have been the first paper owned, edited, and published by a woman and on which all work, including typesetting, was done by women. It was successful until the troubles preceding the rebellion of the Southern States when loss of subscriptions crippled resources, and nervous strain brought on its owner a severe illness. During this illness of Miss McDowell the paper was sold to New York publishers.

Four years later she suffered paralysis of one leg, from which she never recovered, but she was able to walk with the aid of surgical appliances and a cane and to pursue her chosen duty of aiding women in every way. To further this work for some years she conducted a column in the Philadelphia *Sunday Republic* in women's interests, using the money thus earned in many helpful ways. She received a small annuity from a deceased relative's estate, but not more than enough to maintain herself in modest comfort.

After giving up her newspaper work, Miss McDowell was for some years secretary of the John Wanamaker Insurance Association at the Wanamaker store. While in this situation Mr. Wanamaker wrote her, on her birthday, in 1887, that he "would establish a library for the convenience of our womenfolk" and with her permission it would be "known as the McDowell Free Library, in honor of a woman who spent her life as a worker for women."

Miss McDowell lived for many years on Third Street, below Walnut, and later at 535 North Thirty-fifth Street, Philadelphia, where she died after years of suffering. John Wanamaker, who had long encouraged her in her efforts in behalf of women, took time from his busy life to attend the funeral services, where he addressed those who had come, on the subject of her life of endeavor.

MRS. ALBERT W. FORD

ELIZA SPROAT TURNER

1826–1903

AMONG the outstanding leaders in progressive social movements in Philadelphia during the last quarter of the nineteenth century, Eliza Sproat Turner occupied a conspicuous and honored place. At least five well-known Philadelphia organizations and institutions owe their inception largely to Mrs. Turner's leadership: the New Century Club, the New Century Guild, Drexel Institute, the Children's Country Week Association, and the Consumers' League.

The annals of the New Century Club name her "the first and chief of the founders." She served as its third president and for twenty-six years was a most valued member. Her wise counsels, her practical common sense, and her friendly wit frequently saved the day in heated discussion, and her tact and sense of humor took the place of Roberts' *Rules of Order*.

Mrs. Turner saw the need of evening classes for women and girls employed during the day, and was made chairman of a committee to organize and establish classes under the auspices of the club. These were successful from the outset, and formed the nucleus of the present New Century Guild, a flourishing club of nine hundred women, most of whom are in business or professional life.

Drexel Institute in a very direct way owes its origin to Mrs. Turner. One year she applied to Mr. Drexel for money for the support of the classes of the Guild. He listened with interest to her account of the work done in the limited space, with limited means, and said,

You have proved to your own satisfaction that the teaching of household industries is desirable and acceptable to a limited number of young people. For the next year you may draw upon me for all you may need to increase your facilities, and if you prove that there is a considerable demand by a considerable number of people for such instruction I will build a school.

Mrs. Turner, through the success of the New Century Guild classes, proved the demand to Mr. Drexel's satisfaction so that he built Drexel Institute.

Mrs. Turner's heart went out to the children in the hot, dusty, crowded city streets, and she began to take them, in little groups, for a week at a time to her country home. One by one she interested her neighbors, until many needy children found joy and health in hospitable homes in the vicinity of Chadd's Ford, where Mrs. Turner lived in summer. In 1875 she organized the Children's Country Week Association, which has completed sixty-five years of service, and has given many thousands of Philadelphia mothers and children the joy of at least one week in God's great outdoors. The Children's Country Week idea has now extended to virtually every large city in the United States, and even to some on the other side of the ocean.

When a committee was formed to organize the Consumers' League in Philadelphia, one of the first women turned to for assistance was

Mrs. Turner. In her large sympathy for wage-earning women, the league commended itself to her as offering a new opportunity to help women on lines hitherto unfamiliar to social workers, and from that time until her death she gave to it her best counsels and unfailing support.

Mrs. Turner identified herself with the woman suffrage movement in 1870, when the Pennsylvania Society was formed, and never lost interest in the cause, though she died long before its fruition. Her inspirational leadership touched many lives through the printed page, for she contributed to the daily papers and to the magazines of her day hundreds of bits of verse and prose that reflected her bright optimism and high purpose. A collection of her poems, *Out-of-Door Rhymes,* was published by the New Century Guild after her death.

On June 20, 1903, Mrs. Turner passed to the higher life, full of years, of love and of honor; but the organizations that she sponsored live on in increasing usefulness.

A. EDITH MEYERS

WELTHA L. SANFORD

1828–1916

MISS SANFORD's school was opened in Philadelphia in 1857 and continued until 1891. Her aim was the formation of character, as she considered that the first step in education to fit her pupils to meet the exigencies of life. Study and accumulation of knowledge, of course, were in the curriculum, and the importance of influence exerted by good example was constantly stressed.

The motto of the Alumnae Association founded after her retirement is "Largeness of Vision, Sweetness of Spirit, Working with God," and the beneficiary was also her choice, an endowment fund for the supply of surgical appliances for the children's ward of the Philadelphia Home for Incurables.

LAURA BELL

HARRIET JUDD SARTAIN

1830–1923

⚜

HARRIET JUDD SARTAIN, one of the pioneers in breaking down the barriers of prejudice which existed against admitting women to the medical profession, was born in Waterbury, Connecticut, February 3, 1830. Her earlier education was received in the schools of Waterbury, whence, in 1843, her family removed to Michigan in the pioneer movement from New England of that time. She finished her seminary education in that State.

Doctor Sartain, then Miss Harriet Judd, studied medicine in Philadelphia and Cincinnati, graduating from the Eclectic Medical College of the latter city in 1854. She began the practice of medicine in Waterbury in the same year and attracted much congratulatory attention from the local papers for her advanced position. On December 11, 1854, she married Samuel Sartain, young artist and engraver, eldest son of John Sartain, who introduced mezzotint engraving into America, and removed with him to Philadelphia to begin the practice of her profession.

Doctor Sartain was the first woman member of the Homeopathic County Medical Society, being unanimously elected by that body in 1870, thus paving the way for the admission of other women members. In the following year she was elected to the State Homeopathic Society, and in June of the same year became a member of the American Institute of Homeopathy. The election of Dr. Sartain together with two other women candidates, one of whom was her student, closed the notable contest over the admission of women to that Society. A contemporary of Dr. A. R. Thomas, she numbered among her colleagues and staunch supporters such men as Van Lennep, Neidhard, Dudley, and Charles M. Thomas; and although a member of what a former generation frequently regarded as an antagonistic school of medicine, she was respected and esteemed by her colleagues of the "regular" school, counting among her warm friends notable men like Agnew, Weir Mitchell, Leidy, DaCosta, and many others. Thus, by her skill, her sympathetic and charming personality, and the high standard of ethics which she unflinchingly maintained, Dr. Sartain won for herself recognition among all schools of medicine, and paved the way for the woman of today to take her acknowledged place in the profession. Aside from the time devoted to her extensive practice, which was notably the largest private practice of any woman physician in the city, she found time to prepare and read important papers relating to her specialty, the diseases of women, before the various societies of which she was a member.

In addition to the study of her profession, her familiarity with general literature and her love and almost encyclopedic knowledge of poetry, which she memorized without effort, impressed one with the versatility of a remarkable mind. Doctor Sartain was one of the founders of the Women's Homeopathic Medical Club, and as its first president retained this office for many years, even after her retirement from active practice. She was also one of the founders of the New Century Club of Philadelphia.

Retirement from a large and active practice was caused by a severe attack of grippe during the epidemic of 1889, but returning health in spite of subsequent milder attacks vouchsafed her more than thirty years of life, full of cheerful and helpful service to all with whom she came in contact. As the result of a slight fall, which proved, however, to have caused a fracture of the hip, in spite of physical and mental vigor most remarkable for her age, she finally succumbed on February 8, 1923, in her ninety-fourth year.

Dr. Sartain had three children: Edward, who died in infancy; Amy (Mrs. J. Howard Gaskill), and Dr. Paul J. Sartain.

LUCRETIA L. BLANKENBURG
PAUL J. SARTAIN

KATE PLUMER BRYAN

1831–1898

KATE PLUMER BRYAN was the daughter of the distinguished theologian, Dr. William S. Plumer, and the wife of Samuel Smith Bryan, a descendant of George Bryan, member of the first Continental Congress. She was born in Petersburg, Virginia, September 29, 1831, and died in Titusville, Pennsylvania, on February 16, 1898.

Not only as a matter of inherited family tradition, but from deep personal conviction, Mrs. Bryan became actively engaged in church work. She was especially interested in the part of that work which reaches out to groups which have not had the privilege of Christian ministrations. The Synod of Pennsylvania of the Presbyterian Church requested her to head a committee to organize the Presbyterian women of Pennsylvania in work for home missions. On November 8 and 9, 1882, the first such committee was organized at Carlisle. It is interesting to note that Miss Alice Robertson, in later years a congressman from Oklahoma, was a member of Mrs. Bryan's committee.

In 1883 Mrs. Bryan reported to the synod that organizations of women pledged to home missions had been formed in all of the Presbyteries under the State Synod, and asked that her committee be discharged. Instead the synod, recognizing the value of this movement, expanded the committee into a permanent organization, later known as the Pennsylvania Women's Synodical Society for Home Missions of the Presbyterian Church. Mrs. Bryan served as its president until an illness in 1894 compelled her retirement.

It is notable that her leadership resulted in one of the earliest and most thorough pieces of state-wide organization of women in Pennsylvania. Her devoted service to this state is widely known and recognized as being exceedingly valuable and popular. In Guines, Cuba, there stands a school for girls erected by the women of Pennsylvania in memory of Mrs. Bryan's work.

HELEN MERRICK SEMPLE

REBECCA HARDING DAVIS

1831–1910

IN the literary world of her day Rebecca Blaine Harding Davis earned a distinctive place as one of America's first realistic novelists and essayists. In Philadelphia she was known, also, as the brilliant wife of L. Clarke Davis, editor of the *Public Ledger,* whose home was the Mecca for many interesting people. She rounded out a life of rich experiences as the guide, councilor, and friend of her two brilliant sons, Richard

Harding Davis, dashing war correspondent and novelist, and Charles Belmont Davis, dramatic critic and essayist.

Rebecca Harding was born June 24, 1831, in Washington, Pennsylvania, the daughter of Richard and Rachel Leet Wilson Harding. In her early childhood her parents removed to Alabama and shortly afterward to Wheeling, West Virginia, thence to Virginia, where she lived until her marriage. She was largely self-educated. Descriptions of this time show her as a warm-hearted, sensitive child. The life of the industrial community of Wheeling made a deep impression on her. Although the fiction of her day was mostly of the ultraromantic and oversentimental type, she found herself impelled to portray the grim struggle for existence she saw around her.

When she was thirty James Russell Lowell published in the *Atlantic Monthly* her first short story, "Life in the Iron Mills," which attracted a great deal of comment because it was almost Russian in its realism. This was followed soon afterward by a serial, *A Short Story of Today,* later issued in book form as *Margaret Howth.* These two stories were distinct landmarks in the evolution of American fiction, for she deliberately chose her characters from everyday people unlike most of the novelists of her day. Soon the products of her prolific pen were in great demand by the leading periodicals.

On March 4, 1863, she married L. Clarke Davis, and for the rest of her life lived in Philadelphia. Their first home was at 1429 Girard Avenue, where Richard Harding Davis was born, but later they moved to 230 South Twenty-first Street. Their summers were spent at Point Pleasant, New Jersey. Later Mrs. Davis lived at the country estate of her son, Richard, at Mount Kisco, New York. All these places are associated with many outstanding personalities of the day, attracted by the brilliant hospitality of a mother surrounded by an interesting family. Many stories are told of her informal buffet suppers in the Twenty-first Street home. Here she would serve waffles, frizzled beef and smoked salmon, with homemade biscuits and preserves, brandied peaches and other delicacies to the lanky Edwin Booth, the talented tribe of the Drews and the Barrymores, Ellen Terry, Henry Irving, and many well-known writers, statesmen, poets, and scientists. Through this brilliant company moved Mrs. Davis, unperturbed by her household duties, and with a distinct genius for encouraging sparkling conversation.

Until very late in life she continued to contribute to magazines, and in 1904 published an autobiographical volume entitled *Bits of Gossip,* a lively commentary on her times. She was a prolific writer of popular fiction. Her leading titles were *Dallas Galbraith, Waiting for the Verdict, Berrytown, John Andross, A Law Unto Herself, Natasqua, Silhouettes of American Life, Kent Hampden, Doctor Warwick's Daughters,* and *Frances Waldreaux.*

Her husband, her sons and daughter Nora literally worshiped her. The elder Mr. Davis consulted her frequently on editorial policies, while her son Richard wrote her almost daily and frequently returned to her home to share with her details of his fabulous career as a journalist and world traveler. Her other son, Charles, reflected still another phase of the mother's personality—a love of the theatre about which he wrote with charm and undoubted authority.

She died at Mount Kisco, September 29, 1910.

C. F. Hoban

ANNA HALLOWELL

1831–1905

Anna Hallowell, the daughter of Morris Longstreth and Hannah Penrose Hallowell, was born in Philadelphia in 1831. Her deep interest in education placed her in many prominent and worthy positions. One might almost say that this interest began in her early youth in a school for colored children which she held in her home on Sunday evenings. Her great interest in the enslaved colored race led her to sympathize with and attend the celebrated trial of the fugitive slave, Daniel Dangerfield. Soon followed the Civil War which engaged her time and her strength in caring for the sick and wounded, not only in the general hospitals but in her own home, to which shelter many of the soldiers were carried.

Anna Hallowell was a pioneer in education. She was a charter member of the Woman's Hospital and the Woman's Medical College. She formed the Sub-Primary School Society, which, with the financial aid of a few friends, supported a number of kindergartens for some years and led to the adoption of the free kindergarten system by the Board of Education. She was the first woman appointed to the Board of Education, on which she served fourteen years. Her influence was felt in introducing cooking and sewing into the schools, and it was owing to her efforts that the James Forten Manual Training School was established. For seventeen years she was chairman of the Women's Committee of County Visitors of the State Board of Charities. She was also on the board of directors of the Drexel Institute. Her keen desire for the higher education of women is well expressed on a memorial tablet in the cloisters of the library of Bryn Mawr College: "She stood for all that is best in education and all that is highest in citizenship."

She was a director of the Society for Organizing Charity, one of the founders of the Children's Aid Society, and chairman of the Committee on Education of the Civic Club. She advanced the improvements in the St. Mary Street district by introducing a kindergarten and an industrial school, and laid the foundations of the Starr Garden. This active life came to an end in 1905. On May 11 of that year a memorial meeting was held when letters and minutes were read and addresses made by representatives of many of the associations with which she was connected. To quote the chairman of the Committee of Visitors of the State Board of Charities: "I know of no other woman in our city's history who did as much for the advancement of the city's welfare and on so many different lines as Miss Hallowell."

Lucretia L. Blankenburg
Emily Hallowell

ELLEN MURDOCH WATSON

1831–1913

It is not given to many people to achieve two careers, but an example of such a life was that of Ellen Murdoch Watson. Though born at a time when careers for women were the exception rather than the rule, it was her lot to round out two periods of service to her country and state.

Ellen Murdoch was born in Pittsburgh, March 31, 1831. She was the daughter of John and Jane Robb Murdoch, whose home, the old Murdoch farm, is now part of the Squirrel Hill district of residential Pittsburgh. She attended the country school located on what is now Wilkins Avenue. When twelve years old she was sent to Miss Gillette's School in New York, making the long trip by stage and canal and remaining there for two years without seeing home or family.

From the time of her mother's death in 1852, when she was twenty-one, until the Civil War, the care of her father's home fell in a large measure on her shoulders.

When the war broke out she was one of the first to enlist in the United States Christian Commission. She served as a nurse during the war, witnessed many of the important battles, and was one of the agents to whom the people of Pittsburgh sent their supplies for distribution on the field. She served in various capacities at Fortress Monroe, Harrisons Landing, Nashville, and City Point on the James River. Clara Barton was a friend of hers with whom she corresponded.

In after life she wore at her throat a silver pin representing an open Bible, the badge of her heroic service for the Christian Commission on the field of battle. Another valued possession was a silk badge presented by the Hundredth Pennsylvania Reserves and bearing the inscription, "The Soldiers' Friend, Ellen Robb Murdoch."

But fine as her war record was, it was only one chapter of her busy life. In 1867 she married William Watson, a prominent glass manufacturer of New Castle, Pennsylvania. Two children were born to them, William Robb Watson and a daughter, Ellen Murdoch Watson. Because of Mr. Watson's ill health they went to Pittsburgh to live in 1873. Before her husband's death in 1880, Mrs. Watson had begun her work for the cause of temperance, for which she is best known. For nearly forty years she devoted her time and means to that work, writing, speaking, and distributing literature. Friends furnished means to supplement her own gifts, thus enabling her to do a surprisingly large work.

She was an officer in many organizations—the Woman's Christian Temperance Union, the Woman's Christian Alliance, the Anti-Saloon League, state secretary of rescue work of the Woman's Keeley League and the Sabbath Observance Alliance. For more than twenty years she was corresponding secretary of the Pennsylvania Synodical Temperance Committee, and for eight years temperance secretary of the Allegheny County Union Missionary Society. Both of these offices she held at the time of her death.

With all her public service she never ceased to be a modest, gentle, home-loving woman. She loved flowers, and her gardens were remarkable as one of the show places of the city. She had a boundless sympathy for the suffering and unfortunate. Her home was a haven to those in trouble, and its hospitable doors were ever open. "I'll just let you run around tame," she would say, meaning the guest was not to be treated as "company."

With a beautiful face, a winning personality, keen wit and an ever-ready anecdote, she was always the center of attention, while she won all hearts by her gracious and gentle manner.

She never lost the zest of living. She signed many of her letters "Yours hopefully," "Yours for the best that we can do," and like phrases. She was in her usual health and full of enthusiastic plans for her work to the morning of her death, December 2, 1913.

One of the last things she wrote in her little daybook, where she recorded the worthwhile things she heard or read, were these two lines: "Give to the world the best you have and the best will come back to you." So it had been with her.

AGNES E. RHEY

LOUISE E. CLAGHORN

1832–1898

LOUISE E. CLAGHORN, daughter of John W. and Elizabeth Cromble Claghorn, was born in Philadelphia, January 15, 1832. Her father was one of the directors of the Sanitary Commission during the Civil War, and Louise became his active assistant in planning for the proper care of the wounded men.

A strong sense of obligation to the soldiers in the ranks, and a realization of the duty that rested upon the citizens at home to provide for the orphan children of the men who were killed, aroused the passionate patriotism of Louise and her distinguished friend and co-worker

Mrs. Edwin W. Hutter, also of Philadelphia. More than once they went together to the front to minister to the comfort of the sick and wounded soldiers.

Their combined self-sacrifices and notable service were officially recognized by President Lincoln when he requested, after the battle of Gettysburg, that Miss Claghorn and Mrs. Hutter be sent immediately to the battlefield to organize systematic care of the wounded men.

An almost unbelievable opportunity for a highly dramatic action was seized by Louise Claghorn and Mrs. John W. Forney when they delivered to the Union League of Philadelphia the first news of Lee's surrender at Appomattox. Says the *Chronicle* of the Union league:

It was on the evening of April 10th that Mrs. John W. Forney and Miss Louise Claghorn, sister of James S. Claghorn, treasurer of the Union League, were returning from a visit in a friend's home. Rushing along the street came a telegraph boy bursting with excitement and shouting: "Lee surrenders!" "Where are you going with that telegram?" they asked. "To the Press," gasped the boy. The ladies followed him and got the telegram after a copy was made for the Press office. They ran with it to the Union League.

That faded sheet bears the endorcement of J. Gillingham Fell, President of the League.

Lincoln's funeral cortège brought his body to Independence Hall on April 22, 1865, where it lay in state surrounded by flowers. At midnight on the day of the funeral services here Mrs. Hutter, Miss Adeline Sager, and Miss Claghorn entered Independence Hall and reverently deposited on the coffin of the illustrious dead a beautiful cross of white flowers.

For many years Miss Claghorn served as one of the managers of the Northern Home for Friendless Children in Philadelphia, which was originally organized as a Home for Orphans of Soldiers and Sailors.

Louise Claghorn died suddenly on October 29, 1898, while engaged with others in work, at the headquarters of the Red Cross Society of Philadelphia, for the returning sick soldiers of the Spanish-American War.

WILLIAM C. CLAGHORN

SUSAN EVELYN DICKINSON

1832–1915

⚜

SUSAN DICKINSON, author, journalist, and champion of women's suffrage, was born in Wernersville, near Reading, in 1832, her family moving to Philadelphia soon after. Her parents were strict orthodox Friends, and she was educated in the Friends' schools in Philadelphia. At the age of seventeen she became a teacher in a Friends' school and was already writing poetry for papers and periodicals, using several pen names. Within a few years she was signing her own name to articles. Her first book was a memoir of a young friend, written for the Presbyterian Board of Publication. She later entered the newspaper field as a biographer and obituary writer on the New York *Herald,* with which publication she remained many years.

While her mother, to whom she was devoted, remained a Friend and wore the garb of that denomination, Miss Dickinson became an ardent Episcopalian, and a prominent member of St. Luke's parish in Scranton.

She had two brothers, Samuel, an Episcopal clergyman, and John, a Methodist minister and an instructor in Stanford University. Both brothers preceded her in death. When her sister Anna came into prominence as a public speaker, and in 1857 made her debut as an advocate of antislavery, and with her addresses on temperance, slavery, war issues, and other topics attracted country-wide attention, Susan accompanied her on a tour of the country as her secretary.

In Civil War days, and for decades afterwards, Susan occupied a high place in the journalism of the country. She was a correspondent for the New York *Tribune.* Her writings carried great weight. She contributed to other papers and to the leading periodicals of those days. On every occasion that offered she championed woman's rights and equal suffrage. Few women of this country possessed her powers as a newspaper writer, or her great mentality. Her memory was truly wonderful and she was, moreover, possessed of a fund of information on most of the important happenings of the last half-century. Her pen, like her purse, was always at the command of the needy.

She came into close contact with the most distinguished men and women of her time. Horace Greeley, Henry Ward Beecher, and other great figures of that period were her friends, and she retained very clear recollections of Lincoln.

In her small body she carried the soul of a crusader. She was the foe of injustice, the friend of the oppressed. She was as intensely devoted to the abolition of slavery in her young days as was her father's lifelong friend, the poet Whittier. Her Quaker blood was stirred deeply by wrong or cruelty wherever practised. She was always ready to say the word, or write the paragraph that would carry comfort to some sufferer or assist a worthy cause.

About 1880 she was sent from Philadelphia to West Pittston, Pennsylvania, to write a story of the coal fields. She liked that part of the country so well that she decided to remain there. She made her home in West Pittston until about 1900 when she removed to Scranton. She became associate editor of the Scranton *Truth,* and later a contributor to the other Scranton papers as well as the Wilkes-Barre *Record,* the Pittston *Gazette,* and for New York and Philadelphia papers.

After more than half a century of prominence in journalism and in all movements for the advancement of women, Miss Dickinson died November 16, 1915, and was buried in the beautiful cemetery in Honesdale, Pennsylvania.

DEBORAH WALLBRIDGE CARR

SARAH C. F. HALLOWELL

1833–1914

BUSINESS as well as social qualities distinguished Sarah C. F. Hallowell. Far-sighted and level-headed, as constructive in her plans as she was able in their execution, she left a record of accomplishment that has been equaled by few Pennsylvania women. She was so keenly alive to the needs of her community that her activity was confined for the most part to the things that lay nearest at hand, with the result that Philadelphia owes much to her forceful personality and quietly effective influence.

Sarah Catherine Fraley was born in 1833, the daughter of Frederick Fraley, for many years the President of the Western Savings Fund. Through her family connections she grew up in the best traditions of old Philadelphia and was familiar to an unusual degree with its varied activities. Her marriage to Joshua Longstreth Hallowell in 1855 closely identified her with the antislavery movement. For the most part, however, she lived the usual life of a wife and mother in the mid-Victorian era until her husband's death in 1873. Left with several children, she continued to carry on the home and turned to writing as a profession.

She was active in the hard work of the Centennial Exposition and was soon asked by the Women's Executive Committee to take charge of their newspaper, the *New Century,* printed in their building. This attracted widespread attention as a striking exhibit of women's activities, for it was conducted entirely by women, who made up its whole staff, including editors, reporters, correspondents, and even compositors.

After the close of the exposition Mrs. Hallowell became connected with the *Public Ledger,* where she continued on the editorial staff from 1877 to 1895. While her work was concerned primarily with the household, a woman's column, as it were, she developed a wide human interest, contributing frequent articles in the literary page and editorials on many topics.

The woman's movement enlisted her most earnest coöperation. She was one of those who appeared before the State Constitutional Convention of 1872–73 asking that women be given equal property rights, equal rights in the management of schools and the choice of representatives when they were taxpayers. Thirty years later she appeared before a legislative committee to urge the curtailment of the powers of the sectional school boards, which were constantly in conflict with the Board of Public Education.

It was largely through her leadership that one of the oldest existing organizations of women, the New Century Club, had its beginnings in 1877. Some of the women who had worked together for the exposition of 1876 had come to realize the value of united effort. As one of them wrote at the time, the club offered them "an opportunity to use to better advantage than heretofore the scattered feminine ability existing in our community but often sinking into discouragement for lack of recognition or dissipated for lack of any means of combination."

As the new president Mrs. Hallowell soon proved the wisdom of her venture. There were difficulties, of course, and much carping criticism. Dues were paid in cash for lack of checking accounts. The charter was signed by unmarried women lest husbands become involved or embarrassed. One good father of old lineage insisted that his daughter join the club in order that he might find out what these women were doing at their meeting place across the street from his home.

Meanwhile Mrs. Hallowell was shepherding her little flock with rare judgment. An experienced clubwoman of today might well be aghast at the mental bill of fare provided for the little group the first year. Two classes in French, one in German, and one in Greek literature, besides six lectures on the "Antiquities of Man" was only a part of the nourishment provided for the avid "female" minds.

With characteristic zeal Mrs. Hallowell also began immediately to use the latest possibilities of her organization to meet some of the needs of the community. Lectures on cooking were inaugurated that soon led to the formation of a cooking school association.

Another undertaking was to provide short outings for poor mothers and children, which quickly grew into the well-known Country Week Association. It is interesting in this connection to note one of the good clubwomen reporting in a spirit of cheerful inexperience that mothers and children too dirty to be welcomed at farmhouses were taken for an afternoon at the Zoo.

Still another project successfully carried out was the Legal Protection Committee, of which Mrs. Hallowell herself was chairman for a number of years. This furnished legal aid to working women threatened by injustice of one kind or another.

Many other undertakings were sponsored or supported by Mrs. Hallowell. She was a corporator of the Woman's Medical College, a manager of the Woman's Hospital, a founder of the first training school for nurses, a member of the Women's Congress and associated among other groups with the Sheltering Arms, the Pennsylvania Forestry Association, the Contemporary Club, and the Colonial Dames of America. She died in 1914.

ANNA LANE LINGELBACH

HARRIET LANE

1833–1903

AMONG distinguished Pennsylvania women and one who occupied the exalted position of mistress of the White House was Harriet Lane, niece of James Buchanan, fifteenth President of the United States, whose administration dated from 1857 to 1861.

She was born in Mercersburg, Pennsylvania, being the daughter of James Buchanan's sister Jane, the wife of Elliott T. Lane. At the early age of nine years Harriet had become an orphan, with her uncle James as her guardian. He had her carefully educated in excellent schools and watched with pride as she early developed into an intelligent handsome woman.

From her girlhood she was accustomed to meet distinguished persons who assembled in the Washington home of her uncle, when Secretary of State in the Cabinet of President Polk, and at Wheatland, the Buchanan home in Lancaster. She was the accomplished and admired young hostess for local friends and foreign visitors.

Mrs. Ellet describes her as "a blonde with deep violet eyes, golden hair, vivacious expression and a mouth of peculiar beauty, and withal distinguished for dignity and grace in every movement."

In 1852 she accompanied her uncle on his mission to England as Minister to the Court of St. James's, an experience that afforded her remarkable opportunities to adjust herself to the high duties to which she was destined to be called in her own country. She always said that these years spent in England were very happy ones, made especially so by reason of the outstanding and flattering hospitality extended to her as the niece of the American Minister.

It was in 1860 that the Prince of Wales, Albert Edward, made his historic visit to the United States and was entertained at the White House for several days. The royal visitor afterward sent to Miss Lane a set of engravings of Queen Victoria and other members of the royal family.

Jefferson Davis, who was not friendly to Mr. Buchanan, more than once remarked that "The White House under the administration of Buchanan approached more nearly to the idea of a Republican Court than the President's house has ever done since the days of Washington." This brilliancy was in no small degree owing to Harriet Lane.

She was married in 1866 to Henry Elliott Johnston and spent her married life in Baltimore. When she passed away on July 3, 1903, she bequeathed the Nation $100,000 for the erection of a monument in Washington to the memory of her honored uncle, James Buchanan. This monument, located in Meridian Hill Park, was unveiled on June 26, 1930.

GERTRUDE BOSLER BIDDLE

ELIZABETH COOPER VERNON

1833–1865

"Left! Right! Left! Right!
One! Two! Three! Four!"
SHARP, clear and staccato, regular as the ticking of a clock, came the voice of the drillmaster marking the rhythm as raw recruits learned the cadence of military marching.

"Comepanee-e-e-e! Halt!" Incisive as a sword stroke shrilled the command, its echo instantly drowned in the rattle of grounding muskets. In the ensuing silence one became conscious of something strange and incongruous in the bugle quality of the martial voice, suddenly identified its soprano tone and perceived its source, Elizabeth Vernon, of Media.

Neither the slight young woman of twenty-eight nor the men were merrily rehearsing a stage play. Quite the contrary. They were intent upon the grim business of war. The men were learning the rudiments of military evolution preparatory to enlisting in the Federal cause against the Confederacy after Abraham Lincoln's first call for volunteers in 1861.

The young drillmistress was the daughter of Dr. John Wilkins Cooper, of West Chester, who had been a lieutenant in the war with Mexico and who had taught her as a child the manual of arms and the elementary movements of the drill. When the Civil War broke out she was the wife of David A. Vernon, of Media, editor of the

Delaware County *American*. The call for volunteers found plenty of response in the community, but no one seemed to be qualified to teach them to drill.

Mrs. Vernon hearing of this spoke up at once, revealing her qualifications for the task, and, adding, "Bring the boys here and I will teach them the drill." The boys were anxious as well as willing, and immediately began their training upon the wide lawns of the old Haldeman house, still to be seen on the Providence Road opposite the old Friends' Meetinghouse in Media.

Among the recruits were Mrs. Vernon's husband and the entire staff of his newspaper. This contingent became a part of the 124th Pennsylvania Infantry and went to the front on May 17, 1861. Later it took part in the fierce battles of Antietam and Chancellorsville, carrying always the flag made and presented by Mrs. Vernon. This battle-scarred banner is now preserved at Harrisburg.

Mrs. Vernon died on May 31, 1865, being then only thirty-three years old.

HENRIETTA VERNON DAVIS

CAROLINE EARLE WHITE

1833–1916

CAROLINE EARLE was born in Philadelphia in 1833. Her father was Thomas Earle, a distinguished member of the Philadelphia bar, and her husband, Richard P. White, was also an able Philadelphia lawyer.

From her earliest youth, she was interested in the subject of kind treatment of dumb animals. After her marriage she was distressed by the suffering of the mules that in those days were used to drag the freight trains on Market Street. These poor creatures were lashed with cowhide whips. This made Mrs. White declare that she would never rest until a society was formed to prevent such suffering. The Royal Society for the Prevention of Cruelty to Animals of England, then in existence, had been organized in 1822, but nothing of the kind existed in the United States until Henry Bergh, under the greatest difficulties and opposition, organized the New York Society.

The Civil War prevented the accomplishment of Mrs. White's intention at first, but at its close she visited Mr. Bergh in New York in the hope of establishing a Pennsylvania branch. He gave her much practical advice and information. As a result she had papers printed which read as follows:

"We, the undersigned, citizens of Philadelphia, cordially approve of the formation and incorporation of the Society for the Prevention of Cruelty to Animals, and promise to support it by every means in our power."

Her next step was to visit lawyers, judges, merchants, physicians, clergymen, and other prominent men, many of whom signed this pledge. Mr. Richard Muckle, then treasurer of the *Public Ledger,* being already much interested, was an efficient aid in the enterprise, while S. Morris Waln showed his interest by contributing $6,000 to assist in the formation of the society. Having obtained a number of signatures, Mrs. White called a meeting of the signers at the Board of Trade rooms in Philadelphia, where the Pennsylvania Society for the Prevention of Cruelty to Animals was organized. Mr. Wilson Swain was elected president. This was in 1867. The following year the society was incorporated.

At that time, as women did not take a leading part in public work, Mrs. White, though responsible for the founding of the society, did not expect to take an active part in administering its affairs. It was soon recognized, however, that the aid of women was a necessity and Mr. Waln, who had succeeded to the presidency, asked Mrs. White to found a woman's branch, which she proceeded to do. On April 14, 1869, about thirty ladies met in the parlor of Mr. Waln's residence and organized the Woman's Branch of the Pennsylvania Society for the Prevention of Cruelty to Animals. This title has since been changed to the Women's Pennsylvania Society for the Prevention of Cruelty to Animals. Mrs. White was elected president and remained in that capacity until her death at Nantucket in 1916.

Mrs. White was also instrumental in the organization in Philadelphia of the society to protect children from cruelty.

She was a pioneer, indomitable, untiring, always courageous; but the compassionate and devoted women who helped her in those early days must not be forgotten. Together they were a goodly company.

MARY F. LOVELL
MRS. JOHN H. EASBY

ELIZA BUTLER KIRKBRIDE

1835–1919

⚶

ELIZA OGDEN BUTLER was born on November 11, 1835, in New York City. Her father, Benjamin F. Butler, was Attorney-General in the Cabinet of President Jackson.

In 1866 she married Dr. Thomas Story Kirkbride, internationally known as a leader in the modern care of the insane. Dr. Kirkbride had been, from 1840, superintendent and physician-in-chief of the Pennsylvania Hospital for the Insane in West Philadelphia. Mrs. Kirkbride shared his interests wholeheartedly. She became identified with every forward-looking movement for the benefit of her adopted city.

The Philadelphia Vacant Lots Cultivation Association had its origin in a meeting called by her to consider some practical action for the unemployed in 1897. The Octavia Hill Association, which did so much to educate Philadelphia in the need of better housing, held its board meetings in Mrs. Kirkbride's drawing-room during the years that she was its secretary.

But it was in the Civic Club that she found full scope for her deep interest in problems of government. In 1896 Miss Mary Channing Wister, who with Miss Cornelia Frothingham had founded this club, proposed the formation of children's leagues like those organized by Colonel Waring, Commissioner of Street Cleaning, in New York City. She asked Mrs. Kirkbride to become chairman of a committee "on the extension of good citizenship," and this office Mrs. Kirkbride held until the day of her death, twenty-three years later.

The committee's plan of work was a simple one. It first obtained permission from the Board of Public Education to hold monthly meetings of not more than twenty minutes in any school to which the principal might invite them. The children elected their own officers and conducted their own meetings. A Civic Club member attended as a guest and had the privilege of speaking for ten or twelve minutes on some subject connected with good citizenship.

From small beginnings in five schools of the Seventh Ward the number of leagues gradually increased. The bonds of sympathy between principals, teachers, children, and Civic Club members were constantly strengthened. Mrs. Kirkbride, as chairman, not only planned for and held together a varied group of committee members, as well as visiting widely scattered schools, but was herself the speaker at a large proportion of the league meetings.

In the spring of 1919 the Civic Club wished to make some public testimonial to Mrs. Kirkbride's work, but she was unwilling to have the plan carried out. The recognition which gave her keenest pleasure, however, came on October 21, 1919. The new course in civics had been introduced in the public schools and the question arose whether the League of Good Citizenship should be discontinued. Principals and teachers from schools where the league was in operation bore testimony to the helpfulness of the work and their wish for its continuance.

With fresh zeal Mrs. Kirkbride continued the monthly round of league meetings. On November 11, 1919, her eighty-fourth birthday, she took a long trip by trolley to a school in Germantown. On her return she was suddenly taken sick, and, after a brief illness, died on November 17.

Among many touching tributes to her memory none was more perfect than that of a memorial meeting planned and carried out by the children of the McCall School, one of the earliest in which the League of Good Citizenship had been organized. Seven years after her death, a new school accommodating 1,800 children was opened at Seventh and Dickinson streets and named in her honor.

ELIZABETH B. KIRKBRIDE

MARY LOUISA WALKER ROBERTS

1835–1911

BLOCKADE-RUNNING during the last days of the Civil War was a grisly business fraught with almost certain disaster; an adventure to make strong men quail and turn back; unmitigated terror for a woman. Yet Mary Louisa Walker Roberts essayed it, and succeeded. Neither love nor lust for gold inspired her; compassion for the suffering had her by the hand and steeled her heart. Her ship was not laden with powder and shot; its holds, instead, were stuffed with bandages and medicines for the wounded warriors of the Confederacy. It was the last vessel to run the gauntlet of the Union fleet and dock safely in a Southern port.

Mary Louisa Walker, later Roberts, was the second daughter of Isaac and Eliza Ann Brooke Walker, and was born on June 2, 1835, in Sadsbury Township, Lancaster County. Her father, later known as the historian of Lancaster County, was a great-great-grandson of Lewis Walker, of Valley Forge, whose holding of a thousand acres was purchased direct from William Penn. It is worth noting that Lewis Walker erected for his home the first stone residence at Valley Forge; the edifice being used in Revolutionary times by General Washington as his headquarters.

When the Civil War broke out, Mary Louisa Walker was on the eve of being graduated from Baltimore Female College. She had, in fact, just finished preparing her dress for commencement when the first Union Army came tramping by on its way to invade Virginia. Nearly all of her schoolmates were Southern girls and she herself was imbued with a feeling that states' rights was the paramount issue in the impending strife. She therefore cast her lot with the Confederacy and at once proceeded to Richmond to volunteer her services. She was assigned for duty as a nurse-in-chief of Howard Hospital, at Richmond, serving without pay.

As the war proceeded and the Union fleets tightened their grip on Southern ports, supplies of all kinds became almost unobtainable. Finally it became imperative that outside aid be smuggled in somehow. It was then that Miss Walker volunteered for the undertaking.

She embarked on a small vessel at Wilmington, North Carolina, which, after a desperate effort, managed to win clear of the Federal warships, but only after being so damaged by shot and storm that it was forced to run for haven in the Bahamas instead of making for Canada, as intended. However, she managed to get to Halifax in the late autumn of 1864, and by personal appeals in Quebec and Montreal raised money and medical stores. Assembling her cargo, she freighted it on sleds five hundred miles down the frozen St. Lawrence River to get it aboard ship. The hardship was incalculable, but was borne cheerfully, and eventually the cargo was landed in Havana.

There the Confederate consul poured cold water on the enterprise with news that the Union blockade had become so tight not even a rowboat could sneak through. But Miss Walker was not to be daunted, and managed to persuade a very reluctant sea captain to try it "just once—at Galveston."

Fourteen hundred miles of turbulent water were safely astern when the heavily laden mercy ship hove to, to prepare for the final desperate test. The vessel was given a coat of whitewash. The crew was dressed in "whites." Miss Walker, also in white, took a prominent position on the vessel's bridge where she would be easily seen. The idea was to simulate a pleasure craft. The ruse worked, but for a time it was touch and go as the "yacht" moved in between the blockading men-o-war, so close Miss Walker could almost literally look into the black muzzles of cannon and see the shells in place, any one of which could have blown her and her mission to eternity.

After Lee's surrender, Miss Walker was escorted to her father's home near Gap, Pennsylvania, by Colonel Kelso Spear, chief of staff to General Gordon, afterward Governor of Georgia and United States Senator. Four years later, June 16, 1869, Miss Walker became the bride of Colonel John Coleman Roberts, of Kentucky, and with him moved to Texas. But first they purchased the "Henderson Place" at Gap, which they always used as a summer residence. Mary Louisa Walker Roberts died at her home, Elm Grove, Bremond, Texas, on February 2, 1911, and was interred in the graveyard there beside her husband and daughter.

HELEN NOBLE WORST

ELLEN HOLMES VERNER SIMPSON

before 1837–1897

BORN in Pittsburgh, the daughter of James and Elizabeth Verner, Ellen Holmes Verner married the Rev. Matthew Simpson. She went with her young husband to live for two years in Meadville, Pennsylvania, and then to Greencastle, Indiana, where he was called as president of the small and struggling Indiana Asbury College, since developed into the great De Pauw University.

Leaving a home of affluence, she made the long and difficult journey into the West, traveling over the roughest roads, without comforts of any kind, to arrive in the rude town of one-story houses, medieval in its lack of conveniences. She entered into the interests of college life there with undaunted courage and energy, making a home for the students, many of them older than the youthful president, caring for them in sickness, joining in all their festivities with joyous spirit, happy and bright in the present, full of hope for the future, for hers was the "home heart of the meadow-lark and the vision and spirit of the eagle."

For nine years she was their comfort and friend. Sickness, sorrow, and the death of her little boy came to her there, but she still kept her buoyant spirit. Later she went to Cincinnati, where her husband became editor of the *Western Christian Advocate* until elevated in the General Conference of Boston in 1852 to the office of Bishop in the Methodist Episcopal Church. They returned to Pittsburgh to take up their residence, but yielded after a time to the desire for the midwest and lived in Evanston, Illinois, where Bishop Simpson acted as president of Garrett Biblical Institute.

Here again college life claimed the best efforts of Ellen Simpson, and she made herself felt among the many students. When Fort Sumter was fired upon, a flagpole was raised and she gave it its first flag, proclaiming loyalty to the cause of the Union.

Here the path of Frances Willard, then a young girl, crossed hers, and it was through her wise counsel that that great leader entered on her notable career. Miss Willard always gave to Mrs. Simpson the full credit of bringing her into active service.

The lake winds of their western home were so severe that in 1863 Bishop Simpson chose, from among a number of cities which urgently desired him, the city of Philadelphia, receiving as a gift from generous laymen a house at 1807 Mount Vernon Street, which was completely furnished by friends of the church from New York and Baltimore. From that home they moved in 1882 to the residence at 1334 Arch Street, where they spent the remainder of their lives.

It was during the more than thirty years in Philadelphia during which she accompanied the great and distinguished Bishop on many journeys, in Europe, Mexico, and throughout the United States, that Mrs. Simpson was claimed by interests of church and city. Her ability was readily recognized. In 1876 she was selected as one of the thirteen women to represent the original states on Mrs. Gillespie's staff of Centennial women. She devised the plan for obtaining sketches and pictures of the work of all charities in Europe and America supported by women. More than eight hundred associations responded, and this collection for the Centennial Exposition, representing women's work in the world, is still preserved in the permanent exhibition.

Her activities were many and varied. She aided in organizing and was first president of the Bible Readers Society. She sponsored the silk culture, but declined its presidency, although deeply interested in the experiment. She organized the Women's Auxiliary of the Methodist Hospital and was the first president. She also organized the temporary home for the poor in West Philadelphia, and the Home for Aged in Camden. She was actively engaged in the Indian Association, and many of its meetings were held in her home. She was vice-president of the Woman's Christian Temperance Union, of the Women's Foreign Missionary Society, and of the Home Missionary Society, whose presidency she declined. She was a trustee of the American University and a director of the Philadelphia Museum of Art.

Perhaps her crowning work was the Home for Aged, of which she was president thirty-two years, and its close neighbor, the Methodist Episcopal Orphanage. This she founded in 1879, making the first subscription herself, and holding the presidency during her life, which terminated in the Christmastide of 1897. These two great institutions to which she gave unceasing devotion and untiring work for those past the midday of life, and the shelter and care of little children without regard to creed, stand now on the edge of Fairmount Park, Philadelphia, noble monuments of work well and faithfully done.

Not only in tablets of stone do her name and memory dwell, but also in the hearts of many less fortunate who came to her for help. To every woman, girl, and child who sought her, she gave freely of attention, sympathy, and substance. So that it may truly be said of her, "She hath dispersed, she reacheth forth her hands to the needy."

MRS. JOHN FRISBEE KEATOR

SARAH ELIZABETH DYSART

1837–1909

☙❧

SARAH ELIZABETH DYSART was born in a beautiful old home at Tipton, Pennsylvania, December 6, 1837, and died there February 1, 1909. She came of that indomitable English and Scottish stock that has made Pennsylvania a great state.

The daughter of William Patterson Dysart and his wife, Elizabeth Bell, she was descended on her father's side from William Patterson, an officer in the Revolutionary War, and from his father, Arthur Patterson, a member of the Colonial Assembly. On her mother's side, she was descended from Edward Bell, ironmaster, inventor and owner of enormous tracts of coal and timber land, and from James Martin, a member of the old Presbytery of Donegal in 1776, and later pastor of an extension charge which included East and West Penn Valley and Warrior Mark.

Sarah attended the Lititz School for Young Ladies. During a memorable visit to Harrisburg she heard Abraham Lincoln, standing on the roof of a portico, make an impassioned appeal for nurses. So stirred was she by the need voiced by that eloquent pleader that, though untrained, she offered her services as volunteer nurse to the Government and labored faithfully during the whole period of the war.

She served in the hospitals at Harpers Ferry, Nashville, Chattanooga, and Gettysburg. Often after an engagement she went out over the bloody battlefield to help the wounded, or to find and bring back to the hospital some soldier who had been under her care. For many years she kept in an old chest in the attic at Tipton part of a uniform of one of those boys who never came home.

In a day when the wounded needed everything and there was no Red Cross organization and no antiseptic during operations and amputations, she worked with inspired courage and energy, and did much to bring order and health into the fearful conditions prevailing in the hospitals and to sweep away the misery of criminally careless nursing. The appreciation of the soldiers was shown when they, out of their little store, collected enough money to buy her a gold watch as a testimonial of their love and loyalty. The medical officers presented her with the Twelfth Army Corps badge, a gold cross with a crown set with pearls. The Tyrone Division of the Daughters of Veterans of the Civil War named their post for her and annually decorate her grave on Memorial Day.

But great as she was in the service of her country, she was even greater in that home over which she presided with such gracious hospitality for many years. Whenever trouble or illness or death came, she was the first one wanted by every member of her family. As untiring church worker and a firm believer in temperance, she gave her love and care not only to parents, brothers, sisters, nieces, and nephews, but encompassed in her warm-hearted humanity the poor and needy and suffering of a large outlying neighborhood. No call for help was left unanswered and day or night she would go to give assistance to the sick and to comfort the dying.

Among her many gifts she possessed an unusually lovely voice. She studied in Baltimore, where later she was invited to sing in one of the great choirs of that city. But all that was changed when the war came. After that she sang by the bedside of the wounded and dying soldiers in the great hospitals where she labored. Years afterward she would sometimes meet old soldiers who had known her during the war who remembered her for her singing.

In spirit she never grew old; lovable, companionable and sympathetic she was. With a gift of entering into all the joys and sorrows and interests of others, including those of the younger generation, she was friend and standard-bearer. In her life she reaped the love which goes to those with generosity of heart.

CORNELIA I. MORRELL
MARY FLEMING HOLLIDAY

ANNIE HEACOCK

1838–1932

᪥

ANNIE HEACOCK, widely known educator and pioneer suffragist, was born January 16, 1838, in Jenkintown, and died February 1, 1932, in Wyncote.

She was a daughter of Joseph and Esther Hallowell Heacock and moved with her parents in 1856 to the locality then known as Chelten Hills. She was graduated in the first class of the Girls' Normal School of Philadelphia and was a charter member of the New Century Club, of which she was later elected an honorary member. She was also a member of Abington Friends' Meeting.

In 1863, during the Civil War, in company with a party of Northern school teachers, she went to a plantation near Beaufort, South Carolina, and there taught Negro refugees. She was present at Fort Sumter when the flag was again raised over it in the presence of a distinguished company, including Henry Ward Beecher and William Lloyd Garrison. It was on that evening that the assassination of President Lincoln occurred.

In 1869 Miss Heacock became a teacher in Friends' Central School and later established, with her sister-in-law, Mrs. Joseph Heacock, the Chelten Hills School.

She was active in reform movements, first in the abolition of slavery and later in woman's suffrage.

ELLWOOD HEACOCK

SARA A. REED

1838–1934

Sara A. Reed's ancestors first arrived from England in 1630, settling in the vicinity of Boston. She was a direct descendant of Colonel Seth Reed, who commanded a regiment in the Revolutionary War, fought at the battle of Bunker Hill and later became founder of Erie.

Born in Ashtabula, Ohio, she came to Erie when only seven years of age. During her life there she came to be recognized as a leader in the finest endeavors of life, whether cultural, patriotic or philanthropic. Miss Reed was one of a small group of citizens who, in October 1871, incorporated the Erie Home for the Friendless, Erie's first organized charity institution. She was the president for forty-five years, a foster mother to successive generations of homeless children and a faithful protector of hundreds of aged women. A charter member of the Young Women's Christian Association, Erie Art Club, Presque Isle Chapter, Daughters of the American Revolution, having been regent of the latter for sixteen years, she was a member of twenty-five different societies until 1926, when failing strength made it necessary for her to resign from some of them. But she retained her keen interest in them to the very end.

As she had always been a great reader and traveler, both in this country and abroad, she organized in 1879 a travel study class, which continued for many years. All countries of the world were studied for their art, literature, music, history, and customs. Biographies played a leading part. Through this class three generations of Erie women benefited by its educational influence. In the eighties Miss Reed began an evening class for stenographers, teachers, and other women who could not come during the day. This was probably the first business women's club of Erie. Nor did she overlook the younger generation; she had classes for young people right up to the time of the First World War.

Famous leaders whose ideals impressed the whole world were guests in her home. Among them Ralph Waldo Emerson, Bayard Taylor, and Clara Barton.

She was the author of the following books: *Dora Bently, Belated*

Passenger, After Fifty Years, A Romance of Arlington House, and
Her Grandmother's Glory.

In 1927 the mayor of Erie dedicated March 16, which was Miss
Reed's eighty-ninth birthday, as Sara A. Reed Day, requesting all citizens to honor her by flying the American flag. The request was most
heartily responded to. Early in the morning, with proper ceremony,
members of the American Legion raised the flag on the lawn in front
of her home, and at sunset it was lowered by United States marines.
On this great day in her life, she received friends and representatives
of all societies, including foreign ones, all day long and late into the
evening.

She died January 27, 1934, at the age of ninety-five.

MRS. JAMES BURKE

MARY S. GARRETT

1839–1925

EMMA GARRETT

1853–1893

THE inspiration and lifework of Emma Garrett and her sister Mary S.
Garrett was to teach deaf children to speak, and thus prepare them
to live in the world with other people. The very idea was theirs at
a time when it was believed impossible. They first taught, with in-
finite patience, enough children of pre-school age to prove their theory. Thinking people were beginning to realize that the segregation
of the deaf leads to intermarriage and, more or less directly, toward
perpetuating this affliction in humanity.

After a long period of experimenting, their success was such that
in 1884, at the request of Henry Belin, Jr., Judge Alfred Hand, and
other philanthropists, Emma Garrett went to Scranton to establish
the Pennsylvania Oral School for the Deaf. She was principal of the
institution for seven years, during which time a second building became necessary. Miss Garrett won a medal for this school at the Paris
Exposition.

By Act of Assembly in 1891, Pennsylvania endorsed this work and provided for the establishment of the Home School which has become famous at the corner of Belmont and Monument avenues, Philadelphia, thereby making the Commonwealth a pioneer in appropriating money for this purpose. From this home were sent each year into the public schools children who would otherwise have become a charge on the state for special schooling. This Home School for the Deaf, for years the only one of its kind in the world, attracted favorable attention in other countries, especially in England.

After the death of Emma Garrett, her sister Mary continued faithfully to carry on the work until her death, in 1925, at the age of 86.

It was largely through the efforts of Mrs. Frederick Schoff and Mary Garrett that Pennsylvania secured its Juvenile Court Law in 1903.

Widespread interest was aroused in the theories and methods of the Garrett sisters for the training of deaf children to speak, and their names appeared on many programs dedicated to child welfare. They initiated and led to an almost unbelievable result a service that was so remarkable that their school seemed a miracle of achievement.

ADA C. S. SAYEN

MARTHA SCHOFIELD

1839–1918

A STIRRING monument to a Pennsylvania heroine stands today in the city of Aiken, South Carolina. The memorial is the Schofield Normal and Industrial School, a boarding school for Negro children, established in 1868. Behind these walls and within her journal comes to light the thrilling story of a young Quakeress, who gave fifty years of her life that the tremendous sacrifices of the Civil War might not have been in vain.

Martha Schofield was the young Quakeress. She was born February 1, 1839, on a farm near Newton, Bucks County, Pennsylvania. Her parents, Oliver and Mary Schofield, were active members of the Society of Friends, and early inspired their children by a loyalty to worthwhile political, educational, and moral affairs. In her teens, Martha Schofield watched with eager eyes the black-skinned figures who lodged in the family kitchen and were smuggled by her father to the next Underground Railway station, on their way to the Canadian border. She soon took her part as an abolitionist and an alert worker in activities of human interest.

She began her career, at the age of nineteen, as a capable teacher in a New York school, but the arrival of the Civil War changed her vocational service to that of visiting nurse at Summit House, a hospital near her new home in Darby. Four years of war in her youth made her believe, at the age of twenty-three, that "we who are well ought never to complain." She felt the sufferings of those who wrote to her from the front, those whom she inspired by her daily visits, more keenly than her own suffering.

When the end of the war came, she was stirred by the realization that great work must be done in the South before those who lived could dream of peace. Millions must have shuddered at the agonized cry of the liberated, homeless blacks. Only a few went forward to answer that call. Among the Pennsylvania women who responded was Martha Schofield, who sailed in October 1865, with a small volunteer group bound for Wadmalua Island, South Carolina. She lived with one other white woman under amazingly crude conditions, in order that she might feed and clothe the helpless Negroes huddled in sections throughout the island.

The following year she continued her work on Edisto Island and later at St. Helena Island. Here, however, the deprivations were too great, and a raging fever threatened her with death. For over two months she was unable to leave her bed, but in her diary she writes, "I am confident I will not die, for there is still work to do." During her convalescence she passed her time conducting small classes for Negro children. It is not strange then that in 1868, at the age of twenty-nine, Martha Schofield went to Aiken, and founded the school which is now the Schofield Normal and Industrial School. On one hand, this young woman was faced with the enmity of the Southerners; on the other, the ignorance of the blacks, but she was undaunted by any obstacle. On one occasion, when members of a mob threatened her life, she declared, "You may take my body, but you can't touch my soul."

Schofield School began without any equipment or financial aid. Its young founder soon aroused the interest of friends in the North, and a group of twenty-five women from Germantown, known as the auxiliary branch of the Freedman Commission, were its first supporters. The school today still draws its main support from Philadelphia. After fifty years of her leadership, it occupied two city blocks, a farm of four hundred acres, and had an enrollment of three hundred pupils.

Martha Schofield wrought well, for she saw the wisdom of good, honest industry, and today work done in Schofield Industrial Shops is considered the best in Aiken. Her graduates reflect a high standard of character, as well as ability to do the everyday task. One of her students, Matilda Evans, was among the first Negro women in this country to receive a medical degree. She was entered personally by Miss Schofield at the Woman's Medical College of Pennsylvania. Many other students are known in Aiken, and throughout the South, as leading pastors, teachers, physicians, dentists, and contractors. There is a fineness of character and a loyalty of purpose in Schofield students which is definitely traceable to the founder. She well deserved the worship she received, because she coupled graciousness with strength of will, and common sense with spiritual vision.

They were celebrating the Fiftieth Anniversary of her School, when, on her seventy-ninth birthday, Martha Schofield quietly passed away. Instead of mourning her loss, as the train drew her body northward, a song of praise arose from the hearts of a great Negro band. She had brought peace and joy with their fredom, and now they sought to make her freedom from earth a glad and holy liberation. Across the air rang the words of her favorite hymn, "Steal Away, Steal Away to Jesus."

HANNAH CLOTHIER HULL
MARIA COPE JENKINS

AGNES IRWIN

about 1840–1914

SOPHIA IRWIN

about 1840–1915

❧❦

IT is curious how soon we forget "the dates of wars and deaths of Kings" or even our own dates. What seems to come handiest to our memories is not much good to the writer of a biography.

Lately, for instance, I have been trying to corral some of the fixed biographical items belonging to the careers of those two inimitable sisters, Agnes and Sophia Irwin. In their day, which, after all, was only yesterday, they played a very distinguished part in the life of this city, a part of which the pupils of their great school as the years go by are more and more fully aware. Their characteristics, their voices, and faces even, are still unforgettable; their reputation for wit and friendship and critical humor still forms a standard of distinction for many of us which time has not in the least dimmed. And yet now to dig out the dates and the biographical facts concerning their upbringing and the important episodes of their notable careers has been as difficult as though they had lived and died in obscurity a century or two ago.

When it was decided last spring that "The Book of Honor," that golden, illuminated book now enshrined at Strawberry Mansion, was to be reopened for the insertion of more names of illustrious women of Pennsylvania, and that this time the list was to include the names of women whose services to the State or city were of a later date—that of 1900, in fact—than that formerly fixed within the limits of 1876, I naturally thought of Agnes and Sophia Irwin, whose school and whose influence were well in the ascendant here in the eighties and in the nineties.

But with all the good will in the world from those who had felt that influence, and even from those who had greatly valued and achieved the intimate friendship of those great teachers, the biographical items necessary for detailed history of the career of the two women seemed to have escaped into the past without a ripple.

Actually, what I have to make an article out of, through the industry and energy of Miss Bertha Laws, who is now the headmistress of the Irwin School, and who for some years functioned during the lifetime of the Irwins as the school's secretary, and through the genealogical researches of some of the Baches, cousins of the Irwins, and through Mrs. John Mitchell, who was a valued friend of theirs—an inherited friendship beginning with Dr. S. Weir Mitchell himself—what I have gathered would scarcely fill this column.

I understand, though, that Dr. Edward Parker Davis once wrote a biographical sketch of Miss Agnes Irwin's life, which must be somewhere not wholly ungetatable, if only I knew where. And Miss Repplier's rather fragmentary appreciation is now of course available to the public. Also toward the biography necessary for the distinguished women's series, I now know all the parental steps from Benjamin Franklin and Deborah, his wife, by which the two Irwin sisters could regard him humorously and not without complacency as their great-great-grandfather. Feature by feature there was a good deal in Miss Agnes Irwin that was reminiscent of Franklin. And both women had a sense of humor and shrewdness and an emphasis on the facts of life which were recognizable tokens of their mental inheritance from that worldly sage.

The family tree runs thus: Sarah Franklin, daughter of Benjamin, married Richard Bache; their seventh child, Richard Bache, married Sophia Dallas, and among their children was Sophia Arabella Dallas, who married William Wallace Irwin, the mother and father of five Irwins, Agnes and Sophia Dallas Irwin among them.

William Irwin came, I seem to remember, from the west of Pennsylvania, the Irwins of Pittsburgh being well-known folk. He was at one time so recognized for his ability in governmental circles down in Washington as to be made American Minister to Denmark, where, I learn, from the few data on that episode, that Sophia Irwin was born. This would, I judge, make the date of his ministry at Copenhagen in the 1840's. Owing to I know not what family arrangement, later on Sophia, as a youngster, spent some years with her mother's cousins, the William Dallases, at Westminster, Maryland, where she was sent to school to the convent at Emmitsburg, the Dallases of that branch of the family being Catholics. Agnes, meanwhile, was a pupil in Washington at a dame school of the old-fashioned sort kept by a Miss Brooks, a lady of impeccable manners and morals of the "prunes, prisms and pyramids" pattern.

This experience of both sisters in the formalities of an older tradition had its effect, no doubt, on their own future requirements in their own school. For in spite of all of their casualness and shrewdness and plain-spokenness, these two women required a code of manners and a formality of address and discipline of polite gesture from their pupils which in the eighties and nineties was somewhat of an anachronism even in the private schools of that day. The modest curtsy and the rising for one's elders and betters and demureness of dress were not obligatory in most other schools, but it was in theirs.

It seemed to have been about 1860 that the Irwin family, at least the mother and the five children, regathered in New York, where Agnes Irwin taught for a time in Mrs. Hoffman's school, then the fashionable one in the town and where Sophia went on with her schooling, probably in that same polite and limited circle. I think it was about 1869 and at the suggestion of Dr. S. Weir Mitchell that Agnes came to Philadelphia to take over the Penn Square Seminary, a private school for girls which eventually became the Irwin School, a school which has long been familiar to the girls and parents of later generations, and which has been during the memory of most of us, at Twentieth Street and Delancey Place.

In 1894, when Agnes Irwin became the dean of Radcliffe College, at Cambridge, her sister, Sophia Irwin, who had long been associated with her in the Delancy Place school, became its sole directress and remained as such until her death, less than a year after that of her sister, in 1915.

These short and simple annals seem strangely inadequate when one considers what a unique and spirited part these two women played in the history of education not only in this city but in the country during the last quarter of the nineteenth century and the early part of the twentieth. Much was happening to our ideals concerning the functions and the preparation for teaching, many changes were being demanded in the curricula of schools and in the tests of the pupils for whom the schools were being changed. Those two women, in spite of the conventionality and tradition that must have circumscribed the schools which they knew in their youth, were so important in their chosen profession of teaching and so keenly aware of all the choices and chances and changes through which they were living, that it seems incredible that their actual life program could be summed up by so few dates and by such scattered fragments of biography.

The whole system of higher education for women, the change from oral examinations to written examinations, the college-entrance requirements, the different systems of marking and grading, the varying accents on the importance of one study above another, the shifting of the value placed upon mathematics, upon languages, upon science, the specialization on art and upon physics and chemistry, the change in position in subject of literature and history and modern languages, the requirements for college-trained teachers, the changes in schedules for vacations and for school hours, the shift from private finishing schools to post-graduate courses and all the new programs for athletics and for country day-school schedules—all these changes, as well as the national organization of the teaching force into committees and conferences, headmistress associations and summer schools, happened within the active professional careers of those two remarkable women.

Though they moved with the tide, they still held their own with an independence born of culture and of character and of position, so that their own sense of authority made them impervious to the mere demands of a passing fad and singularly aware of what goals would outlast the experimental stage and what would be scrapped by time. Meanwhile, they turned out into a changing world group after group of girls who have proved singularly able to meet the demands of their time and circumstances with a distinction and character which they rightly enough credit to the inspiration of those two women who for over forty years set a standard for private-school education in Philadelphia and for high thinking and brilliant conversation and distinguished friends in the country and the world at large.

Sarah D. Lowrie

SARAH HUTCHINS KILLIKELLY

1840–1912

☙❧

SARAH HUTCHINS KILLIKELLY, author, composer, teacher, lecturer and philanthropist, was born in 1840 and lived all but ten of her seventy-two years in Pennsylvania.

Her great-grandfather on the maternal side was Captain James Brown, of Carlisle, who was with General Washington at Valley Forge. Her grandmother was from Carlisle and her grandfather, Squire Robert Brown, left Carlisle to become a wealthy landowner in Armstrong County. There he built for his daughter a beautiful home on the Allegheny River at Kittanning, upon her marriage to the young vicar of the Protestant Episcopal Church, the Rev. Dr. Bryan Bernard Killikelly.

Sarah was but a child when she learned to play the organ for the services at St. Peter's in Butler. She was organist later at Trinity Church at Freeport, St. Michaels at Rural Village, at New Castle, at McKeesport, Grace Church at Mt. Washington, Christ Church at Leacock, All Saints at Paradise, Grace Church at the Cornish Gap Mines, and other parishes in Pennsylvania.

In Pittsburgh she established a young ladies' school. She composed and gave music lessons and was organist at Calvary Church. She gave historical lectures on foreign countries, in Pittsburgh and its vicinity, and she was editor of the woman's page on the Pittsburgh *Dispatch*. Her lectures on the Victorian era, written during the Diamond Jubilee of Queen Victoria, were read before the Society of Science, Letters, and Art in London which awarded her the Gold Crown Prize and made her a Fellow. Hardly a hospital in Pittsburgh but depended on her judgment and energy to carry on. It is said that the policemen all knew her and called her "Miss Sally." In sections of the city where the sick asked for her, she would be found offering her sympathy and aid. Her last great interest was a philanthropic school which may be said to have been the immediate cause of her death. Her heart had had too long and great a strain. Broken in health, she went to visit a niece in Washington, where she died May 14, 1912.

Miss Killikelly wrote a short history of Pennsylvania and a comprehensive history of Pittsburgh. She edited *The Skein of Life* by the Rev. W. R. Mackay, for the benefit of his family, and wrote three volumes of *Curious Questions*. She was in constant correspondence with the leading literary figures of her day, such as Whittier, Mary Drew, daughter of Gladstone, and others. She was a member of the Archaeological Department of the University of Pennsylvania, Society of American Authors, Society of Indian Authors, American Historical Association, Archaeological Institute of America, League of American Pen Women, and was a life member of the Daughters of the American Revolution and of the Twentieth Century Club, Pittsburgh.

MRS. HARRY A. HORNOR

ELLEN MARY WEBSTER PALMER

1840–1918

For Ellen Mary Webster Palmer life had one great purpose, the gay but compelling adventure of plucking boys out of drabness or danger or devilment.

They say, "Mrs. Palmer discovered boys." And the vivid phrase lighted her field of valor.

Something of her militant heritage from Simon Dewey, made Baron of Stone Hall in 1629; something of Ethan Allen and of Admiral Dewey, her relatives, stirred in her blood. Something of her family's Vermont background struck out sturdily.

Ellen Webster had been a school teacher and a music teacher, so after her marriage to a socially prominent attorney of Wilkes-Barre, she carried her teaching urge into Sunday school.

Then, here in her new coal-valley home, different from the Plattsburg of her birth, Ellen Palmer saw pitiable, poverty-ridden little ten-year-olds, who worked and swore and swaggered like men.

They were the little laborers from the mines near by, in the days that were innocent of any health and education, hour and labor laws for breaker-boys and door-boys and mule-boys. Then a conviction possessed her that long weekdays of work, even with Sunday psalm-singing, were not the good life for small boys. She came to realize that they could not live-by-the-sweat-of-their-brows and mine-whistles alone. She realized that "boys will" not necessarily "be boys," for these young neighbors whose hours and conditions of servitude in the mines and breakers and hazards and hardships that crowded out all wholesome, normal boy-ways. She knew that it wasn't fair, it wasn't decent, it wasn't Christian.

In spite of vocal and vigorous opposition, she begged the use of a small room. She set up a bookshelf, a workbench, and a melodeon and she combined jolly songs with tools and tales of heroes in an afterwork night school. She wrote a poem for every occasion and was herself not the least of the attractions of her "B.I.A." For the group soon took on the dignified name of BOYS' INDUSTRIAL ASSOCIA-TION.

Ellen Palmer had "discovered boys" back there in the days when offensives began; when individuals were gripped by a driving fret about the unfair and unhealthy way of life for whole groups about them. She lifted the small mine-working boy and his doings into view. What she discovered she held up for others to help her bring into a more reasonable, wholesome and safe haven. More and more boys came.

The absence of science and system in her methods would not be tolerated in 1940. The 1940 routine in boys' clubs and camps, play-grounds and libraries; the 1940 projects for the junior delinquent and social legislation; 1940 cannot accept as wholly true such a manger-birth of its own noble notion of the worth of a small boy.

It is of little real importance that Mrs. Palmer's husband helped to make Pennsylvania history; nor that her children are in *Who's Who in America*. It may not be true, nor is it relevant to claim that Ellen Palmer was the first since the First to suffer little children to come; nor that Wilkes-Barre was the home of the very first Boys' Industrial Association. What matter!

That which graces her place in the archives of Pennsylvania women is Ellen Palmer herself. Her sense of responsibility, to right cruel wrongs to small boys; her own faith that power would be given her to do it; her own love, finding love; her own conviction of the use and joy of her labors; her never flagging laughter and rhyme; her amusing persistence, and the final great accomplishment of her pur-pose.

Her work began fifty years ago. Today on the "River-bank" of her home town there stands the monument of a gentlewoman looking into the upturned faces of two small breaker-boys. Once a year some there are who come to do honor to the memory of her place in their own lives. Soon it will be just another good-fairy story; so—once upon a time, long, long ago there lived a Lovely Lady of the miner's lamp who "discovered boys."

There: that's some of the good of "the good old days."

FANNIE SAX LONG

BLANCHE NEVIN

1841–1925

BLANCHE NEVIN was born at Mercersburg, Franklin County, Pennsylvania, September 25, 1841. Her father, John Williamson Nevin of Scotch-Irish descent, a man prominent in the Presbyterian Church, allied himself to the German Reformed Church in 1840 in accepting the call to the chair of dogmatic theology in the Theological Seminary of that church. As theologian, teacher, and preacher he attained eminence at home and abroad. Dr. Nevin went to Lancaster in 1855, where he assumed the presidency of Franklin and Marshall College and, with his family, took a leading part in the activities of the city.

Blanche Nevin always considered Lancaster her legal residence, but later bought Windsor Forges, near Churchtown, the home of her maternal grandparents, endeared by happy recollections, and from there revived the generous hospitality of earlier days until her death on April 20, 1925.

She studied art in Philadelphia, Rome, Venice and Florence, spending much time in Italy, traveled extensively abroad and made worldwide friends and acquaintances.

Her marble statues of Maud Müller in 1875, Eve and Cinderella in 1876, besides various heads and busts, show her ability. She was selected as the sculptor to make the statue of General Peter Muhlenberg, one of the two Pennsylvanians in the Hall of Fame in the Capitol in Washington. She left many heads and figures of distinguished personages in perishable plaster. To the city of Lancaster she gave two drinking fountains, one surmounted by a life-size bronze lion, the other a marble cross ornamented with flowers, in memory of her mother. Painting she indulged in principally for amusement.

In charity she distinguished herself by seeking medical aid for crippled children in her neighborhood, and by impulsively entering the arena of the Sino-Japanese war in offering untrained service as a nurse.

She dashed off many verses and small poems, some of which were printed for private circulation. She was a brilliant conversationalist, quick in repartee, keen in wit and humor. Children adored her and were entranced by her stories and power of mimicry. She was akin to them in naïve, impulsive spontaneity, unconsciously ignoring the conventionalities of ordinary life, and by her impulsive forgetfulness of the usual standards she was dubbed erratic and eccentric. To those who knew her she was a loyal, lovable friend, an inspiring companion and one who left a memory which will long be cherished.

Mrs. Herbert Hartman

C. F. Hoban

SARA LOUISA OBERHOLTZER

1841–1930

The name of Sara Louisa Oberholtzer is associated with school savings banks, the project which began to spread rapidly under her hand in all parts of the United States in the nineties. The idea came from France and Belgium, and was given a trial in Long Island City by a Belgian, J. A. Thiry, while he was a school commissioner in that place.

It was brought to notice in a meeting of the American Economic Association which Mrs. Oberholtzer attended. She made the scheme her own from that time onward, visiting officers and teachers of schools and officers of banks, devising, with their aid, the system by which the notice of thrift and economy and saving for a "rainy day" was put into the consciousness of millions of children. At the time of her death in 1930, several millions of dollars were on deposit in banks in all parts of the country to the credit of American school children.

Mrs. Oberholtzer was a daughter of Paxson Vickers, a granddaughter of John Vickers, and a great-granddaughter of Thomas Vickers, who owned earthenware potteries in Chester County, the products of which are nowadays esteemed as relics in American collections. They were Quakers from England. At least one of her forebears was on the *Welcome* when Penn landed here in 1682.

Her earliest recollections—she was born in 1841—were of the Underground Railroad and the movement of fugitive slaves to freedom in Canada, her girlhood home having been a station on the route. She was the author of a novel, *Hope's Heart Bells,* dealing with the Quaker people in southeastern Pennsylvania.

Mrs. Oberholtzer lived in Philadelphia for forty years, and died there at the age of eighty-nine. From that city she went out to address groups of men and women in the various states in her efforts to extend the school savings banks system. Boards of education, school principals and teachers were to be persuaded that it was a feasible plan to ask for, receive and bank the children's money in the interest of thrifty habits. To convince them was not easy. Banks at first could not be found to receive small sums and worry with the accounts. In a few years they contended with one another for the school deposits when it was realized that the scholar would, in all likelihood, continue business relations with the bank after coming to maturity.

Ellis Paxson Oberholtzer

EMILY SARTAIN

1841–1927

Emily Sartain, painter, etcher, and engraver, was intimately connected with the development of art in Philadelphia, and more particularly with the emphasis on the education of women in its various branches. As principal of the Philadelphia School of Design for Women from 1886 to 1919 she displayed a remarkable executive ability which placed the school among the first of its kind in the country.

Her especial contribution to pedagogy lay in the development of instruction in the applied arts.

She was the daughter of John Sartain, who introduced into the United States the art of mezzotint engraving, granddaughter of John Swaine and great-granddaughter of Edward Longmate, able English engravers. Belonging to a family where the artistic temperament was so strongly marked and which in her generation included Samuel and William Sartain, who were widely known as engravers, painters, and etchers, she was the first and for long the only woman engraver in mezzotint on either side of the Atlantic.

In 1881 and 1883 she was awarded the Mary Smith Prize at the Pennsylvania Academy of the Fine Arts for the best picture by a woman in the annual exhibition. In 1882 she became art editor of the Philadelphia illustrated journal, *Our Continent,* and of an edition de luxe of *New England Bygones,* by Ella H. Rollins, carrying on her studio work at the same time. In 1886 she accepted the invitation of the board of directors of the Philadelphia School of Design for Women to become its principal, and infused into its work a high degree of vitality, bringing it abreast of the art movement of the day. Several years later she was elected a director of the public schools of her native city.

For the Columbian Exposition in Chicago in 1893, she did most effective work as chairman of the committee of women artists who decorated with mural paintings, etc., the women's room of the Pennsylvania State Building. She also served as one of the judges in the fine arts department, the first time a woman ever received such an appointment in an international exhibition. At the Buffalo Pan-American Exhibition in 1901 some of her oil portraits received honorable mention.

In 1899, Miss Sartain was invited to London to speak before the International Council of Women upon the opportunities offered in this country to women trained in applied design. The following year she was appointed to represent the United States in Paris at the International Congress on Instruction in Drawing. She fulfilled the same office again in 1904 at a later meeting of the same congress in Berne, Switzerland.

Further distinctions which came to her in her own city were membership on the board of directors of the New Century Club, of which she was a founder; the presidency for a number of years of the Plastic

Club, which she had also helped found, and a term as president of the Browning Society, during which she illustrated the correlation of painting, music, and poetry. Miss Sartain's long and active life came to an end on June 18, 1927, in her eighty-sixth year.

HARRIET SARTAIN

ANNA DICKINSON

1842–1932

ON October 25, 1842, in the home of John Dickinson, merchant of Philadelphia, and his wife, Mary Edmundson, member of a well-known Delaware Quaker family, a daughter was born who was destined to render brilliant and patriotic service to the nation. Anna Elizabeth was the name bestowed upon this child. She was the youngest of five children and but two years old when her father died, leaving his family without adequate support. Mrs. Dickinson met the situation with courage, managing to clothe and educate her children through taking boarders and teaching in a private school while practicing self-denial at every turn.

Anna entered the Westtown Boarding School at the age of twelve. Two years later she became a pupil at the Friends' Select School in Philadelphia, where her excellent mind, studious habits, and retentive memory brought her admiring recognition from teachers and fellow pupils. Mrs. Elizabeth Cady Stanton, in her sketch of the life of Anna Dickinson, dwelt at length on her brilliant imaginative mind, her love of books, and her passion for oratory. Said Mrs. Stanton:

When Curtis, Phillips, or Beecher lectured in Philadelphia, Anna would perform any kind of work to make enough money for entrance to the lecture hall. On one occasion, she scrubbed a sidewalk for twenty-five cents that she might hear Wendell Phillips speak on "The Lost Arts."

At seventeen she left school, young and penniless, to seek a position that would enable her to support herself. Everywhere she found that boys were paid more than girls for the same type of service. This she regarded as an unjust discrimination against her sex. When barely eighteen years of age she spoke on "Women's Rights and Wrongs" at a meeting of the Association of Progressive Friends. Her youthful face, black curls, large bright eyes, and musical voice, together with her subdued and impressive manner, commanded at once the admiring attention of her audience.

Next to her love for her mother, the strongest influence in her early formative years was found in the home of Dr. Hannah Longshore, mother of Mrs. Rudolph Blankenburg, who became young Anna's most trusted confidante and adviser. In the Longshore home she met sympathetic encouragement and a welcome so cordial that she became a constant visitor, growing to depend upon the wise guidance that was ever ready for her need.

Just before the beginning of the Civil War, she obtained work in the mint at Washington, but later, growing too vehement in her criticisms of General McClellan, she was dismissed. However, she continued her public speaking through that winter on the "Political Aspects of the War," a subject that made her available in party politics, a field in which her extraordinary ability and charming youthful appearance attracted widespread attention.

William Lloyd Garrison, having heard her speak at West Chester and Longwood, Pennsylvania, invited her to his home in Boston. The influence of Mr. Garrison secured for her an invitation to deliver her first lecture in Boston from the pulpit of Theodore Parker on a Sunday morning. Though she was but twenty years of age, and afterwards said that the greatest trial of her platform life was her fear of that first Boston audience, she received the highest encomiums from the press and the people, together with requests for the delivery of the same lecture in other New England cities.

During the summer of 1862, she made a study of the government hospitals, and in the fall delivered her lecture "Hospital Life," at Concord, New Hampshire. In her audience sat the secretary of the Republican State Committee. At the close of the lecture he said to a friend: "If we can get this girl to make that speech all through New Hampshire, we can carry the coming election." In the four weeks preceding election she spoke twenty times, always to crowded audiences. At the close of the campaign, the governor-elect made personal acknowledgment that her eloquent speeches had secured his election.

New Hampshire safe, all eyes were turned to Connecticut, where the Republicans were completely disheartened. Anna Dickinson was sent into that state for a two weeks' speaking tour on "The National Crisis," and did much to galvanize the Loyalists to life and reëstablish popular sentiment. Said Ida Tarbell in writing of these campaign speeches, "It is not too much to say that it was Anna Dickinson who turned the tide. Her usefulness to the Union cause during the war cannot be questioned."

Her distinction as one of the great patriotic orators of her time was well recognized. Invitations poured in upon her from the most distinguished groups in the country. Her famous appearance at Cooper Institute, New York, took place in 1862, with Henry Ward Beecher presiding. For more than an hour she held and electrified her audience, closing with a beautiful peroration. Before dispersing, the audience called for Mr. Beecher, but he arose and with great feeling and solemnity said: "Let no man open his lips here tonight. Music is the only fitting accompaniment to the eloquent utterances we have heard."

Among the incessant and flattering invitations that reached her desk the one which typified the highest tribute to her genius was the summons to Washington, in 1863, by an invitation from both houses of Congress to speak at the Capitol. Her acceptance of that invitation was written from 1710 Locust Street, Philadelphia, suggesting January 16 as the date, and stating that all of the proceeds from the engagement should be devoted to the help of the suffering freedmen. President and Mrs. Lincoln were in the immense and distinguished audience that assembled in the Capitol upon that occasion.

While oratory was her passion, she also entertained an ambition for a dramatic career. She wrote several plays and participated in their presentation. While she was always accorded recognition for scholarship and literary polish, neither as an actress nor playwright could she attain the standard she enjoyed as a public speaker. Through her writings in drama and fiction and her popularity on the rostrum, she earned large amounts of money, and contributed generously to various causes, especially to war sufferers.

Pennsylvania has not produced a more notable woman, nor one who gave herself more loyally to the public service than Anna Dickinson. She withdrew from public life years before her death, which did not come until 1932.

GERTRUDE BOSLER BIDDLE

MARY E. MUMFORD

1842–1935

⚜

For many years an outstanding figure in civic, educational, charitable affairs and a pioneer organizer of women, Mary E. Mumford was looked upon as a "Philadelphia institution" and one of its notable women.

When in 1881 a wave of municipal reform swept over this city, Mrs. Mumford was asked to stand as a candidate for the sectional school board of her district, the Twenty-ninth Ward. She was elected and obtained the right of official protest against some of the methods then in practice. During her six years of service on this board she was instrumental in introducing manual training for boys and a course in cooking and sewing for girls. Going on from the sectional to the central board, she served there until her resignation in 1900. During this period she is credited with many of the improvements which took place, such as the introduction of a college preparatory course in the Girls High School, the institution of child-study classes for mothers and teachers, recognition of the importance of child psychology, as well as several other improvements in ideas and methods.

She was an outspoken foe of mechanical methods in the administration of the public schools, and her high ideals, warm sympathy, and intimate contacts made her the personal friend of teachers and scholars alike. Her keen interest in education led her to further work in women's clubs and child-welfare organizations. It was during her presidency of the New Century Club that the clubhouse on South Twelfth Street was built. In 1890 she was one of the founders of the General Federation of Women's Clubs, in whose counsels and work she was active many years. She was eventually elected an honorary vice-president for life.

It was her active interest in child welfare which led her and her husband to the foundation of the Twenty-ninth Ward division of the Philadelphia Society for Organized Charity, and it was through the Mothers Congress, of which she was also a founder, that she pioneered in the establishment of the Juvenile Court, home and school associations, mothers clubs and day nurseries. Mrs. Mumford served on the board of the Woman's Medical College of Pennsylvania from 1891, being its president from 1893 to 1912, and remaining on the board until 1920.

Mrs. H. O. Peebles

MARY ELIZABETH WILLSON

1842–1906

Mary Elizabeth Bliss, gospel singer and song-writer, was born in Clearfield County, Pennsylvania, May 1, 1842. She was one of four children, one of whom died in infancy. The three remaining children were Phoebe, Mary Elizabeth, and P. P. Bliss, the noted song-writer. While they were still young the family removed to Tioga County, Pennsylvania, where Mr. Bliss bought a tract of timberland and built a modest home among the forest of hemlocks and maples.

Mary Elizabeth and her beloved brother roamed the neighboring hills, calling, singing, shouting to each other, in their carefree, happy youthful days. Many times in after years Mrs. Willson was heard to say: "All my power, strength, naturalness of voice, came from the grand old hills of Pennsylvania, for there is where both my brother and I received the foundation, health, lung power and most of our training to be able to sing."

When Mary Elizabeth was fifteen years of age she accompanied her brother into the adjoining county of Bradford, where he taught a select school. In 1858 she began teaching school. She taught until the year 1860, when she became the wife of Clark Willson, of Towanda. Mr. and Mrs. Willson adopted a daughter and later had four children born to them.

In the first sixteen years of her married life she and her husband spent considerable time teaching music, holding musical conventions, and giving concerts. On December 29, 1876, her great sorrow came when her devoted brother, P. P. Bliss, and his wife were swept to their death in the Ashtabula Bridge disaster.

The work that her brother was doing before his untimely death had a marked effect upon Mrs. Willson and was an incentive for her to follow in his footsteps. Many of the gospel songs that he wrote are still popular in evangelistic meetings. Mr. Bliss's songs were of the type that the people could understand and sing; their melody, martial note, joyousness, and hope produced the religious exhilaration desired.

P. P. Bliss, like his sister, received little musical training in his early days. Most of his youth had been spent on a farm and later in a lumber camp. Music was in his soul and he imparted this to his sister. It is recorded that she exerted a marked influence upon his early life and was part of his inspiration for many of his gospel songs. He was at the height of his success with the evangelists Moody and Sankey when the disaster that claimed his life occurred. The train upon which he and his wife were riding plunged through a bridge in Ohio. Following the catastrophe Mrs. Willson was so greatly affected that she said she never could sing again for sheer entertainment. She decided to devote her time to carrying on her brother's work.

Very soon Mr. and Mrs. Willson were called to do evangelist work by Major Whittle, a co-worker of Dwight Moody and of P. P. Bliss. They went to Chicago, where they had a most wonderful influence. In 1878 Francis Murphy called them to sing in his temperance meetings. The principal cities of the United States were visited. Thompson Weed in an article in the New York *Tribune* pronounced her "The Jenny Lind of Sacred Song."

In 1882 the gospel temperance workers spent several months in Great Britain. Mrs. Willson sang to audiences in Liverpool, Birmingham, Glasgow, Manchester, Aberdeen, Edinburgh, and Dublin. She also wrote several hymns during these campaigns, among the most popular being "Glad Tidings," "Papa, Come This Way," and "My Mother's Hands." In addition she compiled two volumes of sacred songs, *Glad Tidings* and *Sacred Gems,* during these gospel temperance movements.

After the death of Francis Murphy, Mr. and Mrs. Willson confined themselves strictly to gospel work, Mr. Willson preaching and Mrs. Willson singing. This brought them in continual contact with such religious workers as Moody, Sankey, McGranahan, Beecher, Talmage, and many others.

February 15, 1906, at Towanda, Pennsylvania, Mrs. Willson was called to meet her Redeemer.

Mrs. E. M. Muir

AUGUSTA McCLINTOCK LONGACRE

1843–1928

❦

Augusta McClintock Longacre was born in 1843, the daughter of the Rev. John McClintock and his wife, Caroline Wakeman. Her father was then a professor at Dickinson College, Carlisle, where she passed her early years.

Carlisle, on the border between North and South, became a refuge for Negroes who had escaped from Southern plantations, and as Dr. McClintock was a strong antislavery man and used his influence to aid these fugitives, his daughter learned early to champion the cause of the poor and oppressed race.

Dr. McClintock was sent to Europe in 1860 as head of the American Chapel which had been established in Paris. As the struggle between North and South became inevitable, his family was the center of the group of Unionists who were making every effort to diffuse a clear understanding of the issues.

To those who came under the spell of her charm in later years it is not hard to picture the vivid and fascinating girl with a voice of marvelous musical quality. She rendered notable service to her father in his difficult task at the French capital in those troublous times. On Monday evenings Dr. McClintock's house became the meeting place for all Americans in Paris. Both father and daughter had unusual tact, which was greatly needed to keep a tranquil atmosphere and make these meetings a success.

After her family's return from France, Augusta McClintock married James M. Longacre, in 1865, and came to live in Philadelphia. They had four children, and Mrs. Longacre gave the greater part of her energy and devotion to her family.

She had always a lively interest in the early life of this nation, as was natural, since her forebears had taken active part in Colonial and Revolutionary affairs; when leisure was found in later life she devoted her time to original research on Colonial life and customs. Appointed by the Pennsylvania Society of the Colonial Dames of America to the chairmanship of its Committee on Historical Research, she made so comprehensive a study of the beginnings of the iron industry in the state that the result was a book entitled *Forges and Furnaces in the Province of Pennsylvania,* a most complete authority on that subject.

To those who knew her, she was a woman of arresting personality, with the commanding presence and the fine dark eyes which gave even to a casual acquaintance a hint of the mental power which enabled her to influence so strongly those with whom she came in contact. She died in January 1928.

MARY QUINCY ALLEN DIXON

MARY FRANCES LOVELL

1844-1932

MARY FRANCES WHITECHURCH was born in London in 1844, and was five years old when her parents brought their family to this country. Her father, Robert Whitechurch, was an engraver on steel and followed his profession in Philadelphia. On September 13, 1864, Mary married George S. Lovell, a wholesale clock dealer. They lived in Bryn Mawr until Mr. Lovell's death in 1897. Mrs. Lovell then moved to Jenkintown, where she lived until her death on June 25, 1932, leaving no descendants. Her closest relatives were nieces and nephews.

Mrs. Lovell was a great American humanitarian. Her creed, her life motive is expressed in the words "Cruelty is never justified." She gave generously and continuously, day after day and year after year, of her time, her money and her energy to the defense of the tortured and oppressed. Her whole life was spent in the endeavor to relieve by action and by precept every form of suffering and cruelty inflicted upon man or animal.

She was a living link with the early days of the humane movement. In 1859 she helped to establish the Woman's Pennsylvania Society for the Prevention of Cruelty to Animals, and for many years was the honorary president and corresponding secretary of this organization. She founded its Montgomery County branch, and was its president for fourteen years. To Mrs. Lovell and to Philadelphia belong the credit for starting the movement which resulted in "Kindness to

Animal Week." She was a director of the American Humane Association from its incorporation in 1903, and a member of its Executive Committee. From 1905 to 1907 she was secretary of the national organization.

For forty years Mrs. Lovell used her pen in the interests of antivivisection, serving as associate editor of the *Starry Cross,* the literary organ of the American Antivivisection Society, located in Philadelphia. As a young woman she became interested in the Woman's Christian Temperance Union and remained all her life an earnest supporter of the views held by that society. She founded the Dickens Club of Philadelphia, of which she was also president.

NAOMI MERKET STUBBS

ANNA LEA MERRITT

1844-1930

ANNA LEA MERRITT was born in Philadelphia in 1844, and died at Hurstbourne Tarrant, Hampshire, England, in 1930.

Brought up under Quaker discipline, Anna, eldest daughter of Joseph Lea and Susanna Massey, received small encouragement to study art, but her unusually good general education included the classics, science, languages, and foreign travel. Social and family duties often kept her from the drawing and painting which she so loved. Moreover, Philadelphia then offered few opportunities for instruction. She profited well by six lessons from a German artist in Dresden in 1869, painting a portrait of her sister which was exhibited at the Royal Academy in London. This success encouraged her to take a studio there, where Professor Henry Merritt, a noted art critic and expert on methods, gave her helpful advice. Eventually she became his wife. Her grief over his death after three brief months of married life is memorialized in her best-known picture, "Love Locked Out." This was the first picture by a woman painter to be bought for the National Gallery from the Chantrey Bequest.

Friendships, distinguished people, and filling orders for portraits consumed her time, but after her father's serious losses in business and her husband's death in 1877 she worked under the pressure of financial anxieties and painful illness.

Though recognized and successful in her chosen field, her goal was not achieved without effort. Hewing out a path to a professional career was pioneer work, cutting through tradition's tangled undergrowth at every step. She produced more than 162 portraits (some of them double or group portraits), 163 subject pictures, some 14 large mural paintings, many etchings, and several books with illustrations. Her talents were acknowledged during her lifetime by medals and awards from the Centennial Exposition, Philadelphia, 1876, and the World's Fair in Chicago, 1893, where she did mural decorations for the Woman's Building. She exhibited at the Royal Academy from 1871 to 1915.

When no longer able to keep up her London house she retired to a picturesque village in Hampshire, Hurstbourne Tarrant, where she tended a charming garden dominated by a gigantic yew tree. Her illustrated books, *A Hamlet in Hampshire* and *An Artist's Garden,* were published by the Century Company. She edited her husband's memoirs and wrote her own informally for the benefit of her family. These cast many illuminating sidelights on social life and conditions in old Philadelphia, London, Continental Europe, Ireland, and Egypt.

She had personal experience of three wars—the Civil War, when as a girl she worked for the wounded and met Lincoln and Grant in Philadelphia; the Franco-Prussian War, when, in charge of an invalid sister, she escaped the siege of Paris only by prompt action, courage and good sense, and the World War, which shadowed her last years.

EDITH EMERSON

LUCRETIA LONGSHORE BLANKENBURG

1845-1937

⚜

LUCRETIA LONGSHORE was born on May 8, 1845, on a farm near New Lisbon, Ohio, adjacent to that on which Mark Hanna was born. When but a baby of six months she made the long trip to Philadelphia by carriage, where her mother, Hannah Myers Longshore, attended the first class in the Woman's Medical College in 1850.

In those days so fierce was the opposition to women doctors that police guarded the hall during the graduation exercises, while little Lucretia, then six years old, sat on the platform. Her mother was Pennsylvania's first woman physician.

When Mrs. Longshore announced in 1851 that she intended to take up the active practice of medicine, it created a national sensation. It was the bitter antagonism that developed when her mother began lecturing on medical subjects concerning women that impelled her daughter to inject her own dynamic personality into the struggle for equal rights for women. At the same time it served to start her on a career which was to make her at the end of her life America's oldest active clubwoman. She participated in women's club affairs for more than sixty years.

She was born in stirring times. Slavery was a bitter issue. Her memories of the antislavery movement were vivid. Thus she grew up in an atmosphere of political and social reform. In 1867 she married Rudolph Blankenburg, later Philadelphia's reform mayor, whom she loyally aided in his efforts at civic and political betterment. "There is no man in the world who can take the place of Rudolph Blankenburg!" she exclaimed when Mayor J. Hampton Moore, presenting one thousand dollars with the "Outstanding Woman" award, jocularly expressed fear she might "go off and get married."

Mrs. Blankenburg was a member of the group which began organizing the charities of Philadelphia in 1878. She was one of the early and vigorous promoters of the woman's suffrage movement, and, in 1892, began a sixteen years' presidency of the Pennsylvania Woman Suffrage Association.

In 1898 she turned to the General Federation of Women's Clubs work as a new field for suffrage propaganda, and was honorary vice-president of the federation. As a member of the Women's Health Protective Association, she helped promote filtration of Philadelphia's water supply. She battled to have fenders put on street cars, and for vestibule protection for motormen. She was instrumental in having police matrons assigned.

Chairman of the Smoke Nuisance Committee, she led the campaign to abate unnecessary smoke in the city. She was one of the prime movers to get women on the school board. She was president for thirteen years of the Associate Committee of Women of the School of Industrial Art, and did outstanding work in the New Century

Guild for working girls. In 1920 Mayor Moore appointed her to the committee charged with looking after Independence Hall.

In a book, *The Blankenburgs of Philadelphia,* "by One of Them," Mrs. Blankenburg reviewed the battles of her husband to clean up the city government, and traced the social and political development seen with her own eyes from girlhood to recent years.

Among the honors she received from her contemporaries was the Fame Award of the Philadelphia Club of Advertising Women, in 1930. The esteem in which she was held was reflected in 1935 when some three thousand women gathered in Convention Hall to join in a mass tribute to the venerable civic leader at a dinner in honor of her ninetieth birthday.

Mrs. Blankenburg loved the old-fashioned styles of dress, and the old-fashioned ideals, but she had ultramodern views on some things, and a sympathetic understanding of youth. On her seventy-ninth birthday, in the day of "flappers," she termed herself "an incorrigible optimist when it comes to youth, and I know the young people of today will turn out all right."

An independent Republican, she laid her whiplash on the Vare regime and in later years under Roosevelt assailed "inflated dollars," crop destruction, the NRA and other "alphabetical agencies." In line with her views that "the good old days" were not necessarily the best, she expressed the opinion that "we have outgrown the Blue Laws."

Active until the very end, she spoke only a few days before her death at a public luncheon. Mrs. Blankenburg, the "Grand Old Lady" of Philadelphia, died at the age of ninety-two in 1937.

Nicholas B. Wainwright

JANE CAMPBELL

1845–1928

Jane Campbell, author, historian, lecturer, and pioneer suffragist, was a member of an old Philadelphia family, a daughter of John and Margaret Hughes Campbell. She founded the Woman Suffrage Society of Philadelphia and served as its president for twenty years, planning most of its educational campaigns. She was Pennsylvania's representative on the governing board of the National Woman Suffrage Association.

She was interested in the Woman's Club movement, which she sponsored, and was present at most of the organization's meetings. For a quarter of a century she was secretary of the American Catholic Historical Society and a charter member of the Site and Relic Society of Germantown. She was a contributor to the columns of the Philadelphia *Record* and wrote many folk tales for child readers. During the World War she wrote articles on the activities of the Red Cross Society.

She was also editor of the magazine *Woman's Progress* and an authority on old-time music. Her knowledge of early American history and costumes was wide and varied. Two volumnes of Danish ballads and folk songs, which had been published in the *American Scandinavian Review* and other periodicals, were translated by her.

In 1923 the Jane Campbell Memorial Scholarship at Pennsylvania State College was founded. For years she was an active member of the New Century Club of Philadelphia and conducted its famous Monday Morning Class. As a speaker she had few peers, winning her audiences by her irresistible charm. She did much to further the cause of woman suffrage by gaining many converts. She had superb common sense as well as a rare sense of humor and an inexhaustible public spirit. She was identified with the development of the city's interest in art, letters, and music.

On February 12, 1928, she died at eighty-three years of age.

MARY S. DICK

MARY CASSATT

1845-1926

IN the special section of the Chicago Century of Progress Art Exhibition where the works of the ten greatest American painters of all time were exhibited, Mary Stevenson Cassatt was the only woman represented. She was somewhat a shadowy figure to us in this country, for she had spent most of her life in residence abroad, but she was the sort of cosmopolite who retained a passionate love of her native land.

She was born in Pittsburgh, the daughter of Robert S. Cassatt, a banker, who subsequently moved to Philadelphia. Alexander Cassatt, president of the Pennsylvania Railroad, was her brother. Her early childhood was spent in France, whence she returned to Philadelphia and studied at the Pennsylvania Academy of the Fine Arts—the only formal art training she ever had. At the Academy she was a highly individualistic student with undoubted early talent. This institution has always regarded her as one of its most important alumnae, granting her in 1914 its gold medal of honor.

Inspired by her studies here she went back to Europe in 1868 and there studied the great masters of the Italian Renaissance, their influence on her art being manifested frequently in her Madonna-like interpretation of her mothers and children. She settled down in Paris in 1874, where she studied under Manet, Degas, and with Renoir. Their influences are found in the brilliant color of her work. She had come to France at a momentous period of French art when Edouard Manet and his friends had broken away from the French Academy to hold their own exhibitions, thereby rearing up the new school of Impressionism. It was Degas who persuaded her to exhibit with this new group. Although most of them painted landscapes, Mary Cassatt painted figures.

She was a distinct individualist always, in her art as well as in her life. A friend of the French Impressionists, it cannot be said that she belonged to that school or, in fact, to any school of painting. Although personally very retiring, she became a picturesque figure in the American art colony of Paris. She maintained an apartment in the French capital, and a chateau in the countryside, where her hospitality became legendary in its quiet picturesqueness. She died in Paris in 1926 at the age of eighty-one years, having lived to see her works receive genuine acclaim.

Her paintings hang in many famous galleries of the world. She is represented in the Wilstach collection in Memorial Hall, Fairmount Park; in the Metropolitan Museum, New York; the Corcoran Art Gallery, Washington, and in the galleries of Chicago, Detroit, and Providence. Several of her canvases are in the French national art collection in the Luxembourg; a further French honor was given her in 1904, when she was made a chevalier of the French Legion of Honor.

Always Mary Cassatt refused to accept the usual shibboleth that France is the only home for American painters. Just a few years before her death she said most emphatically:

Tell the American artists to stay at home and root themselves in America and to be true to their own conviction and ideals. When I was young it was necessary to come to France. We had so few good painters and our museums were so insufficient. Now all that is changed and the young American, if he is truly serious, can work at home.

It was not only as a painter that Mary Cassatt achieved distinction. Her dry-point and color etchings are of the highest order, noted for their exquisite, sensitive line and delicate texture. Throughout all her art there was evident a remarkable intellectual and spiritual quality which has earned her a permanent place in the history of art and the devotion of art lovers the world over.

FRANK HALL FRAYSUR

JOSEPHINE MILLER

1845–?

OMINOUS silence hung like a pall over the field of Gettysburg in the early morning of July 1, 1863. The Union and Confederate armies were there, facing each other about to join in inevitable battle.

Down in the valley beside the Emmitsburg road stood a little one-story house, a steady column of smoke from its chimney indicating that life went on as usual inside. Occasionally snatches of song in a girl's gay voice drifted through open windows to the ears of soldiers trudging past. Evidently the occupant was indifferent to or ignorant of what was about to occur, that shot and shell must riddle the flimsy walls which jutted up in what was sure to be hotly contested ground.

General J. B. Carr, of the Union Army, passing along the turnpike, took all this in and stopped to issue a warning to those within to flee to safety. His hail was answered by Josephine Miller, the eighteen-year-old adopted daughter of Mrs. Rogers, who owned the house. She was alone. Before she would do what the General asked, she said she would wait until the batch of bread, then in her oven, was baked.

When the batch was done, it occurred to her that the soldiers marching steadily past her door looked hungry. She would serve the bread to them. It seemed a shame that men so starved should not be fed. So Josephine decided to stay right where she was and bake another batch. After that it was too late for flight, and besides she was too busy baking bread and giving water to the wounded even to think about it. The little house shook under the impact of bullets as the battle swept around it. Through it all batch after batch of bread was baked and handed out. There were always men to eat it. It didn't make any difference what color uniform they wore; they were hungry or hurt or both. Josephine fed them and tied up their wounds.

When it was all over, seventeen bodies were removed from what was left of the little dwelling—wounded men who had crawled there for succor, found it, and died. Others, more fortunate, lived to bless the name of Josephine Miller.

MRS. FRANCIS S. SHELLY

JENNIE WADE

1845–1863

ON the afternoon of the 26th of June, 1863, there occurred in Gettysburg the serious invasion of Pennsylvania by the Confederate Army. On July the first the great battle of the Civil War opened and continued without interruption through the second and third of the month.

A heroine, eighteen years of age, whose name is not often mentioned in connection with the tragedy of those several days, perished in the din of that fray.

Both before and during the battle she was busily engaged in baking bread for the National troops who sadly needed food. Unfortunately, the small house which contained the kitchen of her home was in the range of the soldiers of both armies. The Rebels sternly ordered her to leave the premises, but this she as sternly refused to do, saying: "Until the battle is over, I wait. I wish to help."

It was while she was engaged in her patriotic service that a Minié ball pierced the heart of young Jennie Wade.

GERTRUDE BOSLER BIDDLE

ANNE HOLLINGSWORTH WHARTON

1845–1928

ANNE HOLLINGSWORTH WHARTON was born at Southampton Furnace, Cumberland County, Pennsylvania, December 15, 1845, the daughter of Charles and Mary McLanahan (Boggs) Wharton. She was descended from an old and notable family, the founder of which, Thomas Wharton, an Englishman, was an early settler in Philadelphia. A son Joseph, from whom Anne was also descended, married a granddaughter of Samuel Carpenter, Treasurer of Pennsylvania, and built Walnut Grove, a handsome country house with extensive grounds sloping to the Delaware. There, soon after his death, was held the famous Meschianza Ball in 1778. For five generations from the time of their coming to America her Wharton ancestors were successful merchants and importers. Her father became well known in the iron trade.

Anne was graduated from a private school in Philadelphia and began as a young girl the writing that was to occupy so much of her life. Some of her earlier work was for newspapers and periodicals, much of it in the form of children's stories, but her books began to appear while she was still in her early twenties. *St. Bartholomew's Eve* was published in 1866, and *Virginia* in 1869. Several of her later volumes were based on observations abroad, with more or less of historic interest, such as *Italian Days and Ways, An English Honeymoon, In Chateau Land,* and *A Rose of Old Quebec.*

The field in which she became best known, however, and the one which she made particularly her own, is that of America in Colonial and Revolutionary days. The material for these publications she obtained through much careful study and research, both at home and in

England. The result of her long-continued work on the manners, customs, and society of America in the seventeenth and eighteenth centuries was embodied in several interesting volumes. These included *Through Colonial Doorways, Colonial Days and Dames, A Last Century Maid, Life of Martha Washington, Salons Colonial and Republican,* and *Social Life in the New Republic.* One of the best of her books, particularly because of its account of Sulgrave Manor and the Washington background, is *English Ancestral Homes of Noted Americans.* She was associate editor of *Furnaces and Forges in the Province of Pennsylvania,* and wrote *In Old Pennsylvania Towns.*

She ultimately became known as an authority on genealogy. In 1880 she published *The Genealogy of the Wharton Family.* Her keen mind and versatile taste led her from history to its kindred subjects, one phase of which found expression in *Heirlooms in Miniatures,* as well as in magazine articles on artistic and literary subjects.

In 1893 Miss Wharton was a judge of the American Colonial Exhibit at the World's Columbian Exposition at Chicago. She was one of the founders of the Pennsylvania Society of the Colonial Dames of America, and was the first historian of the national society, an office that she held for some years. She received the degree of Litt. D. from the University of Pennsylvania. Miss Wharton died July 29, 1928.

ANNA LANE LINGELBACH

MATILDA HART SHELTON

1846–1894

MATILDA HART SHELTON was born in Philadelphia in 1846. She had intense interest in civic work in her native city, and was for many years engaged in various local activities.

She was a life member of the Pennsylvania Museum and School of Industrial Art, and became a member of the Associate Committee of Women of the Museum in 1888. She served as secretary to that body, and resigned the position only when the pressing duties in connection with her work for the World's Columbian Exposition at Chicago, in 1893, demanded all of her time. Mrs. Shelton was also one of the twelve original managers of the School of Art and Needlework, and later became its secretary.

Her executive ability and tact, as well as her whole life's training—having traveled extensively abroad and at home and having a wide acquaintance with leading women connected with women's interests—fitted her for the appointment, made by Governor Pattison, to be Commissioner of Women's Work of the Board of World's Fair Managers for the State of Pennsylvania. As such Mrs. Shelton had charge of the furnishing of women's rooms of the Pennsylvania State Building and was appointed hostess for the building, but later resigned the position. She was in charge of the installation of the exhibits of woman's work and was also a member of the Board of Lady Managers of the World's Fair. Mrs. Shelton was also president of the Committee of Fine Arts, Painting, Sculpture, Architecture, and Decoration.

The Board of Lady Managers had in its hands all the interests of women in connection with the exposition, as well as entire control of the Women's Building. There were exhibits of women's work from twenty nations.

Her health, undermined by the strain of long hours and heavy responsibilities during her eight months of work at the World's Fair, broke down and brought on her untimely death. During the last few months of her life she had a map of Pennsylvania hung in her bedroom so that her active mind might review the work connected with the collecting of the many exhibits of women's handicraft from the various counties of the state.

MRS. FREDERICK H. SHELTON

ANNA E. BROOMALL

1847–1931

DR. ANNA E. BROOMALL, daughter of John M. and Elizabeth Booth Broomall, was born in Upper Chichester Township, Delaware County, Pennsylvania, on March 4, 1847. She was a descendant of John Broomall, who came from England to East Bradford Township, Chester County, in 1681. Her ancestors on both sides of her family belonged to the Society of Friends.

For a short time she attended a small private school in Chester; then she went to the Kennett Academy at Kennett Square, and was graduated from the Bristol Boarding School on June 20, 1866. Her first ambition was to study law, a tradition of her family, but she eventually decided to take up medicine, and entered the Woman's Medical College of Pennsylvania, in Philadelphia. She was graduated from there in 1871.

Dr. Broomall studied at the Vienna Frauenklinik, where she took courses on the skin, throat, and nose. She became professor of obstetrics at the Woman's Medical College of Pennsylvania in 1879 and, holding this position for twenty-five years, maintained a department second to none in the United States.

During 1877–78 she was a resident physician at the Woman's Hospital, Philadelphia, where she made a reality of the nurses' training school, which had been founded in 1861. In 1883 Dr. Broomall established an office for private practice in Philadelphia. It was due to her efforts that women were appointed medical officers in Pennsylvania. In 1888 she inaugurated the Out-Practice Maternity department at the Woman's Medical College, said to have been the first institution of its kind in America. Dr. Broomall was a pioneer in abdominal surgery in the 1880's. When she first started operating, the manager of the hospital stipulated that one of the men consultants should always be present, but this requirement was soon abandoned.

She entered into many lines of activity within the city of Chester. After her retirement from practice, she became a member of the Delaware County Historical Society in 1915, and the following year was elected a member of the council. The office of curator of the museum and library was established in 1923 by the society, to which position she was elected and which she held to the time of her death on April 4, 1931. Chiefly through her efforts, with the aid of Governor William C. Sproul, the historic old Courthouse, erected in 1724, was restored as a shrine of the founders of the state and nation.

Dr. Broomall published matters of public interest and historic value which would otherwise have failed to be recorded, and many manuscripts, photographs, and drawings relating to the history of Delaware County are preserved as a monument to her memory. She devoted much of the time during her twenty-eight years of retirement to the collection of these historic documents, which she had bound into seventy volumes and bequeathed to the Society.

Dr. Broomall was a member of the various state and county medical associations, the Delaware County Institute of Science, Delaware County Botanical Society, and other organizations.

It was her request that when she died there should be no funeral services and that she be cremated. Her ashes were placed in the Broomall lot in the Media Cemetery.

In 1929 a committee headed by her nephew, Judge John M. Broomall, 3d, established as a memorial in her honor the Broomall Department of Obstetrics as an integral part of the Woman's Medical College and Hospital at Falls of Schuylkill.

MARY B. LUCKIE

EDITH BROWER

1847–1931

FOUNDER of the Wyoming Valley Woman's Club with headquarters in Wilkes-Barre, Edith Brower was a writer, lecturer, and promotor of idealism in private and public life in her community.

As Wilkes-Barre grew past the village stage into a city, she saw the community's neglect of littered streets, unkept yards, uncared-for riverbanks, and lack of parks. She set about to remedy these conditions. Through the organization of the women in sympathy with her ideals into the Town Improvement Society, which later became the Sociological Club, then the Civic Club, and later the Wyoming Valley Woman's Club, she achieved many reforms which did much to make Wilkes-Barre beautiful and civic-minded.

As a musician she was well known for her personal talent, but especially for her interest in and assistance given to other musicians and in the promotion of musical understanding and appreciation in her locality.

Ever ready to welcome newcomers to the city, she made herself known to them and introduced them into congenial circles where they might feel at home and really become a part of the community.

Her work among the foreign-speaking women, with whom she held classes in the study of English and of English literature, brought her in touch with a variety of people of high intelligence whose opportunities were widened through her efforts.

As a writer and speaker, Miss Brower found a ready audience. Her musical criticism and magazine articles were widely published. Through her critical work she became acquainted with the early poems of Edwin Arlington Robinson at the time of their first publication. Her instant appreciation of the value of Robinson's work did much to contribute to the beginning of the general recognition of his poetry, and led to a lifelong friendship.

An idealist, Miss Brower found life-long delight in all beauty, in art, literature, music, and natural surroundings. Born in New Orleans, which her parents left when she was nine months old, she spent the remainder of her long life in the Wyoming Valley. Miss Brower was a direct descendant of Jan Brouwer, who came to New Amsterdam in 1637, whose children changed their name to its present form. Her mother was a member of the Lion Gardiner family of New York, and was one of three sisters famed for their beauty.

About ten years before her death in 1931, Miss Brower prepared her recollections for a series of lectures before the Wyoming Historical Society entitled "Little Old Wilkes-Barre as I Knew It." Full of charm and vitality, these memories give a vivid, personal description of community development typical of many localities in our country.

FRANCES DORRANCE

SARA YORKE STEVENSON

1847–1921

SARA YORKE STEVENSON, a pioneer in the activities of women in public life, was a leader whose influence was far-reaching along civic and educational lines. Rarely gifted, she possessed a magnetic personality, unusual executive ability, and indomitable energy.

Sara Yorke was born in Paris, February 19, 1847. Through her father, Edward Yorke, she was descended from Thomas Yorke, who came to America in 1728, and settled in Berks County, Pennsylvania, and from Peter Stillé, the pastor of Old Swedes Church in Wiccaco. Her mother, Sarah Hanna, was the daughter of an Irish planter in Louisiana.

At the age of fifteen, Sara went to Mexico, where she lived with her family from 1862 to 1867. Her memories of those years she later published in a book called *Maximilian and Mexico*. Later she came to Philadelphia to live with an aunt and two uncles, all three over seventy years of age, whose quiet household routine must have seemed a strange contrast to her previous existence. However, she soon met Cornelius Stevenson, to whom she was married in 1870. She was an excellent housekeeper and entered with spirit into the social life for which her education in Paris had well fitted her. Fond of music, she sang and had unusual skill in dancing.

After a few years she began to develop more serious interests. She gave her support to the Educational Home for Indian Boys and Girls, and then to the Old Ladies Depository Association, which afforded self-help to indigent gentlewomen. It was not long before she turned to research and became one of the founders of the Archaeological Association of the University of Pennsylvania, from which grew the University Museum. It was she who started the museum building plan. For ten years she was the secretary and then the president of the Board of Managers.

As early as 1894 she lectured at the University of Pennsylvania, and was the first woman lecturer at the Peabody Museum of Harvard University. She was curator at the University Museum for a number of years, and later at the Pennsylvania Museum. At the World's Columbian Exposition in Chicago she was vice-president of the Jury of Awards for Ethnology, while in 1898 she made a trip to Egypt for the American Exploration Society.

She became president of the Oriental Club, had the rare honor of being elected a member of the American Philosophical Society, was the first woman given an honorary degree by the University of Pennsylvania, and was made an Officer of Public Instruction by the French Government. She was the first president of the Equal Franchise Society of Pennsylvania. When the Civic Club was organized she became its first president, and with the help of an unusually fine group of women inaugurated a movement that became national in its scope. From 1894 to 1901 she was the only woman trustee of the Commercial

Museum. She was the first president of the Society of Little Gardens, was president of the Alliance Francaise, and was one of the original members and for twenty-five years president of the Acorn Club.

In 1913–14 she was at the same time the head of the Acorn Club, the Civic Club, and the Contemporary Club. From 1915 to 1920 she was vice-chairman of the Emergency Aid and chairman of its French War Relief Committee, which raised $1,500,000. In gratitude for her work on behalf of France she was given the Cross of the Legion of Honor. From 1908 till the time of her death she was literary editor of the *Public Ledger* as well as the contributor of "Peggy Shippen's Diary." For thirteen years these columns afforded never-failing interest to many whom she could never have reached so effectively in any other way. Her keen wit, wide acquaintance, and rich experience enabled her to wield extensive influence.

On the occasion of her seventieth birthday a large number of the most distinguished citizens of Philadelphia gathered to do her honor at a luncheon, while on her seventy-fourth birthday a group of ardent admirers presented her with a bas-relief of herself, the work of R. Tait McKenzie. On November 15, 1921, she was to have sat next to Marshal Foch at a luncheon, but death on the eve of his arrival put an end to her extraordinary life of activities.

ANNA LANE LINGELBACH

ELIZABETH LLOYD

1848–1917

ELIZABETH LLOYD, who was born near Dolington, Bucks County, December 25, 1848, began to read early in life, and when she entered school at the age of seven she was placed in the third reader class. She became a teacher and served in the schools (principally Friends' schools) of Pennsylvania for a period of thirty years. A literary genius that early manifested itself found expression in reportorial work for a weekly newspaper. Later she wrote articles under the nom de plume of Ruth Craydock.

In the early seventies, she began work on a story for children embodying Friends' principles. While a teacher at Buckingham, Bucks County, she completed the necessary chapters, and from the press came *The Old Red School House*. Newspapers and magazines frequently published her poems. One of the most widely known, "The Song of the Twentieth Century," received from President Benjamin Harrison a special encomium. The lyric was inspired by the President's words: "Christ in the heart, and His love in the Nation, is the only cure for the ills which threaten us today."

On October 23, 1883, Miss Lloyd added to her reputation as an able teacher and writer through the reading of a paper on the schools of Buckingham, at Buckingham Meeting. Miss Lloyd was for many years associate editor of the *Friends' Intelligencer*.

She died at Germantown, May 27, 1917, and was buried at Buckingham.

C. F. Hoban

LOUISE DESHONG WOODBRIDGE
1848–1925

Louise Deshong—Mrs. Jonathan Edwards Woodbridge—was descended from an illustrious French family. Of the fifth generation from Pierre Deshong, who came to the United States in the early eighteenth century, her grandfather, John Deshong, married Mary Odenhelmer; his son, John Odenhelmer Deshong, Mrs. Woodbridge's father, married Emmaline Terrell. He owned many acres in the heart of the city of Chester. Those inherited by his eldest son, Alfred O. Deshong, surrounding the family mansion, have been given to Chester for a public park. On these grounds Mr. Deshong erected and endowed a memorial art gallery to house his collection of paintings, bronzes, and ivories.

Louise Deshong was born in Chester, February 6, 1848, and was graduated from Brooke Hall, Media, June 24, 1865, winning the gold medal for scholarship given by Miss Maria L. Eastman, the principal. She was married in St. Paul's Church, Chester, to Jonathan Edwards Woodbridge, May 23, 1876.

She planned a beautiful home on inherited acres at Fourteenth and Potter streets. There she dispensed hospitality in a house filled with objects of art which she brought from her travels about Europe, Syria, Palestine, and Egypt. This property, she willed, just as she left it, as a home for gentlewomen.

She was a charter member of the New Century Club of Chester, founded in 1893, and president for two years. Her last act, the day she died, was to sign a paper giving land at Fifteenth and Upland streets, for a club house. It is now erected. The furnishing of the platform remains as a memorial to her.

Her greatest literary contribution to Chester was the Afternoons With Science which she organized in 1901 and conducted for twenty-four years in her own hall on Edgemont Avenue. Weekly meetings came to a seasonal climax with coaching trips, botanical and geological, to the grounds of notable estates and other places of interest. These were the first garden days.

Mrs. Woodbridge was a member of the Woman's Auxiliary Committee of Pennsylvania for the Columbian Exposition in Chicago, 1893, and received its gold medal. She was a member of the New Century Club of Philadelphia, Botanical Society of Pennsylvania, University Museum, Pennsylvania Academy of the Fine Arts, Philadelphia Art Alliance, Transatlantic Society of Philadelphia, Atlantic Union of London, St. Paul's Protestant Episcopal Church, Chester, and chairman of the board of trustees of the Young Women's Christian Association of Chester.

She died suddenly on October 31, 1925, and was buried in Chester Rural Cemetery.

A. MARGARETTA ARCHAMBAULT

ANNE HEYGATE-HALL

1849–1936

※

ANNE HEYGATE-HALL was born in Northampton, England, in 1849. Three years later her parents came to America, bringing with them their three little daughters. The father of the little family was engaged in engineering work, but also operated a farm. Soon death called him, and Mrs. Heygate-Hall was left with the care of her family in a strange land.

She settled in Philadelphia and soon after opened in her home, at 1208 Walnut Street, a school in which along with her other pupils she educated her daughters. She was a highly cultivated woman, and her success in this work is sufficient testimony to her courage, energy, intelligence, and intellectual insight in the care of the young.

All of these characteristics appeared in marked degree in Anne, who later, for a short time, attended the public school in the neighborhood, afterward becoming a teacher, then a principal. Here her ability was soon noted and she was appointed assistant principal in the School of Practice of the Philadelphia Normal School, later its principal. This latter position she held for twenty-eight years. Under her administration the school became one of the most notable in the city. Children of privileged families sought admission as their parents wished to place them under the care of this remarkable woman. Thousands of men and women today, now parents and grandparents, remember her wise administration, her sympathetic and inspiring attitude toward the problems of childhood, a task for which Miss Hall was unusually fitted. Her influence over the young women who came to her for guidance in mastering the profession of teaching was notably helpful and discerning. Her tact and kindliness in criticism of their faults, combined with her high intellectual ideals, never failed to inspire in them the wish to overcome their weaknesses and to attain higher standards. Her dignity and impressive personality won the respect of her students, awakened their ambition, and led them to desire to win her praise.

In her middle life she became associated with the Protestant Episcopal Church of St. Mark at Locust and Sixteenth streets. There she was for forty years a member of the parish and her devotion to its spirit and interest ceased only with her death.

One of Anne Hall's characteristics was her sense of humor, a chief mark always of the creative personality. Those with whom she maintained an unbroken friendship in the years of her long life, and they were many, can never forget the amusing sayings, the humorous allusions, the quick turn of thought that made her spoken or written word something to be remembered. She had a genius for friendship and a long roll might be called of those who knew her as a friend and will always honor her memory.

After retiring from her work as a teacher, Anne Hall continued for many years her service to children as executive secretary of the Philadelphia Child Welfare Society. In innumerable activities in connection with this society she continued to give help to those who needed her. As a life member of the New Century Club of Philadelphia, she was active almost to the end of her life, always a welcome companion by reason of her social qualities and her effervescent wit.

She never became an American citizen, owing to the curious and illuminating fact that before the question of "votes for women" had become vital in our national life, the matter was not seriously considered in respect to educators.

During the Great War she associated herself with the Daughters of the British Empire, aiding in their work with her accustomed energy. At the close of the war, with her advancing years and her record of work accomplished, Miss Hall thought it best, apparently, not to alter her status. But from her earliest years she had been true to the ideals of America. Of her it may be fitly said: "They that be wise shall shine forever as stars in the firmament."

PAULINE W. SPENCER

MATILDA CAMPBELL MARKOE

1849–1937

⊁⊰

MATILDA CAMPBELL MARKOE was born in Philadelphia on June 12, 1849, and lived there throughout her long life. When she entered society she captivated everyone, young and old. At the age of eighty-eight the curls were still about her head and behind her ears. Her smile and contagious laugh, her quickness at repartee, her intelligence, and her gay air always gathered a circle of admirers.

While Tilly Campbell lost nothing of her gay manner, she deepened in faith and ripened in intelligence with the years. She gained a full grasp of Christian doctrine and entered with devotion into the worship and activities of the church. Mission work in particular appealed to her.

With the opening of the Civil War she supported the Northern cause and, a few years after the soldiers had returned, married John Markoe, a colonel in Grant's army. During the twenty-two happy years of her marriage Matilda Markoe, hospitable, beloved by all who knew her, developed in mind and spirit. She was an able woman and had a brilliant mind; always a reader, broad in her sympathies, with a good memory, she was an exceptional conversationalist. Her devotion to the church, her interest in theological subjects, her zeal for missions, were evident to all her friends.

Her house on Locust Street in Philadelphia was spacious, open, hospitable, homelike, and easy. Few houses in this country have received a more varied, interesting, and distinguished company. Strangers from other lands, especially England, were brought to meet Mrs. Markoe. Literary men and women, soldiers, men of large affairs, bishops and missionaries, looked her up and received her welcome.

It was a rare missionary bishop who did not come soon after his consecration to receive her encouragement. While she gave most generously of her income and at times of her principal to the routine calls of the church and the missionary budget, she had that rare faculty of discovering or feeling just where an unexpected gift would help and cheer. Many are the missionaries and charitable workers who have found unexpected checks in their mail.

From its inception in 1866, the Indians' "Hope Association," founded to help Bishop Hare, claimed her leadership. She called herself and was called the Grandmother of the Woman's Auxiliary, and there is probably no woman in the church who has attended more of the meetings of the Auxiliary than she. Her interest in the meetings of the General Convention and her intelligence in the subjects discussed were lasting.

For half a century the Island of Mount Desert was a mecca for summer pilgrims from all over the country and from England. She was a trustee and reader for the local library, an officer of the Red Cross, supporter of the Sea Coast Missionary Society, and as keen throughout August to encourage foreign missions and church work as in Lent.

One cannot run over the list of missions, missionaries, parishes, church institutions, and charitable objects in which she had personal interest and for which she gave in thought, prayer, and contribution without seeming to exaggerate, but the records are evidence. Her richest gift to the church and to her friends was her life.

GERTRUDE HOUSTON WOODWARD

SARAH TYSON RORER

1849–1937

SARAH TYSON was born in Richboro, Pennsylvania, was educated at East Aurora Academy, and in 1871 married W. Albert Rorer, of Philadelphia. Her first work as a teacher of domestic science in the city was done under the auspices of the New Century Club, in 1881.

At the end of three years she founded the Philadelphia School of Cookery and Diet. This school grew so rapidly that she soon found it necessary to add a faculty of six special teachers. She then established a course of lectures given once a week to the nurses at the Woman's Hospital and to students at the Woman's Medical College. Gradually a number of evening schools and guilds for interne work for normal graduates were organized. This normal course embraced chemistry and the nutritive value of foods; physiology, theoretical and practical cookery, comparative study of fuels and foods, dietaries, planning and serving of meals, food as it relates to health and disease, hygiene, sanitation, manufacturing, milling, marketing, keeping of accounts, lesson plans, public school methods, demonstration and the art of teaching.

It was in 1886 that the famous *Philadelphia Cook Book* was published, and in that same year Mrs. Rorer formed a partnership with Mr. Finley Acker in the publication of *Table Talk*, a monthly magazine on cookery and the household arts. She retired from its editorial staff in 1893 to join Dr. Leffman, Dr. Charles M. Seltzer, and George H. Buchanan, as co-editor of *Household News*. This in turn was purchased by the *Ladies' Home Journal*, and Mrs. Rorer became household editor of that magazine, serving for fourteen years.

At the suggestion of several well-known physicians in Philadelphia she established a diet kitchen where prescriptions for foods in special diseases could be filled in a scientific manner.

For years Mrs. Rorer was in constant demand throughout the United States as a lecturer. She had charge of the Home Economics Kitchen at the World's Fair in Chicago in 1893, at the St. Louis World's Fair in 1904, and received an invitation to demonstrate her work at the Paris Exposition in 1900.

LUCRETIA L. BLANKENBURG

JENNIE AUGUSTA BROWNSCOMBE

1850–1936

JENNIE AUGUSTA BROWNSCOMBE was born in Honesdale, December 10, 1850, the daughter of William Brownscombe, a native of Devonshire, England, and of Eliza Kennedy, whose ancestors settled in Massachusetts in 1630; her maternal great-grandfather having taken part in the Revolution.

Jennie Brownscombe was educated in the public schools and under private tutors in Honesdale. After teaching there for two years she became a student, successively, at Cooper Institute, at the National Academy of Design, and at the Art Students League, New York.

In 1882 she went to Paris and studied there under Henry Mosier. Afterward she went to Italy, where during five winters she had a studio in Rome. She painted in both oil and water color. Her first sale of an oil painting was from the Academy Exhibition in New York in 1876.

Her work received national and international recognition. She specialized in historical subjects. Her canvas, "The First American Thanksgiving," is in the collection of the Museum of Pilgrim Hall at Plymouth, Mass., and "The Peace Ball" is in the Newark Museum. Her genre "Children Playing in an Orchard" hangs in the school at Honesdale and is the source of pride and delight to the children of the town. Her portrait of Captain James Ely Miller is at Yale University.

In 1900 several of her paintings were included in the Royal Academy Exhibition in London. Among the best of her many canvases owned in England, are "The Gleaners" and "Washington's Return to Mount Vernon." A number of her historical figure-subjects have been reproduced as etchings. She was devoted to her profession and attained a distinguished position in the world of art.

She died in New York City in August 1936, at the age of eighty-six.

Harriet Sartain

FLORENCE EARLE COATES

1850–1929

As a poetess, Florence Earle Coates was known as well in England as she was in this country. As a personality, with her keenness of mind, her ability as a raconteur, her stately suavity of manner, she was a distinguished figure in the cultural life of Philadelphia.

She was born in Philadelphia, July 1, 1850, the daughter of George H. and Ellen Frances Van Leer Earle. Her father, a noted lawyer, was the son of Thomas Earle, the philanthropist. She was an aunt of the recent governor of Pennsylvania. Educated in private schools and at the Convent of the Sacred Heart in Paris, she studied music in Brussels with the tenor, Dupré, intending to devote herself to music and art. In 1872 she married William Nicholson, who died in 1877. She was married again on January 7, 1879, to Edward Horner Coates, financier and publicist, who from 1890 to 1906 was president of the Pennsylvania Academy of the Fine Arts.

Mrs. Coates had many talents which endeared her to her friends. Her home, first in Germantown and later at 2024 Spruce Street, was a picturesque center where one always found brilliant conversation among interesting guests. She and her husband took an active interest in local literary affairs, and were among the founders of the Contemporary Club. She was also president of the Browning Society of Philadelphia from 1895 to 1903, and again in 1907–08. While a lover of art she was in addition an accomplished musician, a talented amateur actress, a magnificent reader and interpreter of Shakespeare, and a strikingly beautiful woman. Her portrait by Violet Oakley, entitled "The Tragic Muse," won the gold medal of honor at the San Francisco Exposition.

From childhood she found her chief delight in poetry. On Matthew Arnold's first visit to this country she met him at the home of Andrew Carnegie in New York where they formed a lasting friendship. When Mr. Arnold and his wife came to Philadelphia they were the house guests of the young Mr. and Mrs. Coates in Germantown. On their subsequent visits to America the Arnolds always stayed at the Coates'. It was Matthew Arnold who encouraged Mrs. Coates to develop her gifts as a lyric poet. The encouragement of this great English poet and critic at a formative time was most fruitful. His influence upon her work was one of indelible felicity. It was not long before her poems were appearing in leading magazines in this country and in England. They appeared in collected editions in 1898 and in two volumes published in 1916. Other volumes of verse were: *Mine and Thine* (1904); *Lyrics of Life* (1909); *The Unconquered Air and Other Poems* (1912); and *Pro Patria* (1917). Some of her best verse is found in the fine nature poetry inspired by her Adirondack summer home, Elsinor, at St. Regis Lake, and among her patriotic poems written during the Great War. Many of her lyrics were set to music.

She was intensely interested in promoting friendship between Great Britain and this country, and was an active member of the Transatlantic Society of America. She was also a member of the Society of Mayflower Descendants and of the Colonial Dames of America.

Mrs. Coates' high ideals and her love of beauty remain for us in her poems, and her personal charm in the portraits by Miss Oakley and by John McClure Hamilton. She died in Philadelphia on April 6, 1929.

Mary Eleanor Roberts

BLANCHE DILLAYE

1851–1932

❧❧

Blanche Dillaye, Philadelphia's first woman etcher, a founder and first president of the Plastic Club and a founder of the Water Color Club, was born in Syracuse, September 4, 1851. She was the daughter of Stephen D. and Charlotte Malcolm Dillaye.

Her early schooling was obtained under her aunt in Miss Bonney and Miss Dillaye's school in Philadelphia at 1615 Chestnut Street. There at the age of eighteen she began her work as an art teacher, later becoming head of the department when the institution changed its name to the Ogontz School. Further instruction in her profession she received at the hands of Stephen Parrish, Pennell's teacher, and under Thomas Eakins at the Pennsylvania Academy of the Fine Arts. For three years, beginning in 1900, she worked under Leandro Garrido. Her favorite subjects were poetic and dramatic nocturnes, and the painting and etching of trees.

With her French-American heritage of nervous energy, Miss Dillaye remained an active force in art circles until her death in her eighty-first year. For many years she had served both the Water Color Club and the Fellowship of the Pennsylvania Academy of the Fine Arts as vice-president, frequently exhibiting in major showings of water colors and etchings, in both of which fields she won renown.

Recognition of the quality of her work first came in 1895 when she won a silver medal for etching at the Atlanta Exposition, though prior to this she had won an award from the Philadelphia Art Club. These honors were followed in 1902 by a silver medal from the American Artists Society, and in 1903 by a silver medal for etching at the International Exposition in Lorient, France. In 1913 she won a gold medal for water color at the Conservation Exposition in Knoxville for "Still Evening in the Little Street." In 1927 a comprehensive exhibition of her work was held in the Plastic Club, where a reception was given in her honor.

Miss Dillaye is represented in the water-color collection of the University of Syracuse and in the Syracuse Museum of Fine Arts.

GERTRUDE BOSLER BIDDLE

KATE CASSATT McKNIGHT

1852–1907

IN 1890 a few Pittsburgh women met to talk over certain conditions in their environment which unescapably reacted upon the health and comfort of their families. This group, known as the Woman's Health Protective Association, was the first civic organization in the state of Pennsylvania. It had as its object the desire for a garbage removal ordinance, a smoke ordinance, and an ordinance against spitting in public places. The first vice-president was Kate Cassatt McKnight. No citizen of any time had a more altruistic soul or a more inspired vision. Without her initiative, her wide acquaintance, and her instinctive knowledge of the right person for each committee, the Health Protective Association would have failed to carry out the high aims of its founders.

After five years of service, the Health Protective Association began to feel that its mid-Victorian name was out of date and its somewhat mid-Victorian methods outgrown. It was therefore favorable to the suggestion that it become the Social Service department of the newly organized Twentieth Century Club. A committee from both agreed, however, that the community had been educated to the point of accepting the widespread activities of a civic club, and it had the happy inspiration to include both men and women, so by a process of evolution the Health Protective Association became the Civic Club of Allegheny County. Miss McKnight was the first vice-president and at the time of her death in August 1907 was president, the only woman elected to that office.

The Civic Club was firmly of the opinion that women should have a voice in the management of the public schools. In answer to its call, Miss McKnight, who was always ready to assume burdens where the community was concerned, shocked society and paralyzed the school board of her ward by becoming a candidate for school director. She was elected and devoted many of her crowded hours to the improvement of the school buildings, looking after finances, and employing teachers. The organization of Children's Leagues of Good Citizenship in her own and other ward schools with the salute to the flag proved a proper corollary to the introduction of the national anthem in the schoolrooms.

The present-day cafeteria in the public schools testifies to the efforts she made to provide wholesome food at the various school buildings with diet kitchens as a substitute for outside bakeries. Courses of lectures, the Parent Teachers associations, efforts to increase the efficiency of the public schools through coöperation with the Central Board of Education, and the consideration of school legislation were successive steps among the numerous projects she developed in behalf of the children and in the interest of better schools.

In a comparatively short space of time her inspiring leadership was responsible for the initiation of many varied movements. During her term of office as president of the Civic Club she organized the Permanent Civic Committee composed of two representatives each from the different women's clubs. Later this committee became the Congress of Women's Clubs of Western Pennsylvania, with an enrollment of thousands of club women who enjoyed a club house of their own.

She was instrumental in the creation of the department of Home Economics in State College, Pennsylvania, where a permanent scholarship in home economics was established by the State Federation of Women's Clubs, of which she was president for four years, 1903–07. She was active in the establishment of public baths and playgrounds in Pittsburgh and Allegheny, and was intensely interested in the success of the public schools. In addition, she was one of the founders of the Twentieth Century Club, the Business Women's Club, and the Juvenile Court Association, the Associated Charities, Consumers' League of Western Pennsylvania, the Young Men's Civic Club of Allegheny, the Newsboys' Home, and the Child Labor Association of Western Pennsylvania.

A charming personality and brilliant intellectual endowments made Kate Cassatt McKnight from early womanhood a prominent figure in the social and civic life of the city of Pittsburgh and the state of Pennsylvania. Few women were more admired and beloved than she or enjoyed greater social prestige and success. Her alert mind and broad vision made her a woman ahead of her time. Her tastes ran to civic, educational, and charitable works, and her position was such that she was able to gratify her ambition to work for the interest of the city which she loved. Her ceaseless activity directed toward the cultivation and revival of patriotism and civic virtue can be traced through an illustrious ancestry. On the maternal side her great-grand-father Ebenezer Denny was first treasurer of Allegheny County and first mayor of Pittsburgh, and her great-great-grandfather was General James O'Hara, first Quartermaster General of the United States Army. On her paternal side her great-grandfather, Joseph McClung, owned one of the first foundries in Pittsburgh. The name of Kate Cassatt McKnight appeared high on the rôles of the Pennsylvania Chapter of Colonial Dames and the Pittsburgh Chapter of the Daughters of the American Revolution.

Miss McKnight's high ideals, patriotism, devotion, loyalty, and faith in the city which her forefathers had founded formed the underlying principles of her work and proved the altar upon which she laid her life as a sacrifice. Her vigorous activities in behalf of the child laborers in the state, her valiant support of Florence Kelly's great work in the Consumers' League, and her last supreme effort to federate the charities of Allegheny County were the depleting forces that weakened her physical strength. It was with sorrowful pride that the city of Pittsburgh through its chosen representatives paused to pay tribute to the priceless value of a living ideal as expressed in those real desires for the common good that were quickened and brought into life by the distinguished service of this gifted woman.

MARIE DERMITT

MARY ARTHUR BURNHAM

1853-1928

ᘏᘔ

As a member of the Women's Committee for the Centennial Exposition, Mary Burnham's natural ability came to the front. In 1877,
with others of that committee, she became one of the charter members of the New Century Club of Philadelphia, the first woman's club
in the state, the pattern for many since formed and the earliest to
possess its own home. Her interest in club affairs never flagged. She
was always ready in emergencies with wise advice and financial assistance.

Successively she was member of the board, vice-president and honorary vice-president, although never accepting the highest office, by
her own wish. The New Century Guild for Business Women is to
a great extent a memorial to her wise belief that similar opportunity
should be provided for those who could not afford membership in
the larger club.

With the beginning of the century, women's interest in political
matters increased, urged on by the great need of reform in Philadelphia city government. The Women's Committee for the City Party
was formed, Miss Burnham taking a leading part on its executive
board as well as doing the active work in her own ward. Later, as
its successor, the Women's League for Good Government, grew to
be a permanent organization, she continued to be a notable adviser
and inspiration in this preparatory work for women's actual partici-
pation in the suffrage.

Through all these years, and until the Nineteenth Amendment
was ratified in 1919, equal suffrage was perhaps Miss Burnham's
greatest interest. In the Woman's Suffrage Party she was always a
loyal member, a liberal contributor, encouraging and advising those
who did the more active work. After woman's suffrage was an accomplished fact, the National Woman's Party claimed a great share
of her attention.

Love of music led her to be one of the original guarantors of the
Philadelphia Orchestra. The Society for Organizing Charity, later
the Family Society, can be proud to remember that largely through

her influence and wise planning it was reorganized on its present basis and Miss Mary Richmond brought to Philadelphia as its director.

Her interest extended to international affairs. Before the First World War, the Peace and Arbitration Society counted her as an eager member, and she continued her belief in peace through international coöperation and justice logically by sponsoring the League of Nations Association. She also joined the Women's International League for Peace and Freedom.

Many other instances could be given of the far-sighted vision and wise judgment which she gave to all sides of civic and national affairs. With wealth at her command she was generous but wise in her giving, thoughtful of individual needs as well as those of large associations. Mary Burnham will ever be a happy memory of a gracious, wholesome life well spent as friend, benefactor, and citizen.

She died at her home on May 2, 1928, at the age of seventy-five.

ANNA BLAKISTON DAY

MARY MATILDA COHEN

1854–1911

MARY MATILDA COHEN, the daughter of Henry and Matilda Samuel Cohen was born in Philadelphia in 1854 and died in 1911.

At the time of her death a very beautiful tribute by Anne Hollingsworth Wharton was read before the Browning Society, which gives a general idea of her life and works. Miss Wharton first spoke of the "impressive memorial service held by the Women's Press Club at which much was said of Mary Cohen's work in religious, philanthropic, civic and literary lines."

She continued:

It remains for me to speak of her work in the Browning Society of which she was the founder and, we may truly say, the direct inspiration that it afforded for men and women of literary taste.

To provide such a meeting ground and to share with the intellectuals of her day, advantages that came to her in a large measure as an inheritance from a mother deeply and broadly cultured, were, I have always thought, Mary Cohen's reasons for leading a Browning Study Class. It was through the influence of Professor Morris Jastrow, a brilliant young man connected with the University of Pennsylvania, that men came to be admitted and the class then became known as the Browning Society. Mary Cohen was its first President. Then as now many persons well known in science, literature and art gladly gave their time for the pleasure and profit of membership in the Society.

Mary Cohen contributed a number of valuable papers on the more serious and profound of Browning's poems.

In 1891, having served many years as President, she declined to be a candidate for reëlection but continued to serve as Vice-President until within a few months of her death. She was the officer to whom all succeeding Presidents turned for advice, and I may add with truthfulness that she never failed them. . . .

Like Abou Ben Adhem, Mary Cohen could say "Write me as one who loves his fellow men," which was the secret of her influence and her happiness, an influence that was always exerted in the Browning Society, and in the various organizations to which she belonged.

She was a founder of the New Century Club, one of the founders of the Contemporary Club, an honorary member of the Pennsylvania Women's Press Association, and was the president of the Hebrew Sabbath School Society founded by Rebecca Gratz.

EVELINA HEAP GLEAVES

LOUISE WELLES MURRAY

1854–1931

WHEN Raphael Pumpelly, the American archaeologist, returned from one of his Asiatic trips, he spent the winter in Athens, Pennsylvania, writing about his exploration. A niece, Louise Welles, became intrigued by his tales of Eastern cities and long-buried civilizations. She determined to devote her life to exploring the history and archaeology of her native Pennsylvania.

Louise Welles, daughter of Charles Fisher and Elizabeth Laporte Welles, was descended from a Colonial governor of Connecticut and from Bartholomew Laporte, son of the French émigrés who founded Asylum, Pennsylvania. She attended the Athens Academy, the Moravian Seminary at Bethlehem, and Brown's School at Auburn, New York. In 1870 she entered Wells College, Aurora, New York, where she was graduated in 1872. She married Millard P. Murray, June 27, 1876.

Excavations for their home in Athens in 1882 revealed an unusual Indian burial plot containing portrait pottery and skeletal remains of great size. For nearly fifty years thereafter Mrs. Murray followed up the theory that the Andastes or Susquehannocks of Captain John Smith's account were the Indians who left these remains; her last publication, on which she was at work at the time of her death and which was published posthumously, was concerned with this theory.

Stimulated by these archaeological discoveries, she founded the Tioga Point Historical Society, which opened and maintained the Tioga Point Museum. In 1898 this institution was installed in the Spalding Memorial Building.

In addition to her educational work with the museum, she carried on independent researches in local history and for this purpose accumulated at the museum valuable manuscript and other primary sources. In 1903 she published her first study, *The Story of Some French Refugees and Their Azilum, 1793–1800;* in 1908 appeared her most important work, *A History of Old Tioga Point and Early Athens.*

In 1921 she contributed articles to the *American Anthropologist* on the aboriginal sites in and near "Teaoga" (Athens). In 1929 she published *Notes . . . on the Sullivan Expedition of 1799,* a series of documents drawn from the Tioga Point Museum and other archives. In 1931 the Society for Pennsylvania Archaeology, of which she was a charter member and second vice-president, issued as its first publication her *Selected Manuscripts of General John S. Clark Relating to the Aboriginal History of the Susquehanna.*

She was a founder of the Athens Library Club and was active in patriotic and historical societies.

JULIAN P. BOYD

IMOGEN BRASHEAR OAKLEY

1854–1933

⚹

FOR the major part of her seventy-nine years of vivid life, Imogen Brashear Oakley, daughter of Basil Brown Brashear and Catharine Whitacre, and wife of John M. Oakley, made her home in Pennsylvania. Until 1897 she lived in Pittsburgh and thereafter in Philadelphia, where on September 14, 1933 she died.

Within her active bodily frame was housed a unique personality, possessed of many talents, all carefully cultivated and patriotically used.

To the public she was best known as a gallant fighter of civic ills. Through her initiative, and with the coöperation of the Civic Club of Philadelphia, of which she was for many years a valued board member, ordinances regulating the smoke nuisance, unnecessary noise, and a safe and sane Fourth of July were enacted.

As a Colonial Dame, her fight for improved naturalization laws extended her field of battle to Washington. Her interest in civil service reform resulted in her serving for ten years as chairman of the Civil Service department of the General Federation of Women's Clubs. Furthermore, she was the only woman member of the Council of the National Civil Service Reform League.

A practical idealist, with a basic artistic temperament, all of her warfare was for furthering movements for beauty in living conditions, for pure air, a clean city, abatement of noise, unmaimed children, reputable new citizens, justice. Always her attack was constructive in nature, through a careful study in advance of her proposed remedy. Her likeable, easy, unafraid, personal approach to legislators won for her their favorable attention.

As editor of the Art Alliance *Bulletin* and as a committee member of that organization, her artistic bent and creative mind made valuable contributions. The Red Cross, too, was the richer for her aid as one of its impressive speakers in times of need.

She was an excellent public speaker, a clear, concise writer, a writer of verse, a reader and student, a world traveler, a thinker, clear, open-minded, fair, friendly, sociable, and loving gala occasions. At the same time she was a devoted mother, who recognized the artistic talent of her gifted son and saw to it that every possible opportunity should be his for its best development.

L. WALKER DONNELL

LOUISA KNAPP CURTIS

1855–1920

LOUISA KNAPP was born in Newburyport, Massachusetts, in 1855, of a family of seven children. I have often heard her speak of her happy girlhood, for there were numerous cousins in Newburyport and she grew up in the midst of a large circle of young people. Her grandfather and uncles were shipowners, and I remember the many paintings of their ships that hung on the walls of my grandfather's home, as well as fascinating oriental objects that filled his house, the result of voyages to India and China.

Business later brought the family to Boston, and as my mother and her sisters were then full-grown, they looked about for something to do. One sister taught piano in the famous Perkins Institution for the Blind. My mother became private secretary to Dr. Samuel Howe, a learned and considerable person in his own right, though then perhaps better known as the husband of Julia Ward Howe. Many a button my mother sewed on his coats when his illustrious wife was lecturing!

My father's early struggles in the publishing world have often been told, but my mother's share in those difficulties is less well known. Father had developed an obstinate throat infection during his years in Boston, and when we moved to Philadelphia he was underweight, a bundle of nerves and far from strong. My mother, whose life always centered in her home, devoted herself primarily to him, making his health and comfort her first care.

She was extremely intelligent, and as she shared my father's every interest, it is not surprising that soon she was editing a woman's department of his paper, the *Tribune and Farmer*. This was carried on for four years. Then came the establishment of the *Ladies' Home*

Journal. My mother was its chief editor for six years. Her knowledge of home economics and her grasp of the whole range of a woman's interests fitted her for this work. When she laid down the editorship there were 450,000 subscribers to that magazine, an astonishing circulation for those times. I have heard her tell that her reason for giving up this work was that I, then aged thirteen, came to her one day and said, "Oh mamma, whenever I want you, you have a pen in your hand." She took this as a reproach, and went at once to my father, saying that he must look for another editor.

When Edward Bok succeeded my mother as editor of the *Ladies' Home Journal,* she did not lose touch with the magazine. My father had always brought his business problems home, and he continued to do so. Mother's warm hospitality was enjoyed by many of his business associates, and authors and writers were frequent guests in our home. My parents were always reading something. They read newspapers, magazines, and books, aloud and to themselves. Dickens was much in our midst, thanks to Mother, and the names of his characters were allotted to many of our acquaintances. Her executive ability was evident in everything she did. She was an excellent cook, a meticulous housekeeper, and could manage groups of people. When she joined a woman's club, a literary society, or a church organization, she invariably became its president in a short time.

My parents were devoted to their church and were regular in attendance. Father was always interested in church music, and many a fine choir was brought into being through his efforts. I remember so well, sitting in a pew as a little girl during the singing of hymns, hearing my father sing the baritone part, always correctly in a pleasing voice, and my mother in her rich contralto singing with evident joy and extremely well—so well, in fact, that always many of the congregation turned around to locate her voice, while I (shame on me!) shiveringly wavered between a feeling of deep mortification that Mother would do anything to call such attention to herself and an intense pride in her performance!

I would say that her salient characteristics were her great-hearted love for humanity in general and for her family in particular, her keen intelligence, her executive ability, her generosity, and a complete lack of ego. From the time she relinquished her editorial work she devoted herself ever more closely to her family and her home, for the happy companionship between my parents did not cease when the goal of business success was reached. They traveled a good deal; went several times to Europe and once to Egypt. As my father was always an ardent yachtsman, they spent much time on the water, especially when at their summer home in Maine. I believe their happiest days together were those in Maine.

Mother was somewhat of an invalid the last years of her life. When her physical activity was curtailed, she did not complain, but devoted herself to a study of the needs of the underprivileged. Many a young person was then helped by her to an education, many a sufferer was given hospital or convalescent care. Flowers from her greenhouses were sent, not in the line of social obligation, but to sorrowing, weary, ill people, many of whom she knew but slightly. Her generous thought for others never ceased until her death in 1910.

MARY LOUISE CURTIS BOK

LUCY DORSEY IAMS

1855–1924

"CITIZEN extraordinary" for nearly half a century, Lucy Dorsey Iams gave herself with devotion and utter unselfishness to advancing good causes, many of which are now written on the statute books of Pennsylvania and incorporated into the common experience of this generation.

She dreamed dreams and saw and realized visions in places where it was thought nothing could be done. She looked ahead to future years when she wrote into the laws of Pennsylvania provisions that would protect the homes of the tenement dwellers. Sanitation, building laws, and public baths would have passed by many in our city's life if it had not been that she saw how they touched the home, the father, the mother, and the child. She saw to it that women in industry were accorded the consideration that the mothers of tomorrow require.

The social need to be met in every city and state were hardly secondary to the bodily needs. The children and women who pass through the Magistrates' courts, desertion and non-support cases, habitual truancy and the Juvenile Court were matters of great concern to Mrs. Iams; and her thought and work as expressed in legislation covered their sundry needs. The Industrial School at Thornhill and the State Reformatory for Women and Farm Colony at Laurelton are monuments to her effort. Prison reform was not a new idea with her. She had a part in every effort to improve facilities for the jail and penitentiary population. It was the one and most absorbing thought of her last days following her appointment to the State Prison Board.

The creation of the departments of Labor and Industry and of Public Welfare and the effort she put into the commission appointed by Governor Sproul for the revision of the Constitution formed a part of her state legislative activities. It was her proposal written into a legislative measure which has permitted women to use the seal of notary public in Pennsylvania. This was long before the days of woman's suffrage for which she later actively campaigned.

Mrs. Iams gave her loyal support to the Federal Government during the World War, and through her inspiration and effort the Pittsburgh Employment Bureau, among the best of its kind in the country, was organized. In peacetime the Federal Children's Bureau and laws governing the immigrant and the steerages; alien admission to this country; federal aid for vocational training and a department of Education with representation in the Cabinet were among the projects she furthered. This list is by no means complete, for her part in the struggle to gain governmental protection of forest and national park reserves and Niagara Falls expressed the side of Mrs. Iams that reached out for the right to play and the opportunity to enjoy the beautiful.

Her outstanding service was twenty-two years as first vice-president and chairman of the Legislative Committee of the Civic Club of Allegheny County, and chairmanships of the Legislative committees of the General Federation and Pennsylvania State Federation of Women's Clubs during that time.

To carry out her multitudinous welfare activities, Mrs. Iams did not walk alone, but joined hands with agencies through whom she exercised her wonderful genius. She fought many battles single-handed, but in the majority of her endeavors she was carrying on through the organized forces in which she believed and in whose name many brilliant achievements were accomplished.

Mrs. Iams was born in Oakland, Maryland, on November 13, 1855, the daughter of Mr. and Mrs. James Dorsey. She came to Allegheny County and settled in Pittsburgh. There she was married August 12, 1877, to Franklin P. Iams, and there she died on October 26, 1924.

MARIE DERMITT

ELIZABETH ROBINS PENNELL

1856–1936

≍

ELIZABETH ROBINS PENNELL, who died in New York City on February 7, 1936, after achieving for herself a distinguished place in the world of letters, was always proud of the fact that she was by birth a Pennsylvanian, although she spent an important portion of her life in Europe. She was born in Philadelphia on February 21, 1856, the daughter of Edward Robins, a banker, and the granddaughter of Thomas Robins, for many years president of the Philadelphia National Bank. It was in the Convent of the Sacré Coeur, Conflans, France, and later at Eden Hall, Torresdale, that she received her education. One of her classmates at the latter institution was Agnes Repplier, destined to become one of her most intimate friends.

Elizabeth was urged, when she reached womanhood, to attempt an author's career, by a relative, Charles Godfrey Leland, the author of the "Hans Breitmann" ballads and an authority on gypsy lore. Through his influence Thomas Bailey Aldrich, then the editor of the *Atlantic Monthly,* asked her to submit an article to him. The result was her first appearance in print with "Mischief in the Middle Ages," which Aldrich praised highly for its scholarly treatment. In after years she produced a biography of Leland, whose encouragement she never forgot. Her venture into magazine work was followed by a book, the *Life of Mary Wollstonecraft.*

In 1884 Miss Robins married Joseph Pennell. She had met him in Philadelphia when the editor of a new magazine called *Our Continent* had asked her to write a series of articles about quaint buildings and sights in the Quaker City to be illustrated by Pennell. Almost immediately after their marriage the Pennells went to Europe and began a literary and artistic career that made them widely known abroad and at home. They were commissioned to furnish for the *Century Magazine* a series of articles, the wife to supply the text and her husband to make the drawings.

One of their assignments required them to ride a tandem tricycle from Florence to Rome, and then to send back to New York a story about it, with pictures. They made the trip, to the astonishment of the Italians, and were arrested in Rome for "riding on a closed thoroughfare." The first book which they issued as co-workers was *Our Canterbury Pilgrimage,* a little paper-covered edition which is now sought by book collectors.

Mrs. Pennell and her husband finally made their home in London, although taking occasional trips to the Continent. Their flat in Buckingham Street, off the Strand, and afterward in Robert Street, Adelphi Terrace, became the center, on their "evenings at home," of literary and artistic London. Whistler, Sargent, Galsworthy, Bernard Shaw, Harold Frederic, Aubrey Beardsley, Barrie, Fisher Unwin and his wife (the daughter of Cobden), H. G. Wells, and many more of the illuminati were glad to accept their hospitality and meet their friends and fellow workers. The two hosts never forgot their American birth and ancestry and new as well as old acquaintances from "the States" were always welcomed.

It was during their residence in London that Mrs. Pennell wrote some of her most important books, including the *Feasts of Autolycus, French Cathedrals* (illustrated by her husband), *Our House and the People in It, The Life of Whistler* (in collaboration with Pennell) and a charming little story from real life entitled *Les Amoureux.* Another book, considered by several critics her best literary achievement, was *Our Philadelphia,* which will be quoted in the future by all chroniclers who may be describing the Quaker City as it was in the Victorian era. During all this time the author was writing art critiques for London journals, attending the opening of art exhibitions, and visiting Paris to see the annual salon.

Shortly before the end of the World War the Pennells gave up their home in London. They resided for a time in Philadelphia and afterward went to Brooklyn, where Mr. Pennell died in 1926. Mrs. Pennell then moved to New York City, where she devoted her time, in part, to editing the *Life and Letters of Joseph Pennell* and to assisting in compiling the catalogues of his etchings and lithographs. She also took great interest in contributing to the Whistler Memorial Collection of the Library of Congress, which her husband had founded and endowed.

EDWARD ROBINS

M. CAREY THOMAS

1857–1935

≫≪

M. CAREY THOMAS, born in 1857, was a pioneer in demanding for women the right to be educated, to take their share of responsibility in the political and economic world and to receive proper recognition of their leadership.

She was gifted with a mind of unusual capacity and a will toward excellence. Graduated from Cornell University, Phi Beta Kappa, at the age of twenty, she was admitted by vote of the trustees of the Johns Hopkins University to the graduate department of Greek, with the condition that she study privately and not enter the regular classes for men. She continued her study in French and German universities and took her doctor's degree *summa cum laude* at the University of Zurich, a distinction not given before to a foreigner or to a woman. Among numerous honorary degrees, she held the only LL.D. awarded to a woman by the Johns Hopkins University.

Her personal achievements are paralleled by the successes to which she spurred other women. She started her career in 1884 as the first dean of the newly founded Bryn Mawr College. As its dean for nine years, president for twenty-eight years, trustee for thirty-two, and president emeritus for thirteen, Miss Thomas insisted on the maintenance of the highest standards in entrance requirements, in faculty work, in graduate and undergraduate schools.

To her may be attributed many of the startling and progressive innovations in women's education—the establishment of the Bryn Mawr Graduate School, with resident and European fellowships; the inauguration of student self-government and the founding of the School for Women Workers in Industry.

In all of her educational work—at Bryn Mawr College; as the first woman trustee of Cornell University; founder of the Association to

Promote Scientific Research by Women and the International Federation of University Women; co-founder of the Bryn Mawr School for Girls, of Baltimore; and worker in the campaign to found the Johns Hopkins Medical School—Miss Thomas worked incessantly for the opening to women of opportunities for higher education and professional work.

In addition to her work as an educator, Miss Thomas took a leading rôle in the political and economic world. She was a valiant worker for woman suffrage from 1906 to its attainment in 1918, president of the National College Equal Suffrage League for sixteen years, and a leader in the League of Women Voters. She was always in the foreground of community life, especially in Montgomery County, Pennsylvania, where she made her home from the opening of Bryn Mawr College to her death. She was an active member of many civic organizations in Philadelphia, among them the College Club, the Acorn Club, the Civic Club, the New Century Club, the Contemporary Club, the Cosmopolitan Club, and the Art Alliance.

Miss Thomas died on December 2, 1935.

CAROLINE CHADWICK-COLLINS

JOANNA WHARTON LIPPINCOTT

1858–1938

JOANNA WHARTON, born in Philadelphia December 16, 1858, was the eldest of the three daughters of Joseph Wharton, portrayed in the Philadelphia *Press* as "the great iron master, patron of education, and littérateur." Her mother was Anna Corbit Lovering, the daughter of Joseph S. Lovering and Ann Corbit whose Colonial country place, beautiful "Oak Hill," near Stenton, later became the country home of their granddaughter Joanna.

Joanna Wharton's childhood years were spent in part at her parents' country home, "Ontalauna," on the Old York Road; in winter at the town house on Twelfth Street near Walnut; and in summer at Newport and Jamestown, Rhode Island.

In 1885 she married Joshua Bertram Lippincott, youngest son of

Joshua Ballinger Lippincott, the Philadelphia publisher. Many literary celebrities of the day, including Mrs. Humphrey Ward, Sir Hall Caine, Sir Gilbert Parker, Sir Ernest Shackleton, John Masefield, and others from abroad, were entertained at "Oak Hill," or in winter at the town house.

There were four children, Joseph Wharton, Marianna (Mrs. William Paul O'Neill), Sarah (Mrs. Nicholas Biddle), and Bertram. When in 1935 Mr. and Mrs. Lippincott happily celebrated their golden wedding anniversary, just as Mrs. Lippincott's parents had done thirty-one years earlier, all of their children and their seventeen grandchildren were present.

Coming from Quaker stock through both parents, Mrs. Lippincott belonged to the Society of Friends, Hicksite branch, attending Meeting at Germantown, Green Street, Abington, and Conanicut Island. Following her grandmother's and her father's lead, she was an active member of the Board of Swarthmore College from 1894 to 1933, and from then until her death was associated as a manager emeritus. Though most interested in Wharton Hall and in the development of the Observatory of the College, for which she founded the Astronomical Research Fund, her enthusiasm extended to all of the College departments. Her keen interest in higher education was also manifested in her contribution of the original Lippincott Library Fund to the Wharton School of the University of Pennsylvania, the School having been founded by her father through gifts to the University dating from 1881 to 1902. Each year she encouraged student enterprise by offering a number of prizes for the most distinguished research theses by members of the graduating class of the School.

She was associated with the work of the Welcome Society of Pennsylvania in restoring Pennsbury Manor, the historic home of William Penn on the west bank of the Delaware River. As a member of the Society's council and of its Pennsbury committee, she was a substantial contributor to their Pennsbury Fund. One of her greatest interests was the Pennsylvania Society of the Colonial Dames, to whose service, as a member of the board, she devoted herself for many years. She was a member also of the Acorn Club. During the World War, like so many Philadelphia women, she did several kinds of war work and participated in many charities.

In 1931 Mrs. Lippincott was the recipient of the honorary degree of Master of Arts from the University of Pennsylvania. She was one of the very few women to hold this degree at that time, and appreciated it especially because of her father's interest in the Wharton School, her husband's long connection with the University as a member of the Board of Trustees and her own association with it as member of the Women's Board.

Two books appeared under her name, *Biographical Memoranda Concerning Joseph Wharton,* published in 1908, and *Speeches and Poems by Joseph Wharton,* published in 1926.

Up to the time of her death, May 16, 1938, following a brief illness at her latest country home, "Melmar," in the Huntingdon Valley, Mrs. Lippincott was just as active as ever. The keynotes of her life had been intense devotion to her family and her friends, continual, generous hospitality, and kindness to those in her service.

JOSEPH WHARTON LIPPINCOTT

KATHERINE MYRTILLA COHEN

1859–1914

KATHERINE COHEN, daughter of Henry and Matilda Samuel Cohen, was born in Philadelphia, March 18, 1859, and died there December 14, 1914. Chiefly known for her sculpture, in which art she was active from 1880 to her death, she was honored by membership in the Fellowship of the Pennsylvania Academy of the Fine Arts, the American Art Association of Paris, and the New Century Club of Philadelphia. She was one of the founders of the Browning Society.

She attended the School of Design for Women and pursued a course of study at various times under different tutors, among them Peter Moran, Sarah Levis, and J. Liberty Tadd; her special branches then being china painting, decorative art work, and modeling. She attended the Academy of the Fine Arts under Thomas Eakins' instruction, and the School of Industrial Art where she followed sculpture under the tuition of John J. Boyle. She thus pursued both leading branches of art; she also studied water color under William J. Whittemore. Later on the famous artist, Augustus St. Gaudens, became her teacher in sculpture. Miss Cohen also added to her studies a course in

Paris under Mencie and other masters, and went a second time to Europe in order to develop still further her knowledge. The results are seen to pronounced advantage in her works.

In sculpture, this artist has produced a number of busts; two representing Venetians, boy and man, which are beautifully wrought; a decorative head entitled "John of Algiers"; "A Viking, or Northman"; "Rabbi Ben Ezra"—a group; portrait busts of several persons, among them Mayer Sulzberger, the accomplished lawyer and scholar; besides statuettes, models, and bas-reliefs.

Miss Cohen's work has been shown at several distinguished exhibitions at the Academy of the Fine Arts and at the Art Club of Philadelphia, the New York Academy, the World's Columbian Exposition in Chicago, and in the Paris Salon. Her paintings as well as her sculpture give evidence of exceptional talent. Among these, chiefly water colors, are "An African Woman"; "Driving Geese at Concarneau"; "Street in Cairo"; and "A Moorish Mosque."

"Miss Katherine Cohen," observes a critic, "shows the stuff of which good sculptors are made." The same remark could be applied to this artist in the field of painting, which calls not only for accuracy and precision but also for beauty of conception, wealth of imagination, and delicacy of treatment. All these requirements Miss Cohen possessed in an eminent degree which enabled her to win a recognized position in the field of art.

EVELINA HEAP GLEAVES

FLORENCE ESTE

1859–1926

FLORENCE ESTE was a radiant daughter of an old Philadelphia family. In youth, desire to express in paint her ecstasy in life becoming dominant, she entered the Pennsylvania Academy of the Fine Arts. Here today live evidences of her personality: water colors in the Academy's collection, and a mural of her inimitable trees that beautifies the arch above the stage in the assembly hall.

In Paris she studied at the atelier Colarossi under Raphael Colin;

later in Brittany she received criticism from Nozal. Soon, however, shaking off all influences that hampered free expression, she spoke in oil and water color with a richness that was utterly her own.

Despite her vivid spirit hers was a life of struggle. Fate in many ways was cruel. It swept away her fortune. It swept away her comrades. It chained her to a foreign soil. But courageously she rose to take her place among the foremost painters of her time.

Florence Este's canvases combine those qualities which mark strikingly that Breton coast where she dwelt so many summers. Her seas have mystery. Her pines reach into the heavens. Topping the long, low stretches of the headlands her houses blink with all the strangeness that is Brittany. Despite her strength in oils—in recognition of which her work is found in the collection of the Luxembourg—one is especially stirred by her mastery of aquarelle. With this perhaps most recalcitrant of mediums she made undying record of the spirit of the Breton coast.

In 1924, at the annual Philadelphia Water-Color Exhibition, Florence Este received the Philadelphia Water-Color Prize, one of the outstanding awards in the field of water-color art. Upon receiving word she wrote, "I have read your letter with amazement and since then joy has come into my heart. To have had this honor given me by an American jury! It is too delightful! I may have some idea of art. I think I have. I know I have. But I am not really much of a water-colorist, you know. Please keep this to yourself most carefully."

Florence Este died in Paris, but it is at Saint Briac that she rests in sleep. There in the village graveyard an inscription tells the story of her life:

FLORENCE ESTE

American Artist 1859–1926
A Painter of this Breton Country

THORNTON OAKLEY

FLORENCE KELLEY

1859–1932

᭐᭐

MRS. FLORENCE KELLEY was known for half a century as a militant opponent of harsh working conditions and child labor, and as a welfare worker who received recognition from high government officials.

She was born in Philadelphia in 1859 and entered Cornell University at the age of sixteen. Following her graduation she studied law and economics at Zurich and Heidelberg. Her admission to the bar of Illinois was a step in her campaign of attack on the child labor conditions in Chicago in the last decade of the nineteenth century.

Her social work was begun in Chicago, where she lived for seven years at Hull House as an associate of Jane Addams. She was deputy investigator for Chicago when the United States Department of Labor made its 1892 survey of slums in large cities. For thirty-three years, until her death, Mrs. Kelley was secretary of the National Consumers League and fostered a nation-wide campaign of public education in the correction of bad working conditions through this organization. Virtually all the aims of a ten-year social program, drawn up by the Consumers League under Mrs. Kelley's direction in 1910, including shorter working days, prohibition of night work, and minimum wage standards for women, have since been realized.

She campaigned vigorously against congestion in the New York slums and for the establishment of a children's bureau at Washington. Newton D. Baker, Secretary of War in 1917, appointed her secretary of the Board of Control of Labor Standards for Army Clothing. She was a former trustee of the National Child Labor Committee and vice-president of the National American Woman Suffrage Association.

Mrs. Kelley died February 17, 1932.

GERTRUDE BOSLER BIDDLE

MINNIE FOGEL MICKLEY

1859–1932

❧❧

MINNIE FOGEL MICKLEY was born at Hokendauqua in 1859. She was the daughter of Edwin Mickley and Matilda Fogel. Her Colonial ancestors were Jean Jaques Michelet, who came from Zweibrueken, in Bavaria, in 1733, and Philip Gabriel Fogel from Hanau, Hesse-Nassau, Germany.

After attending Elmira College, she visited Europe with her sister. In 1892 she became a member of the Daughters of the American Revolution and organized the Liberty Bell Chapter of Allentown, of which she was regent in 1893. That same year, Miss Mickley published the Mickley genealogy. She was fortunate in meeting Dr. Charles Michelet, professor of philosophy at the University of Berlin, with whose assistance the names of all the Mickley families in France, Germany, and Norway in their line from 1444 to 1893 were added.

After her father's death Miss Mickley, accompanied by her mother, made her home in Washington, devoting herself to genealogical research. She was elected registrar general of the Daughters of the American Revolution during Mrs. Fairbank's term of office, and in 1905 and 1906 served as vice-regent of Pennsylvania. Afterward she was business manager of the magazine published by the Daughters of the American Revolution.

She organized the Michelet Chapter of the Daughters of the American Revolution in 1913, a chapter composed of members of the Mickley family. She also organized the Northampton Blues Chapter of U. S. D. of 1812. Of both these chapters she was regent.

Miss Mickley was a member of the Woman's Press Club of Washington, the National Huguenot Society of New York City, the Regents Club of Philadelphia, the Royal Genealogical Society of England, the Michelet Chapter, D. A. R., and the Northampton Blues U. S. D. of 1812. She made several visits to Europe to do research work for clients.

She was a member of the Reformed Church, all of her Colonial ancestors having come to America to enjoy religious liberty. They were Huguenots, Hollanders, Swiss, and Palatines, arriving in the years from 1722 to 1733. The restoration of the tomb of Jean Jaques Michelet and his wife and its conversion into a memorial was arranged by Miss Mickley and dedicated in 1917.

ELEANOR KENT CHANCE

KATE DOUGLAS WIGGIN

1859–1923

Rebecca of Sunnybrook Farm alone would justify the inclusion of Kate Douglas Wiggin in any hall of fame, but she made other very worthy contributions which entitle her to a prominent place among the notable women of Pennsylvania.

She was born in Philadelphia in 1859, and early in life gave evidence of the field in which she would attain eminence. She was a prolific traveler and a keen observer. These characteristics are reflected in her writings. Of equal prominence to her *Rebecca* are *Timothy's Quest* and *The Birds' Christmas Carol*. It is safe to say that both are commonly known to a large proportion of the teachers and school children of the country. Both were translated into eight foreign languages.

Her work in organizing kindergartens which spread from California to the Atlantic coast played a great part in the history of her times.

Perhaps no state in the Union has produced four autobiographers such as Benjamin Franklin, Edward Bok, Maurice Francis Egan, and Joseph Jefferson. In the judgment of many critical readers, Kate Douglas Wiggin's autobiography ranks with these.

In 1881 she married Samuel B. Wiggin of Boston. Although he died in 1889 and she married George C. Riggs of New York City in 1895, she continued to write under her first married name for the balance of her life. Much of her second husband's business was transacted in England, and it was there that she died in 1923.

Although she spent only the first few years of her life in Philadelphia, she retained clear memories of her birthplace to the last. In her *Autobiography* she wrote, "There is fixed in my memory a picture of a great open space filled with trees, a space of winding paths and groups of children that I now know to have been Independence Square in Philadelphia."

C. F. HOBAN

FRANCES ROSE BENÉT

1860–1940

FRANCES NEILL ROSE, daughter of William Rose of Pittsburgh and Mary Lee Mahon of Carlisle, Pennsylvania, though born in Washington, D. C. on October 23, 1860, was a native of Pennsylvania, and was brought to the home of her grandmother, Mrs. John D. Mahon, while still an infant. After this same grandmother moved from Pittsburgh to Philadelphia, Frances or "Fanny," as she was lovingly called by her devoted family circle, grew up in that house where her mother, early widowed, made her home. She was a most lovable and precocious child and when so tiny that she was placed on a table, recited by heart poetry and long passages from Shakespeare. As a growing girl she attended her aunt, Mrs. Sutton's School for Girls in Philadelphia and graduated as the valedictorian of her class.

Few vocations outside the home were open to women in those days and the question of teaching arose when she was twenty. Her first position was as substitute instructor in her cousin, Miss Agnes Irwin's celebrated school in Philadelphia. Then came a request from Dr. Horace Howard Furness, the Shakespearean scholar of his day, that she become the tutor and companion for his small daughter, Caroline, later Mrs. Horace Jayne. Meanwhile, "Fanny Rose" had grown up into a winsome, bewitching blonde with an inexpressible amount of charm.

In the summer of 1882, in company with her mother and sister, she visited Fortress Monroe, Virginia. There she met her fate in the person of an erect, fascinating and highly intellectual young second lieutenant in the light artillery, James Walker Benét. He was the elder son of Brigadier General Stephen Vincent Benét, Chief of the Ordnance Bureau in Washington, D. C. On June 23d, 1883, James Walker Benét and Frances Neill Rose were married and made their first army home at Fortress Monroe, Virginia. Their second station was at Fort

Hamilton, New York City, where a daughter and son were born to them. Here Lieutenant Benét took the exacting examination for the Ordnance Department, a staff corps of the United States Army. At that time an appointment to the Ordnance Department was permanent. Thus, what was then known as the "line" of the army was left behind forever for the more sedate staff posts.

During her husband's varied and executive career of forty years in the service, Frances Rose Benét's life was passed at various arsenals and cities—Springfield Armory; Frankford Arsenal, Bethlehem, Pennsylvania; Watervliet Arsenal, New York; Benicia Arsenal, California; and Augusta, Georgia. In Bethlehem, Pennsylvania, in 1898, a second son, Stephen Vincent Benét, author of *John Brown's Body,* was born. The busy and devoted wife and mother was a natural born homemaker, lending supreme charm to her environment and aiding her husband's official career by every means in her power. In addition to a warm heart and lovely nature, she was highly magnetic, quick-witted, amusing and a delightful conversationalist. Her powers as a raconteur were singular and dramatic and she was gifted from a literary point of view. She wrote easily and brilliantly in both prose and verse for her family and friends on many social occasions and anniversaries but rarely for publication.

Eventually the mother of writers (for her elder son, William Rose Benét early distinguished himself as a poet and her second son's great poem, *John Brown's Body* swept the country in 1929), Frances Rose Benét can best, perhaps, be described as an artist in *living.* There is no doubt that had she chosen to undertake it, she might have gone far as a novelist and short story writer. But she always remarked that she was "too busy *living.*" Her reading to, and with, her children included the powerful in literature, and she was well versed in Shakespeare and the Bible, possessing a marvelous memory.

During the First World War she headed a canteen at Augusta, Georgia, where her husband had his famous Ordnance Camp and gave of her services freely and abundantly. After his retirement from the service in 1921, their home was for two years in Scarsdale, New York, and later in Westtown, Pennsylvania, where her husband died in March 1928. In 1932 Frances Benét spent months in England and France on a trip that yielded her much, mentally and spiritually. Although seventy-two at this time, her mind was as alert, eager, and imaginative as a young girl's, gathering in and giving out to all with whom she came in contact. Indeed, she never, in the slightest sense became old, though invalided in the last two or three years of her life through failing sight.

Her last years—1934 to 1940—were spent at the Westtown Farm House, Pennsylvania, where her loving heart and profound interest in humanity, her unique and interesting narratives of her long, wonderful life, with their humor and power of anecdote, charmed the circle of friends who were privileged to come in contact with her. She rounded out eighty full and rich years and died, suddenly, of a stroke, in Amagansett, Long Island in July 1940. To her children, her grandchildren, great-grandchildren and her legion of friends, the loss of so rare a spirit and mind is irreparable. She has been described as a beautiful and shining personality who "touched nothing that she did not adorn" and no human soul that she did not benefit.

LAURA BENÉT

MARY VAN METER GRICE

1860–1936

MARY VAN METER GRICE was born at Fort Washington in 1860, the daughter of Joseph E. and Catherine B. Van Meter. She married Edwin C. Grice, and as a bride lived in Riverton, New Jersey, where she inaugurated a crusade for better schools, a need made apparent to her in a few years of teaching. The Porch Club and Little Plays were other activities.

On coming to Philadelphia she found larger opportunity and was soon a participant in new movements. In Superintendent of Schools Martin G. Brumbaugh she found hearty coöperation. In the face of opposition Mrs. Grice espoused playgrounds, social centers, and other extra-curricular activities.

In National Parent-Teachers work she realized the benefit in bringing together parents and teachers, and in 1907 founded the Philadelphia League of Home and School Associations, a name she felt had more embracing significance. In three years there were twenty-five thousand members, and the discussion and beginnings of better things for the schools by those early groups were far reaching. It stirs one to appreciate the rare vision, abundant energy, and inspiring leadership of the founder.

Nevertheless she had opposition, but she met it with no bitterness in her heart. "They are sincere," she said, "progress marches, and when they and I are dead those things which I am working for will be consummated."

She was a friend of Jane Addams and other outstanding women who also realized the needs of the times. Those who knew her, see in the widening circle of social forces started or aided by her a never-ending memorial. The rights of children were uppermost for her then, but there was also her work for Americanization, suffrage for women, and the peace movements. She was a militant pacifist. The war meant to her the failure of religion. She said, "We cannot preach the gospel of love and faith and live militarism and distrust God and man." With such expressions she stirred the people and yet was so trusted that she was asked and became hostess at Camp Dix.

Mrs. Grice resigned from the Home and School League in 1919, and from other activities, feeling it in line with age to retire from organizations when there were others younger with newer views able to push forward the work.

She was an early officer of the Civic Club, a charter member of the New Century Club and, in her last (manuscript) book, "Tunnels— Short Cuts to the Light," she tells of the founding in Philadelphia of the General Federation of Women's Clubs. She was a member of the Vice Commission; chairman of the Billy Sunday campaign; appointed by Governor Pinchot to the Old Age Pension and Mothers Assistance Funds; a member of the Birth Control League.

She helped found the Playgrounds Association, Camp Fire Girls, Business Women's Christian League, and worked on the state campaign for increased salaries for teachers. In addition she founded the library in Coral Gables, Florida. She was vice-president of the Women's International League for Peace and Freedom and was with the Emergency Peace Campaign.

Mrs. Grice was a lifelong member of the Church of the Saviour, serving on its Women's Auxiliary. Her brother, the Rev. Allan Van Meter, was executive secretary of the Episcopal Diocese of Pennsylvania. With the Society of Friends she had much in common and belonged to the Fellowship of Reconciliation. One of her last efforts was to forward the coöperative movement in Philadelphia.

Not only in groups did Mrs. Grice's presence inspire others, but she will be remembered in her innumerable personal contacts in which she enriched others' lives with her sweetness of spirit and ever new vision. She gave fullness of service to the world and to members of her family and friends. On May 15, 1936, her active life was translated to the freedom which death meant for her.

EDITH W. PIERCE

CELESTE DE LONGPRÉ HECKSCHER

1860–1928

CELESTE DE LONGPRÉ MASSEY was born in Philadelphia, February 23, 1860, daughter of Robert V. and Julia Pratt Massey, of Irish and French descent. Notable among her earlier ancestors was Louis de Longpré, her great-grandfather, an artist and musician.

She received her early education under private tutors. Her musical predilection became evident at an early age. At ten she had written some pieces for which her singing teacher secured publication. Her musical studies were conducted under Zerdahaly in piano, Albert Lang in composition, and Wassill Leps in orchestration. After producing a number of songs she wrote a suite for violin and piano, "Forest Ride," and the orchestral pantomime "Dances of the Pyrenees." The latter was presented for the first time as a symphonic suite by the Philadelphia Orchestra under Carl Pohlig.

Although ill health caused a suspension of creative activities she was able to resume with further piano and orchestral pieces and a mystical opera in two acts, *The Rose of Destiny,* of which she also wrote the text in 1918.

Mrs. Heckscher for a period was president of the Philadelphia Operatic Society.

On her death in 1928 she left four children, one of whom, Robert Valentine Heckscher, has gained distinction as a poet.

CELESTE HECKSCHER TROTH

MARGARET F. BUTLER

1861–1931

THE first woman to preside over an international congress of physicians was Dr. Margaret F. Butler, professor in the Woman's Medical College of Pennsylvania. This congress was held in Vienna in 1908. Dr. Butler was the sole representative in attendance from the United States.

Margaret Butler was born on a farm in Chester County in 1861. She was the daughter of James Butler and Rachel James Butler and traced her ancestry on both sides to Colonial settlers. The eldest of seven children, she entered school at the age of four, was graduated from Darlington Seminary, and at seventeen was teaching school.

Becoming interested in the Society to Encourage Studies at Home, she took up correspondence courses under Mrs. Seth Low, Mary Kinsmore, and other prominent women. It was Dr. Theophilus Parvin who encouraged her to study medicine, and in 1894 she was graduated from the Woman's Medical College of Pennsylvania, later taking postgraduate courses in Vienna under Politzer and Hyack.

Returning to Philadelphia, she was made professor of the Ear, Nose, and Throat in her alma mater where, beloved by her students and her professional colleagues, she taught till her death on October 16, 1931. She died suddenly while performing an operation in the room where she loved to work—for work and helping others were her joys.

Preëminent in the field of diagnosis and surgery, she was made a Fellow of the American College of Surgery in 1918. On numerous occasions she represented her college in scientific assemblies and through her integrity, skill, and professional good judgment did much toward the advancement of her sex in the medical profession.

MIRIAM BUTLER

HELEN BOAS REILY

1862–1932

HELEN MARGARET BOAS was born in 1862 at Harrisburg. Her parents were Margaret Bates, a native of Ireland, a member of the Church of England, and Daniel Dick Boas, of Reading, a business man active in civic and church affairs who served as warden of St. Stephen's Episcopal Church for many years.

From her mother, who was gifted and talented, she inherited her artistic tendencies. Many beautiful examples of her drawing and painting, and also of her needlework, are to be seen in the homes of her friends in Harrisburg. She was gifted musically and was one of the organizers of the Wednesday Club, Harrisburg's oldest musical organization.

She participated actively in church work, teaching a Sunday school class at St. Stephen's Church for many years. A person of vigorous health, she was also active in sports. She played tennis and was an expert in archery; she drove horses well and was equally at home in the saddle. These were the days of the S. M. B. L. Young Ladies Cooking Club, which was well known for its gay meetings and its cookbook of succulent delicacies. Helen Reily was an organizer and first president of this club.

It is hard to understand just how Mrs. Reily could have given so much time to the community which surrounded her estate at Fort Hunter on the Susquehanna. A steady stream of people was constantly coming to her door, seeking advice and help in their home problems. To these persons she listened attentively and gave help in the most amazing way, thereby becoming a real source of inspiration and guidance to the entire neighborhood.

From the neighborhood her interests stretched to the city of Harrisburg and the entire state. She was president of the Civic Club from 1910 to 1914, and first vice-president from 1914 to 1918. It was at this time she became interested in the Young Women's Christian Association of Harrisburg, serving as president from 1915 until the time of her death. The establishment of a summer camp on a portion of her husband's property, known as Camp Reily, was one of the outstanding contributions Mrs. Reily made to the Young Women's Christian Association.

She was one of the few women members of the Harrisburg Chamber of Commerce. She took part in Red Cross drives and played a prominent part in the welfare drives. Her seventieth birthday was celebrated by the entire organization at one of their luncheons. She was president of the Needlework Guild, one of the leaders of the Pennsylvania Federation of Women's Clubs, and chairman of its information service for many years. On the occasion of the convention of the State Federation held in Harrisburg, October 15, 1934, the officers held a luncheon at Fort Hunter as a tribute to Mrs. Reily's memory.

She died in her sleep on the night of July 26, 1932 with her well-worn Bible beside her. In her will she left a large tract of beautiful woodland to the Harrisburg Country Club, to be used as a public park and to be known as the Reily-Boas Park. She also left another tract of land adjoining Camp Reily to the Young Women's Christian Association of Harrisburg.

SARAH LOGAN WISTER STARR

JOSEPHINE AGNES NATT

1862–1934

BORN in Philadelphia August 31, 1862, Josephine Agnes Natt, daughter of Joseph S. and Isabella Goodheart Natt, was educated in private schools. In 1881 she entered Smith College. There she was soon recognized as a student of unusual ability, character, and genius for friendship.

Eager for experience to test her training, she was the pioneer woman of her family in paid work. In 1890, with the Agnes Irwin School, she began what was to be her life work. Four years later Miss Irwin became dean of Radcliffe and Miss Sophia Irwin succeeded her. When Miss Sophia died in 1915, Miss Natt was made headmistress. Through the years that followed she gave herself to preserving the school's traditions and to continuing its progress.

She was an outstanding executive. It is said that "no detail was too small for her to notice, no problem too large for her to solve." She was a loyal co-worker with teachers, parents, and trustees. Her unpriggish devotion to duty, her unpedantic scholarship, her vigor, humor, justice, and understanding endeared her to her pupils, but it was their daily association with a great personality that gave permanence and power to her influence.

All her days they came to her with their difficulties and their achievements. Her memory held the history of each one, and her pride in them was to her greater than any personal glory. When she visited a post-war school in Athens, her discovery of an Irwin girl teaching nursing was more joy to her than the Acropolis. There are few phases of service to which her pupils have not made a contribution of worth.

Her conviction that an executive should resign while still at her best dictated her retirement in 1928. Always a worker in every civic and national crisis, she dedicated her time and ability to volunteer philanthropy, first with organizations like the White-Williams Foundation, and afterward to the daily labors of the Emergency Aid and the Board of County Relief. She died November 7, 1934.

She was a member of the Board of Trustees of the Agnes Irwin School, the board of the Emergency Aid of Pennsylvania, the Philadelphia Board of County Relief, a director and officer of the College Club, on the Scholarship Committee of the White-Williams Foundation, member of civic and other organizations, among them the Family Society, Philadelphia Art Alliance, American Association of University Women, Head Mistresses Association of the East, Smith Alumnae, Smith Club, English-Speaking Union, Republican Women of Pennsylvania, Geographical Society, and the American Academy of Political and Social Science.

Her life was the story of intense, beneficent activity. In the Josephine Natt Memorial Hall at Wynnewood her portrait looks down on the school she loved. Her greater memorial is and will be in the lives and affection of those who knew her and in the lives of future citizens to whom her influence will descend.

ADELE M. SHAW

JESSIE WILLCOX SMITH

1863-1935

JESSIE WILLCOX SMITH was born in Philadelphia on September 8, 1863, the daughter of Charles Henry and Catherine Willcox Smith. Descended from a Colonial family which had already produced such pioneers in education as Emma Willard, her aunt who for many years was president of the Women's College in Troy, it seemed inevitable that the idealistic young girl, with her alert, progressive mind, should seek a scholarly career. It was indicative of those inner characteristics which guided her destiny that the training of the very young child should appeal to her so strongly that she turned first to the kindergarten, a phase of child education which was developing rapidly in America at that time.

Soon a happy destiny led Jessie Willcox Smith to membership in the inspiring classes at the Pennsylvania Academy of the Fine Arts, under the direction of Thomas Eakins. Later that amazingly imaginative artist, Howard Pyle, became the true guide of her genius. In his classes in illustration at the Drexel Institute she formed delightful friendships with two other young artists, Violet Oakley and Elizabeth Shippen Green. These three highly gifted girls combined their studies, first in the old Love Building at 1633 Chestnut Street, and later in the wooded suburbs near Villanova, where, under the sign of the Red Rose, developed one of those lovely and rare combinations of youthful genius and high endeavor. Devoted to their art, though followed on entirely different lines, they formed a circle whose charming influence in the city was far-reaching, and will be cherished and remembered by the group of friends who gathered round them in appreciation.

Miss Smith's first illustrations of child life appeared in *Collier's* and *Scribner's* and captivated the public mind with their charm of subject, freshness of color, and originality of design. The quaint and winsome little creatures who play hide-and-seek across the canvases of Jessie Willcox Smith, who dance into existence as a Peter Pan or a Christopher Robin, seem to convince one that the artist was born on the edge of the magic forest. What other artist would select this line as a text for an illustration of *Water Babies:* "He felt how comfortable it was to have nothing on him but himself"?

Her illustrations for children's books were executed with immense joyousness. Besides *Water Babies,* she has left what are now rare editions of Stevenson's *A Child's Garden of Verses; Little Women; Heidi;* and the delightful *Children of Dickens,* which will ever enchant the hearts of the young of all ages.

When the expiration of the lease of the Red Rose necessitated a change, the studios, now teeming with activity, were moved to Chestnut Hill, on the beautiful Wissahickon Valley overlooking Cresheim Creek. Here under the apple trees, Jessie Willcox Smith built the home of her dreams, a low, rambling, white house with wide doors and windows letting in the sun, a home of peace and quiet joy, so peopled with the creatures of her imagination that one expected to hear secret laughter in the shrubberies, and little feet running down the garden path to the low-latched green gate. These were indeed busy days, for many were the mothers and children who came to her door to find immortality in her portraits.

Life was now full and rich with industry and experience. Many honors came her way, received always with modesty, for she rejoiced more in others' success than in her own. She received three medals from the Charleston, the St. Louis, and the San Francisco Expositions, and from her own native city, the Mary Smith Prize, given by the Academy of the Fine Arts, and the Beck Award from the Philadelphia Water Color Club.

Though her work made necessary the long, quiet days in her peaceful studio, she took an active interest in all educative and artistic enterprises in the city: in the Plastic and Water Color Clubs, the Art Alliance, and the Fellowship of the Academy of the Fine Arts. She found time for the exacting duties of the Women's Board of the Art Museum, and kept inactive contact with the Society of Illustrators and the Water Color Club of New York.

In April 1936, a year after her death, a memorial exhibition of her work was held in the three galleries and rotunda of the Academy of the Fine Arts. Nearly two hundred drawings, water colors, and portraits were displayed, loaned from private collections and public galleries. The enthusiasm with which the exhibition was received gave her work a high place of honor for all time in the artistic annals of her country. No more beautiful tribute could be paid than in the closing paragraph of the foreword for the catalogue written by her devoted friend, Edith Emerson:

The ideals of Jessie Willcox Smith have been woven into the fabric of contemporary thought, and impressed upon the consciousness of innumerable mothers, who hope that their children will look upon the children she paints. Hers was a brave and generous mind, comprehending life with large simplicity, free from all pettiness, and unfailingly kind. With unerring directness and sure instinct, she touched the heart of the people, and it is there that we must look if we seek to find her special shrine.

ETHEL TAIT McKENZIE

ANNA LEA CARSON

1864-1933

ANNA LEA, daughter of John R. and Anna Robson Lea Baker, was born in Philadelphia, April 29, 1864. Her education was received in private schools in that city. On April 14, 1880, she was married to Hampton L. Carson, a prominent member of the legal profession, and later professor of law at the University of Pennsylvania and Attorney General of the state.

Mrs. Carson's ability and public spirit, accompanied by her gift for leadership, led her to identify herself with many of the civic and humanitarian enterprises of her native city. Among other activities, she served as a manager of the Midnight Mission, as a member of the Committee for the Restoration of Congress Hall, and for many years was a director of the Ladies' Depository Association.

In 1926 at the close of the Sesquicentennial in Philadelphia, she was one of the group of women who undertook the restoration of Strawberry Mansion in Fairmount Park. She there assumed the responsibility of assembling and arranging the furnishings of the large attic which, as a result, became one of the most interesting period features in this early American home.

As chairman of the Associate Committee of Women of the Genealogical Society of Pennsylvania, her genius found its full expression and won for her the honor and admiration of her associates. Greatly interested in the Penn story and the Provincial history of the Commonwealth her ancestors had helped to found, she took an active part in the plans of the General Committee appointed by Mayor Moore for the commemoration of the 250th anniversary of the landing of William Penn in America.

She had many interests apart from this committee and the Historical Society of Pennsylvania, of which her husband was president at the time of his death. She was a member of the Committee on Museum, Pennsylvania Museum of Art, and a frequent donor to its exhibits. One of her collections, believed to be the most considerable of its kind in the country, that of the English eye miniatures of the eighteenth century, has been a loan exhibit of the museum since 1930.

Some time before her death, which occurred June 2, 1933, Mrs. Carson presented the Historical Society of Pennsylvania her collection of works on silhouettes, together with 275 unusual specimens of the profile art. These were collated, mounted, and cabinet-arranged under her own direction.

M. Atherton Leach

ELIZABETH PRICE MARTIN

1864-1932

Elizabeth Price was born October 14, 1864, in Philadelphia. Her father was John Sergeant Price, son of Eli Kirk Price, and descended from a family well known in the annals of Chester County as influential members of the Society of Friends, as notable agriculturists, and as organizers of important and far-seeing community interests.

From her grandfather, Eli Kirk Price, Sr., she had both by contact and inheritance much for which she was eager always to pay a grateful tribute. He was a lawyer of astuteness and with a talent for responsibility. And it was chiefly through his perseverance and acumen that the deeds of the estates which had been condemned to form Fairmount Park were eventually put in order, filed, and became actually the property of the city.

Her young days at home were happy and active; and as a pupil at the Irwin School, presided over by those remarkable sisters, Agnes and Sophia Irwin, and as the child of her mother, a redoubtable head of her own household and a woman who made much of the way things were done after a pattern soon to be lost or mislaid by later housewives, she gained her early experience of people and of standards.

She began early to enjoy being a good neighbor. She also gained experience, for the small street at the rear of her father's house at 1709 Walnut Street proved a likely vantage point for her to try out what was later to be known as social service, but which in that day, and later for her, was always to be just neighborliness.

Her marriage in 1886 to Jonathan Willis Martin, Jr., a young lawyer who was soon to establish a name for himself both in his profession, where he became eventually an honored judge, and in many other interests both sporting and military, gave Elizabeth Price Martin new and fertile outlets for her energies. With the birth and the interests of their children and of their life out on the Bethlehem Pike at Chestnut Hill, their program of existence as notable members of a distinguished social group might have sufficed most good citizens, but not these particular two Pennsylvanians, whose interests were so eminently to be those not only of their state, but of their nation.

Elizabeth Martin's philanthropy had begun in the street at her father's back gate, and received a new impetus during the Spanish-American War. But it was during the World War in 1914 that her leadership in many sides of social service became recognized far and wide. Home relief, farm gardens, Red Cross, Emergency Aid, national defense, Liberty Loans, prison reform, Municipal Hospital reorganization—in such national and civic and church activities she became a leader and adviser, always carrying the heavy end of work on her own shoulders as well as of responsibility of administration. She also gathered a phenomenal group of friends from far and near to work with her, and for her.

Her four most outstanding contributions to her own and to later generations were: the Social Service activities of the Emergency Aid of Pennsylvania, fostered and augmented under her leadership; the conception and organization of the Garden Club of America in a national pattern recognizably her own ardent and faithful and dominant one; the hospitality in Philadelphia by the Women's Sesquicentennial Committee on the High Street of 1926 with its perpetuation of patriotic interests in the historic Strawberry Mansion in Fairmount Park; and her eager support and backing of the idea of The Book of Honor from its inception under the impetus of her leadership almost to the final stages of its successful completion.

Elizabeth Martin died after a brief illness in the spring of 1932 in the heyday of her usefulness.

SARAH D. LOWRIE

BERTHA T. CALDWELL

1867–1915

THE daughter of Dr. William Caldwell and Susan Levergood Caldwell, the latter a lineal descendant of Peter Levergood, Sr., one of the pioneer settlers of the city of Johnstown, Bertha Caldwell inherited the characteristic traits of both her parents—the vigor and mental alertness of the Scotch-Irish blended with the thrift and energy of the early Pennsylvania German. In her flowered the best qualities of both these strains.

Born in 1867, her early education was obtained in the public schools. Graduated in the high school class of 1885, she became a student of the Indiana (Penna.) State Normal School and afterwards taught for several years. Within a few days after a narrow escape from death in the Johnstown flood of 1889, Miss Caldwell matriculated in the Woman's Medical College in Philadelphia. She took a graduate course in the University of Pennsylvania, at the same time being in charge of the medical department of the Indian school at Hampton, Virginia.

Subsequently Dr. Caldwell volunteered as a medical missionary in India, spending one year at Lodiana, and later became head of a hospital for women and children in Allabahad. An episode of her life in India concerns an elephant-back ride through the jungle to the home of an Indian prince whose wife was desperately ill. Upon her arrival she diagnosed the case as one requiring an immediate surgical operation. The obdurate husband objected. Dr. Caldwell promptly sent him out of doors and successfully performed the operation and saved her patient's life.

Having completed her seven years of service in the foreign field, she returned in 1902 to her native city to practise her profession. She became the first probation officer in Cambria County. Her interest in public affairs led to her election as School Controller in 1908, the first woman to attain that distinction.

That nothing of interest in human affairs was alien to her was also manifested by her membership in the Civic Club of Cambria County, in her organizing and teaching Bible classes, following the spiritual renaissance of the city in the year 1913, and in her work as one of the organizers of the local Young Women's Christian Association.

The end of this brilliant and useful career came with tragic and distressing suddenness while she was on a professional mission. On her way to visit a patient on the night of July 31, 1915, she fell through an opening in the footwalk of a city bridge twenty-five feet to the river bed below and died from her injuries a few days later.

The life and work of Dr. Caldwell vindicated the claims of her sex to recognition in fields where men have held almost entire sway, and proved there was a wide field for women which had long lain fallow. Particularly was this true of her work in India where custom and caste forbade male physicians' attendance upon women. Life for her was a great and successful adventure. She went far on hitherto untrodden paths. It was given her to see, in the years between 1885 and 1915, an almost completed cycle in the realms of science. In it Dr. Caldwell played a prominent rôle as a humanitarian, equaled, in the practice of the medical profession in Johnstown, by only one other physician, Dr. Victor Heiser.

CHARLES C. GREER

LAURA H. CARNELL

1867–1929

ひ长

THERE is in the life story of Laura Horner Carnell, A.B., Litt.D., who devoted thirty-four years of her life to the upbuilding of Temple University, a saga of modern American education. She was a very quiet person, tireless in her energies but with a distinct ability for doing tremendous services in an unobtrusive way. The academic pattern of Temple University, as it is today, remains largely of her design.

She was born in Philadelphia, September 7, 1867, the daughter of Lafayette and Rebecca Wood Ayers Carnell. In 1885, she was graduated from the Philadelphia High School for Girls, and attended the Philadelphia Normal School during the following year, thereafter continuing her studies at Cornell, the University of Chicago, and Cambridge University. Upon completion of her education, she taught in the public schools of Philadelphia until 1893, when Dr. Russell H. Conwell, founder of Temple University, first called her to help him with this new project. She had previously been associated with him as a worker in the little Baptist chapel, now Grace Baptist Temple, helping in the evening classes Dr. Conwell had instituted.

Almost overnight these classes had grown into a thriving "people's university," and it was to her that Dr. Conwell entrusted his ideals and aspirations. The first days of her new job must have been bewildering. Dr. Conwell told her he was not exactly sure what she should do. Everything was more or less new—new teachers, new faces, new students. When she finally got a class together, she noticed that among her students she had a Chinese, a policeman, and a little boy with curls, who became a pupil at Temple because his older sister was a student and he wanted to be with her. At that time there were about two hundred pupils in the day classes, and it fell to Dr. Carnell's lot to do a great deal of the executive work of the university.

Dr. Conwell often spoke of her genius and resourcefulness as an organizer. She taught all day long and worked far into the night. "The record of the service which Laura H. Carnell has given to the university," said Dr. Conwell shortly before his death, "could not be tabulated or approximated; it has been the life work of a martyr and a genius." When the classes began to expand she was selected as principal of the women's department. In 1897 she was made acting dean, and with this promotion she became, in effect, the functioning educational head of the university. This position she held until 1905 when she became dean of the Temple University Corporation and lecturer in the history of art. In 1925 she was made associate president. Though keeping in close touch with the students, she was able to do considerable writing on educational subjects; essays, and biographical sketches.

Dr. Carnell traveled extensively, her last trip abroad being a Mediterranean tour in 1927. In Alaska in 1925 she witnessed a veritable gold rush. As an ardent football fan, she rarely missed one of the great games, and attended in addition most of the undergraduate functions, constantly watching out for the welfare of the students entrusted to her care.

She took an interest as well in various civic, religious, and social activities. She was a member of the Philadelphia Board of Education from 1923 to her death and was associated with the National Education Association, American Association of University Women, Republican Women of Pennsylvania, the College of Arts Association, and had been president of the National Association of Women Deans. She was a member of the Civic, New Century, Women's City, College, and Contemporary Clubs in Philadelphia.

For many years she lived with her mother at 2136 North Camac Street, Philadelphia. When Miss Carnell died on March 30, 1929, Dr. Charles E. Beury, president of Temple University, said of her:

"One of the outstandingly useful women in Philadelphia, she quietly and modestly served a great variety of interests with surpassing ability and devotion.

"I question whether Temple University would be in existence today but for Dr. Carnell. I am sure it would not hold its present high place in democratic higher education but for her."

CHARLES E. BEURY
LILLIAN H. KETTERER

ANNA BEACH PRATT

1867–1932

❧

BORN and reared in Elmira, New York, Anna B. Pratt went from public school to Elmira College, where, at nineteen years of age, she received her B.A. degree. The next year she served as professor of history there, and at the age of twenty-one she had the unusual distinction of being chosen a trustee of her college.

Later she studied at the New York School of Social Work, for her real interest lay in the rather undeveloped field of welfare work. A pioneer, she began her work in Elmira. Soon a working girls' club was meeting at Miss Pratt's home. It grew so large that it had to have its own clubrooms. Her plans for the unfortunate were so advanced and received such signal recognition that the people of Elmira soon wanted her as Overseer of the Poor. As this was an elective office and not at the time open to women, her father was asked to be the candidate, with the understanding that he would appoint his daughter as his deputy.

She was the first to suggest and carry out the now familiar plan of uniting all welfare agencies. Then, as secretary of the Women's Federation for Social Service, she sponsored the building erected by this organization, where for the first time all such agencies were housed under one roof. Thus duplication of work was eliminated and greater efficiency obtained.

After nine years of such practical experience in Elmira, Miss Pratt went for a year of graduate study to the University of Pennsylvania, where, in 1916, she took her master's degree. The same year she received the appointment which began her long career of ever increasing activity, accomplishment, and honor as director of the reorganized Magdalen Society—the White-Williams Foundation.

From the first her objective was to provide "for every child a chance to grow to the limit of his ability" by such original, forward-looking plans as the training of student volunteers from the Philadelphia Normal School, Swarthmore College, and the University of Pennsylvania, and the maintenance of a staff of trained workers to administer high school scholarships to able boys and girls of more than fourteen years of age. Three such scholarships are financed by the interest from the Anna B. Pratt Memorial Scholarship Fund, which is still receiving gifts.

Thus Miss Pratt, by completely changing its methods and objectives, transformed an obsolete, restricted social agency into a much greater organization, of the most advanced type in the United States. Not only throughout this country, but abroad, her principles were adopted, her plans and methods copied, her views on mental hygiene, education, every phase of welfare work accepted as authoritative. She was constantly widening the scope of her activities and connections. To further coöperation between parent and teacher, she served as president of the Philadelphia County Council of Home and School Associations and secretary-treasurer of the International Federation of Home and School. She was one of the two woman members of the Philadelphia Board of Public Education, a delegate to the White House Conference on Child Welfare, and an honored member of practically every child-helping organization.

Knowledge, intellectual power, fineness of character, exquisite but very practical sympathy and understanding; limitless, tireless, selfless devotion to the cause of children everywhere—such excellence combined with rare graciousness of personality made her universally admired and beloved.

Miss Pratt died in Philadelphia, January 3, 1932.

RUTH M. WALKER

HELEN MARTIN

1868–1939

HELEN REIMENSNYDER MARTIN, noted for her depiction of Pennsylvania Dutch life, was born in Lancaster, Pennsylvania, in 1868, the daughter of the Reverend Cornelius and Henrietta Reimensnyder. Her father was a Lutheran clergyman. She received her education at Swarthmore and Radcliffe colleges, and, in 1899, married Frederic C. Martin.

She began her career by writing short stories, but the opportunity which provided the first definite opening for her subsequent career as a novelist was when a Philadelphia magazine requested a lawyer of her acquaintance to write a history of his Pennsylvania Dutch ancestry. He turned the work of research over to her, with the result that her imagination was fired by the simple and frugal life of the Mennonites. She soon realized that she had struck a rich field for fiction.

The first of her thirty novels to be published appeared in 1904, *Tillie, a Mennonite Maid*. This, as well as *Barnabetta* published in 1914, was dramatized. The latter, as *Erstwhile Susan,* was played by Mrs. Minnie Maddern Fiske in the starring rôle of Juliet Miller in 1916. Thirty-six years old when she wrote her first novel, Helen Martin confessed that up to that time she had preferred to write about "lords and ladies."

GERTRUDE BOSLER BIDDLE

ALICE BARBER STEPHENS

1868–1931

AN entry in Arnold Bennett's *Journal* records a conversation he once held with the art editor of one of America's leading monthlies. They were discussing Howard Pyle.

"Ah," I said, "Pyle is your greatest man."
"Ye-es," he said, hesitatingly, "a great man."
"Who greater?" I asked.
"Well," he said, stroking his shaven chin, "I guess I should put Alice Barber Stephens a shade higher."

This is not quoted to draw comparisons between two notable artists but to emphasize the commanding position Mrs. Stephens held among the illustrators of her generation.

Born in 1868, she chose her profession in a day when the study of art was still unusual for women, but by dint of immense energy as a student of engraving at the School of Design for Women, and under Eakins at the Pennsylvania Academy of the Fine Arts, she became an illustrator for *Harper's* and *Scribner's* while still a girl. After some years at this work she continued her studies in Paris at Colarossi's and Academie Julien, exhibiting in the Paris Salon in her late twenties.

During an active professional life of more than forty years her output was immense and always of the highest order. Her work was in constant demand by the best magazines and book publishers, and the honors which came to her were many. For her illustrations for George Eliot's *Middlemarch* she was awarded a gold medal at the Earl's Court Exhibition in London in 1899. The same year she won the Mary Smith Prize at the Academy of the Fine Arts and later a medal at the Atlanta Exposition. Some two hundred of her drawings are in the collection of the Library of Congress in Washington.

Through all of Mrs. Stephens' work, in oil, in water color, in charcoal, in her engravings, shone the deep sincerity which those who knew her felt to be her most salient characteristic; sincerity, which, coupled with sympathetic open-mindedness, made her genius as a homemaker and as a friend as great as her genius as an artist. With her husband, Charles H. Stephens, and her son, Owen Stephens, both painters, art was in the very air she breathed.

Those who, through the lovely pages of Lady Burne-Jones' *Memorials of Edward Burne-Jones,* have become intimate with the charmed circle she so vividly portrays could not but feel in Mrs. Stephens a spiritual kinship with that group—the same highmindedness, the same deep seriousness, the same delicious play of humor over all the little contretemps of life. In all that pertained to her art she was more direct, more realistic, and her work, though lacking nothing in dramatic and poetic qualities, struck a more vigorous, modern note; but in mode of living, in drawing about her home an atmosphere of beauty and dignity and grace, one felt strongly the parallel.

Mrs. Stephens died in 1931.

MARIAN GREENE BARNEY

JANE BOWNE HAINES

1869–1937

ᐅᐊ

JANE BOWNE HAINES was born in Cheltenham, Pennsylvania, in 1869. Her father, Robert Bowne Haines, had started the Chelthenham Nurseries in 1852, and so it was but natural that she should acquire a love for trees and flowers at a very early age. Under her father's guidance she became familiar with the names of trees and shrubs and, watching him at work in the fields in summer or in the potting shed in the winter months, she gradually obtained a good technical knowledge of horticulture.

Miss Haines received her education at Miss Stevens' private school in Germantown, and at Bryn Mawr College, where she received her degree of B.A. in 1891, and M.A. in 1892. After holding a fellowship in history at Bryn Mawr she took a course at the State Library School in Albany, New York, and later engaged in library work from 1895 to 1903, three years of which were spent at the Congressional Library in Washington. She was interested in education in general, and industrial and vocational education in particular.

After her father's death, she and her sister took over the management of his nurseries, which then included about ten acres. The business was entirely local, and was largely devoted to raising fruit trees. Because of the success she encountered she came to believe that more opportunities should be provided for women in horticulture. This was a very advanced idea for its time, as the general conception of a woman's place was the home. But with one of her nature, action followed conviction in her plans to establish a school where women could learn gardening and the raising of trees. In 1906 she was corresponding with English gardeners, and the horticultural colleges at Swanley and Kent.

Miss Haines was not only positive but deliberate. She spent more than five years in searching for the exact type of farm she wanted for her project before she finally fixed upon a site at Ambler as the ideal location. The actual school was begun on a very small scale, and in the face of many obstacles. But these did not discourage her, for she was determined to let her plan grow slowly like the great oak trees she so much admired.

The Ambler School of Horticulture was thus founded in 1910. Its object was to give educated women scientific instruction in horticulture, combined with all necessary conditions for actual practice. The course was planned to equip women with the theoretical and practical knowledge that would enable them to manage private and commercial gardens, greenhouses, or orchards. This was the first American training school for women in its field, and has in its development met with the great success it so much merited.

Its steady growth has justified the faith and courage of its founder. To many young women it has offered a healthful and pleasant employment in an honorable and useful profession. Time necessarily has wrought many changes in the curriculum of the school, but the ideals of Jane Bowne Haines remain unaltered to inspire and guide its future.

Her busy and useful career was terminated by her death on September 21, 1937.

JOHN G. WISTER

MARY CHANNING WISTER

1870–1918

❧❧

AMONG the precious possessions of a Philadelphia family is a photograph of a girl dressed in the armor of Joan of Arc and carrying in her uplifted hand the banner which typifies the consecrated career of the Maid of Orleans. Mary Channing was about seventeen when she played the part of Joan of Arc, but even then her young life was taking on some of the qualities of the girl who will live forever. For she had that vision without which the people perish, which went ever before her as a shining ray which she must follow.

She was born in Philadelphia in 1870, the daughter of William Rotch and Mary Eustis Wister. Very early she began to try to improve the lot of those less fortunate. She loved children and animals and those weak and unable to care for themselves, and associated herself with agencies dedicated to their welfare. Before she had graduated from school she was busily at work in the Evening Home for Boys and was teaching a class in her Sunday school, experiences which were to make her a valued member of the Board of Public Education, on which she was later to serve for nearly two years.

In 1893, with Miss Cornelia Frothingham, she founded the Civic Club of Philadelphia, serving twice as its president. Throughout her life she was an active member.

In 1898 she married Owen Wister, a second cousin of her father, and six children came to inspire and gladden her experience. Still, with this added care and responsibility, her interest in the movements with which she was associated never ceased, and she ever found time to be a loyal and devoted friend to those with whom she came in contact. No one who worked with her can forget her radiant presence, her shining eyes so full of a light which can come only from the soul of one consecrated to the good of mankind. From the memorial prepared for her by the Civic Club these words best express the life of this remarkable woman:

Now and then there comes into this troubled world a soul that seems so related to the unseen world by happy temperament, by mentality, perhaps, that it is all ready to do the Lord's work among us; so the world says, in common parlance of such a soul: "She was born good." Such a one was Mary Channing Wister—a very unusual character, born for an unusual work in the city of Philadelphia.

She died August 24, 1918.

ELLA E. WISTER HAINES

ELIZABETH WILSON FISHER

1873–1938

ELIZABETH FISHER, who died in her sixty-fifth year in April 1938, was one of the founders of the Acorn Club and a member of the first Board of Governors of the Woman's City Club of Philadelphia.

She was well known for her activities in behalf of young girls, having assisted in the establishment of the St. James Guild for Girls at St. James Protestant Episcopal Church in Philadelphia. In 1910 she helped open Beaver Camp in Maine, where hundreds of girls from the major cities of the country spend summer vacations.

Greatly interested in photography, Miss Fisher was one of the organizers of the Lantern and Lens Club, an organization of women photographers. For many years she served as secretary of the Pennsylvania Audubon Society and in addition filled the office of vice-president of the Churchwoman's Club of the Protestant Episcopal Diocese of Pennsylvania. At the time of her death she was companion-in-charge of the Philadelphia Chapter of the Companions of the Holy Cross.

Sarah D. Lowrie

HELEN FLEISHER

1875-1931

Helen Fleisher, born the daughter of the late Simon B. Fleisher, a well-known manufacturer, and Celia Fleisher, who was a gifted musician, died in 1931 after an active career in social and welfare work that rose quite above the usual formal and non-personal phases of such activities. Fortunate in her father and mother, she was brought up in a home where a concern for the arts was an abiding thing. One of her brothers, Samuel S. Fleisher, established the Graphic Sketch Club, a place for recreation in and through the arts as well as a creative center of art instruction in all media. Another brother, Edwin A. Fleisher, did the same service for music through his Symphony Club, where young musicians receive a training in instrumental music, covering all the orchestral choirs, and also developing solo performers. Miss Fleisher not only interested herself in all the projects growing out of her family relationship, but on her own account went in strongly for movements looking to individual and community betterment. Her endeavors along this line in the Neighborhood Center and the Community Health Center movement were as training to meet the emergency created by the First World War. She proved one of the most valuable, stimulating, and sympathetic workers in the Emergency Aid—an organization which, during the war and after, had the support of the leading women of the city. Among them all, none was more appreciated than Miss Fleisher, who reflected the indomitable activity and profound human sympathy of a Florence Nightingale.

Familiar with the Girl Scout Movement and all sorts of women's organizations, Miss Fleisher, while working with the Emergency Aid, was largely instrumental in developing sewing rooms throughout the city. It was by reason of her experience in coming in contact with young women trained in these classes that the idea of a trade school for girls as part of the solution of the problem of the untrained and often unemployable girl came to her mind. From the moment that this inspiring idea took its shape Miss Fleisher, in an extremely practical way, together with a group of prominent women belonging to the Home Relief division of the Emergency Aid, opened a trade school for girls. This school was free of charge and was located, in 1915, in Toure Hall, at Tenth and Carpenter streets. The idea and the actuality of it, growing by leaps and bounds, took on a broader outlook. Before the end of the war, a bigger school was opened at Ninth and Walnut streets. Then, through the influence of Simon Gratz, it was moved to the old public school building at Pine and Quince streets, where finally it became a part of the public school life of Philadelphia, just at the close of the war period. Eight years later, in 1926, the million-dollar building at Thirteenth and Green became a realized dream. In this school it was not only Miss Fleisher's conception of the project which counted, but her definite personal touch with all those concerned in the organization, from the faculty to the pupils.

All this was done while Miss Fleisher, despite repeated illnesses and a by no means robust constitution, was doing everything she could for the cultural life of Philadelphia through the Philadelphia Orchestra groups and other art organizations. One of the most picturesque memorials of her taste and artistic interests as well as her knowledge of the fundamentals of American life, was her gift of the Empire Room in Strawberry Mansion in the interests of the women associated with the High Street enterprise at the Sesquicentennial. All these unwearying activities, however, give but a slight idea of the radiant personality that was back of everything she did. Few names of women, which are attached to public institutions in Philadelphia and Pennsylvania, carry with them such a wealth of noble associations as does the name of Helen Fleisher. Not only is this true in connection with educational matters but also in those fields of socio-humanitarian activities where the heart plays as important a part as the head in vitalizing society. Her work gave new hope to all those who came in contact with her stimulating influence; the influence of one who had ideals, who never rested until the practical means of accomplishing them had been faced and the thing sought and longed for actually achieved.

HARVEY M. WATTS

KATHERINE BAKER

1876–1919

KATHERINE BAKER, daughter of J. Thompson and Elizabeth Bordner Baker, was born in Lewisburg, Union County, on October 4, 1876.

She was educated at Bucknell Seminary and at Goucher College. She read law and, upon admission to the Pennsylvania bar, she became her father's assistant in his law office in Lewisburg. In 1904 the family moved to Wildwood, New Jersey. Presently Katherine received recognition in the field of literature, becoming a constant contributor to the leading magazines. The *Atlantic Monthly* for February 1913 contains her "Entertaining the Candidate," which was afterward reprinted in the Atlantic Classics. Her last story, "Enjoy the Day," dealing with her war experiences, was written in Cannes while she was convalescing from an illness, and appeared in *Scribner's Magazine,* April 1919.

In 1917 she had sailed for France to volunteer her services to the French Government as a nurse. After her training under Dr. Alexis Carrel in his hospital at Compiègne, she was sent to the front. Shortly thereafter, in recognition of her service and her complete devotion to the work, she was made an honorary corporal, and as such was entitled to wear the Fourragère, the only woman to be so decorated.

After serving in various hospitals and working in furtherance of the American Fund for the French Wounded, she joined the Flying

Tent Hospital at Cugny. Gradually her health became impaired and she was transferred to Cannes where, two days after her arrival, she was overcome by an attack of pleurisy and pneumonia. This illness was long and grave. She had scarcely recovered when she insisted upon resuming nursing of the wounded in the spring offensive of 1918, despite the warning of doctors that her life depended on a year's rest.

In the summer she joined the American Red Cross and was sent to the front at Bruyères, in the Vosges. There she had charge of a ward in a French hospital by day and walked a mile and a half at night to another hospital to serve as interpreter for wounded Americans. In 1919, her health shattered, she returned to America. Soon afterward she died at Saranac.

The French Government conferred upon her the posthumous honor of the Croix de Guerre. The Katherine Baker Memorial, an orphanage which houses thirty little girls, was built by Americans at Issy-les-Moulineaux, a suburb of Paris, in her memory.

MARY MATLACK RAIGUEL

MAUD CONYERS EXLEY

1876–1926

MAUD EXLEY was born in England on September 18, 1876, the daughter of Robert and Mary Exley of Stonefall Hall, Knaresboro, Yorkshire. When she was seven years old she accompanied her parents to Philadelphia. After receiving her early education from governesses and tutors, she entered St. Luke's Hospital, New York, where she trained as a nurse. Upon her graduation she took special training at Sloan Maternity, New York, and for a while held the post of night superintendent. She was graduated from the Woman's Medical College, Philadelphia, in 1910, and was for a time affiliated with that institution in the department of gynecology.

Her work soon took her to Harrisburg where she established herself in a private practice. She was the first woman to serve on the staff of the Harrisburg Hospital, preceding all others by ten years.

Professional recognition and honors grew steadily, as did the respect and confidence of her colleagues. From the time of her arrival in Harrisburg until her death in 1926, her achievement was one of constantly increasing power and brilliancy. Voluntary contributions from patients furnished the pediatric ward in the Harrisburg Hospital in her memory.

The secret of her abundant life is found in the beauty and nobility of her personal character and in her firmly founded medical skill. She devoted herself whole-heartedly to the study of medical science and, in spite of the onerous duties of a large practice, found time for constant reading and study in her chosen field. To the decisive logic of a well-trained mind she added the sympathetic intuition and tenderness of a woman.

In appearance and personality she was singularly gifted. During the era when the woman physician was characterized by starched collar and tweed suit, she was conspicuous for the beauty and distinction of her bearing and for her great personal charm and magnetism. As the burdens of life increased, personal disappointments and grief were met with high courage; she never lost the buoyancy of spirit or whimsicality that were the delight of her associates. It is with gratitude her friends remember that a sudden short illness spared her the physical suffering she so often saved others. For many who knew her, her singularly radiant and lovely personality still lives and bears witness to Euripides' assertion, "That which is beautiful is ever dear."

EMILY EXLEY

CHRISTINE WETHERILL STEVENSON

1878–1922

THE presentation of her inspiring Pilgrimage Play in California and the founding of the Art Alliance in Philadelphia were perhaps the two outstanding achievements of Christine Wetherill Stevenson's brief but active life.

She was born in Philadelphia, April 12, 1878, a daughter of Samuel Price Wetherill and Christine Northrop. Following her conventional education in that city and its suburbs, she studied art, music, and history in Europe, to which she returned soon after the turn of the century to prepare for a stage career.

On her return to Philadelphia from the second trip, she founded the Plays and Players Club, subsequently becoming its president. Ibsen's works greatly attracted her; among the first plays she put on were *Lady of the Sea* and *The Woman and the Fiddler*. In 1907 she presented at the Adelphia Theatre her own translation of *Sister Beatrice,* in which she played the leading part.

In 1908 she was married to William Yorke Stevenson. They took a folding canoe with them to Europe on their honeymoon and, to the surprise of the villagers, paddled on the Garonne. Upon their return, they settled near Philadelphia in the historic Hummel place, which was built in 1721 by Benjamin Franklin, at Eddington.

She lost no time in getting back to the stage, where she shortly presented *The Feast of Solhaug,* in which she played the leading rôle, following this with a charity performance of *The Flight of Time,* a play and pageant which she herself wrote.

After another trip to Europe with her husband, during which the couple explored Norway and Sweden on the trail of Ibsen, she presented a return engagement of *Sister Beatrice* at the Little Theatre, Philadelphia. She established her studio at 1709 Chestnut Street, where the arduous work of founding the Art Alliance was carried on. Many prominent social leaders and civic workers, as well as artists, climbed the steep, dark stairs to hear the plans for the united center of art which she eventually opened at the old Audenried home, North Rittenhouse Square. Mr. Wetherill took a deep interest in this project of his daughter and, after his death in 1926, his home was bought by the Art Alliance, and dedicated to Mrs. Stevenson through the presentation of the beautiful relief sculptured by R. Tait McKenzie.

The Art Alliance founded, she went to California and presented the Brotherhood Players in *The Light of Asia,* which was intended to be the first of a series of religious plays sympathetically interpreted by devoted theological students. Walter Hampden played Buddha, Ruth St. Denis had charge of symbolic dances, and Charles Wakefield Cadman wrote the incidental music.

The Light of Asia was given in the out-of-door amphitheatre of the Theosophical Society. A canyon was bought to serve as a setting for her final and greatest production, the *Life of Christ*. Henry Herbert and Helen Freeman played the leading parts. She traveled to the Holy Land to study costumes, and intended to tour Europe with the company of Pilgrimage Players when she felt the presentation was as nearly perfect as possible.

She was occupied with these plans and with a dramatization of the life of St. Francis of Assisi, which was to have been the next in her series of religious plays, when death overtook her in the fall of 1922.

In her memory a lighted cross glows nightly over the hills of Hollywood near the setting of the *Life of Christ*.

ANITA W. WARDER

MARION REILLY

1879–1928

MARION REILLY was born in Altoona on July 16, 1879, the only daughter and youngest child of John and Anna Lloyd Reilly. Her father was long associated with the Pennsylvania Railroad and, in 1875–76, represented the Seventeenth District of Pennsylvania in Congress.

Her lifelong interest in education sprang from her own love of learning. She prepared for college at the Agnes Irwin School in Philadelphia during the lifetime of its founder, and took her degree at Bryn Mawr in 1901. She carried on advanced studies in mathematics and physics in the postgraduate school at Bryn Mawr, and spent the year 1907–08 at the Universities of Göttingen and Cambridge. At the latter university she worked with the mathematician-philosopher Alfred North Whitehead, later of Harvard. In 1910–11 she spent another year of postgraduate study in the mathematical department of the University of Rome.

Her scholarly abilities and qualities of sympathetic leadership led to her appointment in 1907 as dean of Bryn Mawr to succeed in office Dr. M. Carey Thomas, who had acted since 1894 as both president and dean. On her resignation as dean in 1916 she was made a director of the college and served as one of its more useful and distinguished members for the rest of her life. She died in Philadelphia January 27, 1928.

Before her death her administrative capacity and knowledge of educational problems were put to the service of many schools and educational associations. She was a director of the Agnes Irwin School, the Bryn Mawr School in Baltimore, and the School of Horticulture at Ambler. She was also very active in the work of the American Association of University Women, and one of the first to bring that body in touch with the women graduates of European universities.

In the years before 1920 she was a leader in both state and national suffrage movements. During the World War she organized and financed the Bryn Mawr Service Corps, which equipped, financed, and sent to Europe a body of social and educational experts for relief and reconstruction work. She was a member of the Committee of Seventy in Philadelphia, of the board of trustees of the Philadelphia Award, the committee which awards the Bok Prize, and was chairman of the Philadelphia League of Women Voters.

In a city of collectors, Marion Reilly became known to connoisseurs as an amateur distinguished in two fields. With her mother, she assembled a choice selection of Japanese prints, and independently she formed one of the finest collections of Napoleon cartoons and prints in America.

MARION PARRIS SMITH

CAROLINE TYLER LEA

?–1930

CAROLINE TYLER BROWN was born in Cambridge, Massachusetts, daughter of James Perry Brown and Ellen Douglas Cowperthwait Brown. Her father was a partner of Little, Brown & Co., Boston publishers, and later of Cowperthwait & Co., Philadelphia publishers. She lived most of her life in Philadelphia.

In 1897 she was married to Arthur H. Lea. Highly educated, possessed of a brilliant mind and strong memory, she had inherited the entire fearlessness of her ancestor, Israel Putnam. Early training in the amenities of social life gave her ease and absence of self-consciousness as a hostess and leader. She was an excellent speaker. Deeply wise, she possessed the unusual power of placing herself outside of any question even if it affected herself, and of deciding it objectively. She had an instant grasp of a situation and resourcefulness in meeting it. Everyone she met trusted her judgment, and she had no enemies.

This rare combination of wisdom and tact made her sought for leadership, but she avoided many honors, feeling that she could accomplish more by counseling official leaders than by administering their offices.

Her chief interest was in the Red Cross, as she appreciated its many great services for the suffering. She was an original incorporator of the National American Red Cross in Washington. She declined the chairmanship of the Southeastern Pennsylvania Chapter, but became first vice-chairman, and remained so for life. In the Mississippi flood of 1927, Washington assigned her chapter a quota of $500,000. As the ranking officer present she set to work with the telephone, and in two weeks she had the amount pledged with so much surplus momentum that the quota was oversubscribed with a total of $649,000.

When King Albert of Belgium, his Queen, and the Crown Prince came to Philadelphia on their visit of thanks to America, Mayor Smith asked Mrs. Lea on a Saturday to arrange for their reception on Monday at the Red Cross headquarters in Rittenhouse Square. With only two days for all the arrangements she had three thousand Red Cross overseas nurses and canteen workers in uniform in the square, received and addressed the King, and was addressed by him as representative of the Red Cross in the region.

Her interest in good government led her to become a member of the Civic Club, of which she was a vice-president thirty-five years. Other offices which she held were those of vice-president of the Emergency Aid and chairman of its Belgian Committee, vice-president of the Pennsylvania Society of Colonial Dames and of the National Society of Colonial Dames, and president of the Acorn Club for eight years. She was also active in the Russian Committee and in the Committee for Education of Russian Refugee Children in Paris and Constantinople, playing in addition an active part in war work in 1917–18, raising and giving money and equipment.

Interested in sports for women, she became active in the Women's Branch of the Philadelphia Cricket Club, and was its president for twenty-five years.

She was the only woman member of the board of the Athenaeum in 116 years, and rendered essential service. She was also a member of the board of the Philadelphia Forum from its organization till her death.

For thirty-eight years she was on the Ladies Committee of the Institution for the Deaf and Dumb and made herself familiar with its operation and needs by frequent visiting. She was also a member of the Lady Visitors of the Germantown Hospital, serving sixteen years. A beautiful quiet charity in which she was actively interested was the Country Nursery of Chestnut Hill, where poor, tired mothers could bring their children from the hot city and find rest and every facility under the care of a trained nurse skilled in social work.

Such a life passed away with the blessing of peace and without suffering on August 14, 1930.

SERENA M. HUTCHINSON

INDEX